PowerBuilder™
Building Client Server Applications

Paul Mahler

Prentice Hall PTR
Englewood Cliffs, New Jersey 07632

Library of Congress Cataloging-in-Publication Data

Editorial/Production Supervision: Lisa Iarkowski
Acquisitions Editor: Paul Becker
Manufacturing Manager: Alexis R. Heydt
Cover Design: George Willett

 Prentice-Hall, Inc.
A Simon & Schuster Company
Englewood Cliffs, NJ 07632

The publisher offers discounts on this book when ordered in bulk quantities.
For more information, contact:

Corporate Sales Department
PTR Prentice Hall
113 Sylvan Avenue
Englewood Cliffs, NJ 07632
Phone: 800-382-3419
FAX: 201-592-2249
E-mail: dan_rush@prenhall.com

Printed in the United States of America

10 9 8 7 6 5 4 3 2

ISBN 0-13-179300-4

Prentice-Hall International (UK) Limited, London
Prentice-Hall of Australia Pty. Limited, Sydney
Prentice-Hall of Canada, Inc., Toronto
Prentice-Hall Hispanoamericana S.A., Mexico
Prentice-Hall of India Private Limited, New Delhi
Prentice-Hall of Japan, Inc., Tokyo
Simon & Schuster Asia Pte. Ltd., Singapore
Editora Prentice-Hall do Brasil, Ltda., Rio de Janeiro

Publisher: Paul Becker

Developmental Editor: W. Tom Ireland

Cover Artist: George Willett

Editor: Lewis W. Heinford, Ph.D.

Technical Reviewers:

    Robert Chu

    Pat Flanigan

    Geoff Herman

Production Editor:

    Janos Gereben

Dedicated to Kathy and George.

Table of Contents

About the Author

Paul Mahler graduated with honors from the University of California at Berkeley with a B.A. in Philosophy of Science. He then pursued the Ph.D. program in Bio-Physics at U.C. Berkeley and the graduate program in Medical Information Sciences at U.C. San Francisco.

After receiving an undergraduate degree, he worked as a rocket scientist at NASA/Ames research center constructing computational models of hypersonic fluid flow in rocket engines. Since then, he has built business information systems for global 1000 companies and provided training world-wide.

Mr. Mahler is a certified PowerBuilder developer and a certified PowerBuilder instructor.

For assistance with training or development, you can contact Paul Mahler on the Internet at pmahler@ix.netcom.com or by mail at P.O. Box 60430, Palo Alto, CA 94306

Acknowledgments

This book results from many people's diligent efforts. I thank everyone who helped. I especially thank Rick Dutta and Don Gangully for giving generous support, Gene Powell for teaching me everything I know about PowerBuilder, Tom Ireland, and Paul Becker for making it happen, George Willet for the great cover, Lewis W. Heniford for turning my writing into English, Robert Chu, Pat Flannigan, Geoff Herman, and Janos Gereben for helping to make it right.

Preface

This book is a fast, practical, "hands-on" introduction to writing client-server applications with PowerBuilder™ version 4.0 from Powersoft.

PowerBuilder is an application development tool useful for building industrial-strength client-server applications.

This book will start you writing your own applications with PowerBuilder. You should be able to get to that point quickly—even without familiarity with PowerBuilder, or client-server software, or relational database systems.

I strongly recommend PowerBuilder training, but you can get started working only with what's presented here. This material can enable you to develop PowerBuilder applications using the database management system of your choice.

Here is the book's structure:

Part One addresses PowerBuilder application development using the demonstration database the comes with PowerBuilder. The floppy diskette in the back of the book contains samples you will need in Part One. You should work through Part One from start to finish.

Part Two presents basic tools and concepts for building applications. You should consult Part Two about topics that appear unfamiliar.

These are the assumptions:

You should be familiar with the operating system and graphical user interface you are using. You should be familiar with common programming terminology and practice. Actual programming experience is helpful, but not essential. You should have already installed a licensed copy of PowerBuilder including the sample programs.

The examples in the text are drawn from the Microsoft Windows version of PowerBuilder. If you are using another operating system or graphical user interface, the screens will look different on your system. However, the examples remain pertinent in each of the supported environments.

Style conventions:

Action verbs (instructions for you to do something) are in **bold** type. The objects of the verbs usually appear in *italic* type. Read the instructions carefully, so that you don't miss any of the steps. "Click" in the text means a single click of the left mouse button.

I hope you find all this helpful. Good luck and good programming!

Paul Mahler
pmahler@ix.netcom.com
The Sea Ranch, California
November 1994

Introduction

A client-server application places a workstation in communication with a central database server. With the common availability of networks and inexpensive workstations, client-server applications have grown ever more popular. This book describes each of the tools you will use to build your own client-server applications with PowerBuilder.

A database can serve as a central repository for enterprise information. For example, a relational database could hold and structure all the sales and accounting data for a business or all the research data for an oil exploration company.

Many people in an enterprise may wish to access such a database. The accounting department, the sales department and the shipping departmentally might all want to access parts of the sales and accounting data.

In the past, a database would reside on a centralized machine, such as a main-frame or mini-computer. Older database managers supported indexed files like ISAM. Newer database managers supported hierarchical or networked database structures. Most modern database managers support the relational model detailed in Part Two of this book.

Also in the past, users would access a centralized database through a terminal attached to the machine running the database management software. These could be ASCII terminals talking to a mini-computer or 3270 terminals talking to a mainframe running ISAM or DB2.

Today, a database resides on a separate machine, a server. The server is available enterprise-wide via a network. The database management software runs on the server. Application software runs on the remote work stations. The applications running on the client workstation accesses the data held on the server by passing requests over the network.

Part I
PowerBuilder Concepts

1-1 Getting Started

Once you learn PowerBuilder version 4.0, you can easily build sophisticated client-server applications.

Learning PowerBuilder may not seem so easy to you right now.

This book makes it easier.

A PowerBuilder application is a program that runs on a computer. The program uses a graphical user interface, for example, Microsoft Windows or Motif. The program can connect to some source of data, for example a database, via a network.

The user interacts with the running program through the graphical user interface. The interaction can be with the keyboard or with a pointing device like a mouse.

For example, the user starts a data entry application by double clicking an icon. The user can then command the data-entry application to open a data-entry window. The command can be made through a menu selection, a keyboard selection or an on-screen button. The user then interacts with the running application through the open window.

A window can have controls like an exit button or a button to retrieve data. The user can click an exit button with a mouse to close a window or can click a retrieve button to retrieve data to display. The user can enter data into fields displayed on the window. The running application can present results to the user as a table, picture, or graph.

PowerBuilder provides all the tools you will need to build these applications.

NEW FEATURES IN VERSION 4.0

Version 4.0 of PowerBuilder adds important new capabilities including

✓ multi-platform support
✓ enhancements to the object-oriented model
✓ improved report writing
✓ improved database access
✓ improved connectivity
✓ additional compiler technology
✓ better version control

With the 4.0 release of PowerBuilder, you can write applications that run in different environments besides Microsoft Windows. New platforms will be added over time and should eventually include HP/UX from Hewlett Packard, AIX from IBM, Solaris from Sun Microsystems, Macintosh System 7, Microsoft Windows NT, and OS/2 from IBM. You can write an application in one environment and then move it to any of the other environments. Moving the application is as simple as re-compiling it in the new target environment. Support for conditional compilation makes it easy to quickly adapt to each new environment.

Please note that the examples in this book are shown with Microsoft Windows as this is still the most common PowerBuilder development environment.

Version 4.0 adds additional support for objects. There is additional support for creating or extending non-visual classes. There is also better support for accessing external objects and classes including DLL (Microsoft Dynamic Link Library) custom tools.

Nested reporting is now supported. With the 4.0 release, you can place a DataWindow object inside another DataWindow object. This is useful in many applications, for example, creating detailed report headers or report detail sections. This capability can also provide for multiple formats in a single report.

Data pipelines let you connect a data source to another data target simply by defining the pipeline connection. Your applications should be able to move up to tens of thousands of rows per minute between applications through these data pipelines. The 4.0 release also provides better built-in support for Oracle 7 stored procedures.

The 4.0 release supports Microsoft's OLE 2.0 (Object Embedding and Linking) architecture. Support for object specifications including Object Management Group (OMG) Common object Request Broker (CORBA) is included in the new release. Various intermediate service toolkits like DCE and Tuxedo are now supported as well.

Release 4.0 incorporates new Watcom compiler technology. The 4.0 release now includes the Watcom C++ object class generator. With this generator, you can build libraries that are C or C++ compliant.

Release 4.0 provides better support for source code control and configuration management. This release supports management of multiple applications and parallel development.

Application versions provide labels for all PowerBuilder objects. Once objects are labeled. it is easy to track, or return to, any past version of the system. You must have the Intersolv PCVS product, which is sold separately, to take advantage of these new contol and configuration features.

OBJECT-ORIENTED, EVENT DRIVEN

In the past, with traditional procedural languages like Basic, COBOL, or C, you as a programmer controlled the operation of a running application. The program would control when windows opened and closed, and would control the cursor's movement from data field to data field. The running program determined the sequence of events. The programmer determined the sequence of events by coding this sequence into the program.

In a modern application with a graphical user interface, the user manages the sequence of events that occur as a program runs. For example, the user determines when the application starts, when a window opens or closes, when enter the next data field is entered, or when the application ends. Instead of the program or programmer controlling events, the user controls events.

In an environment where the user is calling the shots from behind a graphical user interface, writing applications is difficult with a procedural language. It is difficult to write a program for an event driven environment where the programmer must determine the sequence of events.

It is easier to write programs for this event-driven environment with a newer object-oriented language—like PowerBuilder 4.0. It is designed to work with objects and events. PowerBuilder is object-oriented, it has built-in facilities for managing windows events and objects.

So be of good cheer. Writing applications with PowerBuilder is easy. There are tools for creating applications and the objects within applications. There are tools for forging the link to sources of data. There are tools for easily responding to the events that happen as the application is running.

Once you have learned PowerBuilder you can build your own industrial-strength applications—quickly, easily, efficiently.

THE GRAPHICAL INTERFACE

A graphical user interface is an object-oriented, event-driven environment. Windows are objects—as are the controls and other objects that appear on the windows. A picture, an icon, or a graph are all objects.

Users can trigger various events. A user can *click* the left mouse button on a window. Programs can also trigger events; for example, a program can trigger the close event for a window.

PowerBuilder programs respond to these events, such as when a user *clicks* a mouse button. The program must respond to the *clicked* event. The initiation of and response to events controls the operation of a running application.

Objects like windows and controls each have a list of associated events . A PowerBuilder application object has four associated events:

- ✓ open
- ✓ close
- ✓ idle
- ✓ system error

A PowerBuilder window object has many associated events, such as

- ✓ open
- ✓ close
- ✓ move
- ✓ re-size

Some PowerBuilder objects, like data structures or user defined functions, do not have any associated events.

Perhaps the most difficult part of learning to write PowerBuilder programs is learning about events and how to manage events. You must learn the available events for each object and how to write PowerBuilder scripts and functions for the events.

For instance, all windows have an *open* event. Opening a window triggers the *open* event. You can write a PowerScript program for the open event. When the window opens, the script runs. For example, you could include a script that connects to a data source in the open event for the window.

Any graphical user interface is a rich environment with many events. Because there are many events, many functions are available within PowerBuilder to manage these events. Learning each of the events and the functions that go with them is going to take you a while. This book attempts to make the learning easier by demonstrating some of the more commonly-used events and functions.

THE DEVELOPMENT MODEL

If you are used to programming with a traditional procedural language, you must learn a new way to think about programming. This is because PowerBuilder is an object-oriented language. Object-oriented programming is described in greater detail later in this chapter.

You can see what a program does in a traditional language by reading the program. For example, you may have a program that displays a data-entry form that allows a user to enter data. All the operations for displaying and using the form are there in the program. Statements in routines you can print and read describe all the operations for the form.

A PowerBuilder application presents no one place you can go to read a program. There is no one listing you can print and read to understand the program's operation.

You will find with PowerBuilder that you usually do little programming. What programming you do is in scripts written for the events associated with an object.

For example, an event is triggered for an application when the application opens. This is the open event for the application. You can write a script to run when the open event triggers, that is, when the application first runs. For example, you could include a script that prompts the user to name the data source for the application.

Most of the work that you do will be in creating the objects for the application, not programming how the objects react. The tools provided in the PowerBuilder development environment make it easy to create the objects and write the scripts.

THE DEVELOPMENT PROCESS

In the following chapters, you learn how to build a PowerBuilder application. Here is a quick overview of this process. Take a simple data-entry application with one window.

Do not worry about the individual steps now. Later chapters guide you through each step. For now, just concentrate the overview of the steps you will take to create a PowerBuilder application.

An application object contains the entry point for an application. The application object also maintains various high-level application attributes, such as the name of the application.

Application Object — Application Name / Application Font / Library Search Path / Global Variable / Global External Functions

The next figure shows that the application object also has certain associated events.

Application Object — Events / Open / Close / Idle / SystemError

You can use the PowerBuilder script painter to create a script for any of these events. A script controls what happens when an event occurs. The next illustration shows the script painter and a script for the *Open* event for an application. Remember that the samples in this book are from Microsoft Windows and may look slightly different in your environment.

The script shown below connects to a demo database. If it cannot establish the connection, it displays an error message dialog box and exits. If it successfully establishes a database connection, it opens a window named *w_main*.

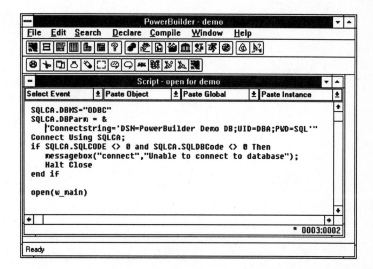

The script line *open(w_main)* opens the main window for the application. This is a call to a built-in PowerBuilder function named *open*, one of the many useful PowerBuilder functions that support you in writing applications.

Having created the application, you must save it. The application object is saved in a PowerBuilder library. When you create the application, you respond to a request for the name of the library; then PowerBuilder creates the library. A PowerBuilder library is a file with a *.pbl* extension (pronounced *pibble*) that contains PowerBuilder objects.

demo.pbl

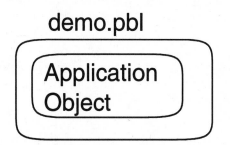

Now that you have an application object and you have saved it in a library, you can add other objects. With the data window painter, you might create a data window object. With a data window object, you select the data to be displayed, then select the format the data is to be displayed in. The following illustration shows the data window painter while creating a data window object.

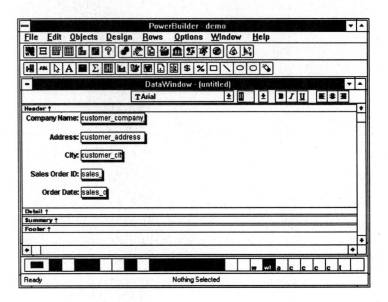

By convention, a data window name starts with the prefix *dw_*. (See the appendix listing the naming conventions for PowerBuilder objects and controls.)

Later, when the running application uses the data window object, data is selected from the source you specify. Your instructions select the data and the format of the data.

Saving the data window object adds the data window object to the library as shown below:

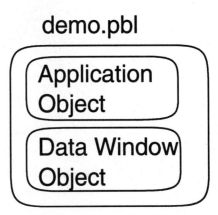

demo.pbl

Application Object

Data Window Object

A data window object allows you to select data from a data source and present to the user that data in a useful format. With the data window painter, you select the data to be displayed, then you select the data display format. However, you cannot use the data window object by itself. The data window object must attach to a window control, as shown below.

You can use the PowerBuilder window painter to create the *w_main* window for the application. This becomes the first window the user sees when the application runs. It is the first window because of the *open(w_main)* function in the *open* script for the application.

The next illustration shows the window *w_main* being created with the window painter. Again, do not worry about the details; just try to grasp the big picture.

With the window painter, you can add controls to the application window. These controls are also objects. The sample above contains several objects, a picture of the Powersoft logo, three control buttons and a data window control. The data window control is where the data window object attaches to this window.

The following illustration shows the Window Painter:

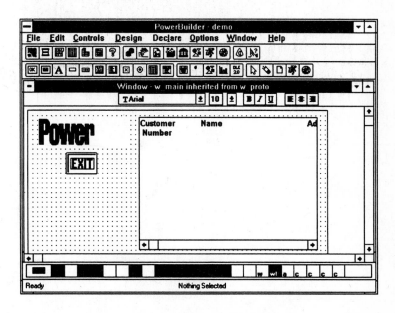

Please note that a data window control is not the same as a data window object. A data window object determines the source and format of data. A data window control governs the use of the data window object. When you build a window you can associate a data window object with a data window control.

To be used in an application, a data window object is associated with a data window control. Actually, a single data window object can recur with different data window controls on different windows. This allows reuse of data window objects throughout an application.

In the example above, the data window object *d_orders* is associated with a data window control on the *w_main* window. The window painter allows you to make this association. You display and control the data window object through the data window control.

Saving the new window places another object in the PowerBuilder library as shown below:

demo.pbl

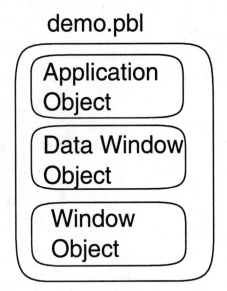

The window and the objects on the window each have their own associated events. A window has many events associated with it including *open, close* or *clicked*. One of the challenges you face is learning the events associated with each of the objects in PowerBuilder and the functions useful in responding to those events.

Do not worry, though. You need not know all the events and functions to start. You can write sophisticated applications after you have learned just a few of the more important events and functions.

Note that the data window control also has events associated with it. All the standard events available for a data window are below.

Clicked	Other
Constructor	PrintEnd
DBError	PrintPage
Destructor	PrintStart
DoubleClicked	RButtonDown
DragDrop	Resize
DragEnter	RetrieveEnd
DragLeave	RetrieveRow
DragWithin	RetrieveStart
EditChanged	RowFocusChanged
GetFocus	ScrollHorizontal
ItemChanged	ScrollVertical
ItemError	SQLPreview
ItemFocusChanged	UpdateEnd
LoseFocus	UpdateStart

Do not worry if there seem to be many events. You rarely write scripts for all these events in a single application. Typically, you script only a few events. You will be able to start writing applications when you have learned about a few of the more crucial events.

Please note that no events are associated with a data window object, only with a data window control. The data window control has events, but not a data window object. This is because a data window object never occurs by itself but only association with a data window control. The data window control manages the operation of the data window object.

You can preview a window from within the development environment. The preview allows you to see the window as it appears later as part of an application.

To complete this sample application requires writing more scripts for other events associated with the other objects in the application. For example, the following is the script for the clicked event for the exit button.

```
// Prompt the user to confirm exit,
// then exit application.

If MessageBox('Exit Application',&
'Exit?',Question!,YesNo!) = 1 then
   DISCONNECT ;
   close (w_main)
End If
```

This script asks the user to confirm the *exit* request then close the window *w_main*. Closing the main window triggers the close event for the application. This, in turn, closes the running application.

This example is a simple application. Little here resembles traditional programming. We have created (1) an application, (2) a main window, (3) controls to manage the application, and (4) a data window control that displays data. Only a few short scripts are needed to manage a few events.

This is typical when writing PowerBuilder applications: create an application, create all the objects you need for the application with the painters, write a few simple scripts that respond to selected events.

This is one of the reasons writing PowerBuilder applications is easy. The amount of work needed is small because of the object-oriented model. You spend most of the time writing an application in creating the objects. Some time goes to writing scripts for events, but the few scripts tend to be short.

With a traditional program written in a traditional programming language, learning the application meant learning the code for the program. A PowerBuilder application requires your learning (1) the objects in the application, (2) the relationship between the objects, and (3) the scripts used to respond to various events.

In a traditional program you must learn how the parts of the program fit together, the program itself, subroutines and functions. With PowerBuilder, it is more important to learn the objects in the application, how they fit together, and how they react to events.

PowerBuilder provides powerful tools to assist you in building applications. You can use the application painter, library painter, or browsers to view the relationships between all the objects in an application and the script painter to view scripts for events. You can use the painters to see the objects themselves.

OBJECT-ORIENTED PROGRAMMING

Object-oriented programming incorporates elements that make writing programs for a graphical user interface easier. PowerBuilder includes tools that make it easier to write object-oriented programs. These tools are called painters. Each of the painters is described in a following section.

In a traditional programming language, you write programs. The programs have modules you call in some sequence. Usually, the program predetermines the sequence. Data passes back and forth between routines in the running program. For example, arguments pass to a function that can perform some action then the function returns one or more values.

The programming model differs in an object-oriented environment where you are writing with an object-oriented tool like PowerBuilder. With PowerBuilder, you create objects. Objects can respond to events. Objects communicate with each other with messages.

Objects And Attributes

A PowerBuilder application uses objects like a window, a control, a drawing or an icon. Objects have attributes. For example, a window object can have attributes including its size or shape or color.

Objects can include other objects. For example, an order-entry data window object can combine a main window, several control objects, and a menu object. Some objects, like menus and windows, come with PowerBuilder. Others you can create.

Methods

An operation that inquires about an object or changes an object in some fashion is called a *method*. In PowerBuilder, methods are created by writing scripts. For example, a script that opens a window or a script that closes a window are methods for that window. In PowerBuilder, the methods are the scripts associated with the various objects.

Events

PowerBuilder scripts can include functions. A function is a named script that accepts input arguments and returns one or more values. These functions can then be reused. PowerBuilder functions are called in methods. PowerBuilder functions can attach to an object or can exist globally within an application.

In a PowerBuilder application, the user rather than the program usually determines the sequence of events for a running application. For example, the user starts the application then opens and closes windows. The user triggers events, for example, by clicking an open button or a close button.

The application itself can also trigger events. For example, a running program can trigger an idle event after a predefined period of inactivity by the user. The program—with no intervention by a user—triggers this idle event.

With PowerBuilder, you can write scripts that determine the response to events. A window object can contain a script to respond to an open event or a script to respond to a close event. These events and the scripts associated with them are available when a running application uses an object.

Messages

While an application runs, objects communicate with each other with messages. The messages sent between the objects in an application control the running application.

Take a window object containing an exit button object. When the application runs and the window displays, the exit button appears. A mouse click on the close button can close the open window.

The user's click on the close button triggers the clicked event for the close button. The clicked event invokes the script for the clicked event. This script sends a close message to the window containing the close button. The window gets the close message; this triggers the close event for the window. The script attached to the close event for the window then runs.

Classes

A traditional programming language provides various built-in data types, such as *integers*, *real numbers*, and *strings*. In a traditional language, you can create a new variable; the newly-created variable has one of the types the language provides. You could use a statement like

```
int a
```

to create a new variable named *a* that has a type of integer. In this example, integer is a type that is built in to the language. In some languages, you can even create new data types then create variables that have this new type.

An object-oriented programming language provides classes instead of data types. A class in object-oriented programming is similar to a data type in traditional programming.

A class definition is a set of attributes and methods combined to define an object. You could have a class definition named *window*. The class definition includes the attributes of a window and the methods that operate on a window. The attributes include the x position, y position, height, width, and window type. The methods could include scripts that control the operation of the window when it opens or closes.

A class is a template for an object. In an object oriented programming language you create a new class. Once you have created the class, you can create objects of that class.

In a traditional programming language, you can create new objects with the built-in data types. In object oriented programming, you can create new objects from any class.

A class library is a collection of classes held in a PowerBuilder library.

Instances

Individual objects are members of a class. When a running program creates an object that belongs to a certain class it *instantiates* the object. An instance is a manifestation of a class definition. For example, California is an instance of the class *state*. A window named *w_dentry* is an instance of the class window.

You could build a window object with the window painter named *w_main* then save the object in a library. In a running application, the script

```
open(w_main)
```

opens the window object; that is, it instantiates the window object. This is a call to a built-in PowerBuilder function named *open*. The open function brings the window object into memory for ready use. You must instantiate an object before it can respond to events or messages.

PowerBuilder provides many built-in classes and functions. One such class is the transaction object, which communicates with a database. This PowerScript fragment instantiates a new transaction object:

```
// define a new object of type
// "transaction"
transaction newtrans
// instantiate an object of type newtrans
newtrans = create transaction
// reference some of the attributes
// of the new object
newtrans.dbms = "oracle"
newtrans.logid = "dba"
```

The Class Hierarchy

PowerBuilder comes equipped with many classes. For example, PowerBuilder provides windows, controls, menus and other classes.

Classes are organized hierarchically. You can examine the class hierarchy with the *browse class hierarchy* selection in the library painter. This figure displays part of the PowerBuilder class hierarchy as shown by the library painter:

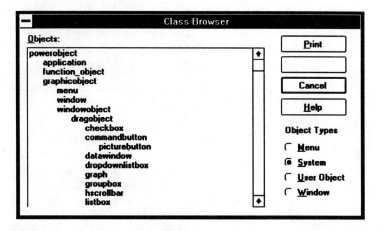

You can create new classes with the PowerBuilder object painters. You can create new

      ✓ classes of windows with the window painter

      ✓ classes of menus with the menu painter

      ✓ object classes with the object painter

You could create several windows classes of your own. These classes expand the class hierarchy:

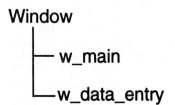

Inheritance

The class *w_main* in this figure is a **child** of the window class. Conversely, the window class is the **parent** of the *w_main* class. Window is also known as the super class of the window *w_main*.

With object-oriented programming, a new class inherits all the features of its parent. Any change made to a class automatically propagates down the class hierarchy.

A PowerBuilder object painter allows you to create a new object that is a member of an existing class. For instance, you can use the window painter to create a new window that is a member of the w_main class.

You can use an object painter to create a new class. A new class inherits all the attributes and methods of its parent. An object that is a member of a new class inherits all the attributes of the parent class. You can add new methods and attributes to the new class. You can use scripts as inherited, or you can extend or override them. With PowerBuilder, you can only create new classes under the windows, menu, and user object classes.

Creating a new object and choosing inheritance creates a new class. A selection on each of the menu, window, and user object painters allows you to create a new object that inherits its features from an existing class, thus creating a new class.

Encapsulation And Methods

Encapsulation hides and protects data. An object encapsulates the data and methods for an object. For example, the size of a window is an encapsulated attribute in the window object. To find the size of the window you must send a message to the window that inquires about the window size.

Only the object can modify the data that the object encapsulates. Other objects can only inquire about the encapsulated data. Other objects can pass messages to an object to request changes, but only the object itself can make the changes.

Polymorphism

Polymorphism means objects from different classes can accept the same message. You could send the message *print* to several different objects. The same message would cause each of the objects to print something.

Think of a small business that ships many different packages. Small packages go by mail, medium packages by courier, large packages by truck, and urgently-needed packages by air. The same message, *ship*, can accommodate each of the objects. The effect is different for each of the objects. While each object gets shipped, the method of shipping is different.

In a traditional programming language different functions must have different names. Trying to create a function that has a name already in use will cause an error at compile time or when the program is linked. In an object-oriented programming language like PowerBuilder, different functions can have the same name.

As a programming example, imagine an application that has a variety of different windows drawn from different classes. Each of the windows presents different data to a user. Some windows might have text, others graphs or pictures. The same message, *print*, can go to any of the different windows. Each window can use a function that will print the displayed data, even though each window is from a different class.

Operator Overloading

A message typically includes one or more arguments. In PowerBuilder different functions can have the same name. For the functions to work correctly, the arguments must be able to take different values for the arguments. This ability to use the same interface for different purposes is an example of operator overloading.

Here are two different functions used by two different objects drawn from two different classes. The classes are a data entry window and a graph window.

```
w_dentry.print(w_dentry, 4, 3)
w_graph.print(w_graph, "x title","y title")
```

The same message is in both cases, *print*. Both functions have the same name, *print*. The function formats are the same, both messages use two arguments. However, the arguments are different types. The first function uses two integer arguments, the second two strings.

The operators are overloaded. In the first case, each operator accepts a number; in the second case, the operators accept a string.

Operator overloading is possible because arguments resolve at run-time. The object receiving the message accepts the arguments of the appropriate type. No error results at compile time, because there is no type checking.

Polymorphism cannot readily occur without this facility for operator overloading. PowerBuilder, of course, supports operator overloading.

CLIENT-SERVER COMPUTING

With the advent of efficient, economical networks and low-cost personal computers, a new computing model has emerged. This is the client-server model.

The client-server model has three components—a server, a network and clients:

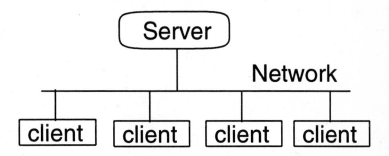

Three Components of Client-Server Computing

A server is a computer that stores and manages data. For example, the server can run a database management system. This database management system holds data for some enterprise. For example, the database can hold all the accounting information for a company or all the reservations for an airline.

The server is responsible for processing any data requests from the user. The server retrieves data based on the request then routes the data to the client. The server is responsible for concurrency control, the maintenance of database integrity, and management of transactions. (If you do not know what these concepts are, please consult section two of this book.) The server is also responsible for data security and access control. Finally, the server provides the storage space for data.

A client machine requests data from the server. The client computer runs a program locally. This program knows how to request data from the server. The program running on the client is responsible for managing the display, interacting with the user, and operating on retrieved data. The client validates data input by the user and generates requests for data from the server.

A network connects clients to the server. Two common networks are Novell and TCP/IP. A Novel network or TCP/IP network can connect all the workstations in an office to a database server. A brief introduction to networks is in chapter 1-15.

A client sends a request for data to a server. The server sends back the data selected in response to the request. The client can make changes to the data. The client can send these changes or additions back to the server to be put back into the database.

The client machine can perform much of the manipulation or processing of data. For example, if the user is entering data into a data entry form, all the entry, validation and correction occurs at the client. When the data is correct, it goes to the database on the server assigned to the database.

The client can also request changes that are then directly applied to the data held at the server. For example, the client can send a request to the server to change all the records that match a certain pattern, or to delete all the records that match a certain pattern.

In a company accounting system, the central computer (a network server) maintains a database with all the accounting information for the company. This central database server connects to a network. Various personal computers or workstations around the company connect to the same network. Each of the separate workstations or personal computers are a client.

The database machine now acts as a database server. Client machines send requests for data across the network. The server retrieves the data requested and returns it by the network to the client.

A smart client machine can manage all the interactions with a user. This off-loads much of the burden of processing from the server to the client.

A PowerBuilder program running on a client machine can display a screen form. The user can enter data into this screen form. The PowerBuilder program running on the client machine uses the contents of the form to create a request for data from a server.

Any data used by the client application resides in the database on the server. If the order entry clerk requests information about orders, that information comes from the database on the server and goes to the client over the network. Any changes made to the orders return over the network and reside in the database on the server.

The client application can display the retrieved data, for example, on a screen form. The client application can also manipulate the returned data and display the results of the manipulation. For example, the application could use data retrieved from the server to write a report that is printed, or show summary information that is computed at the client machine, or display the summary information as a graph.

Distributed Data

In a client-server environment, data can disperse across machines on a network. Several machines acting as database servers can connect to a network. Data can disperse across the servers and across databases.

Accounting, sales and shipping could have separate servers holding their portion of the enterprise information. Enterprise information can all be on one server in one database, on one server in more than one database, or on several servers in different databases.

PowerBuilder lets you build applications that access data from anywhere in your enterprise. Multiple concurrent connections to a variety of database management systems can access the data on any machine. With PowerBuilder, you can develop applications that access remote data on mainframes, mini-computers, or workstations or access local data on a desktop.

Local Data

Of course, a PowerBuilder application can also run on the same machine as the database. In the most simple case, the client and the server are the same machine, and no network is necessary.

PowerBuilder ships with a copy of the Watcom relational database management system. The Watcom relational database management system can run on a personal computer from within Microsoft Windows. The PowerBuilder application running within Microsoft Windows can access the Watcom database engine that is also running from within Microsoft Windows.

Summary

PowerBuilder provides all the tools you need to build client-server applications. You can write PowerBuilder applications that run on a client computer. These applications can communicate via standard network protocols.

The applications can access data locally or remotely from a variety of sources. Servers can run any major database system. Servers can be personal computers running Novell and Microsoft SQL server; workstations or mini-computers running Oracle, Informix or Sybase; or Mainframes running DB2.

THE POWERBUILDER TOOL SET

The next few sections provide a brief overview of each of the tools in the PowerBuilder tool set. Longer descriptions of each of the tools introduced here are in following chapters. Do not worry yet about the details of using any of the tools. The brief descriptions that follow familiarize you with what tools are available, not how they work.

If you have not already, **install PowerBuilder** according to the instructions supplied with the product. Examples in following chapters use the **demonstration database** shipped with PowerBuilder, so be sure to **install** it, too.

From within Windows, **start** PowerBuilder by double-clicking the PowerBuilder icon. A PowerBuilder window similar to this opens. Note that the examples in this book were produced with Microsoft Windows. PowerBuilder running in your environment may look a bit different.

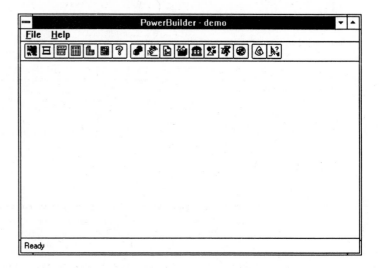

PowerBuilder provides a variety of *painters*. Each painter is a tool for a special purpose. Each icon on the PowerBar accesses a different painter.

If this tool bar is not displayed when you start PowerBuilder, **select toolbars from the File menu**. The following dialog window appears:

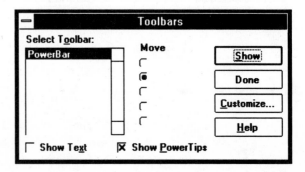

Click on the Show button, and the PowerBar will display at the top of the PowerBuilder main window. **Click on** the Done button to close the dialog window.

Note that you can use this dialog to customize the tool bar. Consult the PowerBuilder supplied documentation for assistance in customizing the tool bar.

You can also access the PowerBuilder tools from the PowerPanel. To access the PowerPanel, **select the PowerPanel item from the File menu, or type ctrl-p.** The PowerPanel appears:

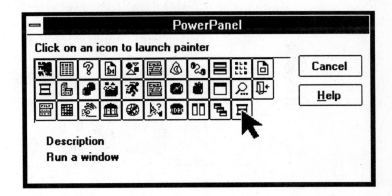

Clicking on an icon starts a painter. Leave the cursor on any icon on the PowerBar for a moment and a description of the painter appears near the cursor. **Click and hold** on any icon to see a brief description of its function as shown above. **Move** the cursor away from the icon and **release** to avoid starting the painter. Continue to **hold** and **move** the cursor *from icon to icon* to see the use of each.

You can move the PowerBar around the screen. **Move** the *cursor* somewhere on the PowerBar— but not on an icon. **Click** the *right mouse button* to display a menu. The menu has selections for left, right, top and bottom. **Select** a preferred *position* for the PowerBar. To return the PowerPanel when the PowerBar displays, type *ctrl-p.*

Each PowerBuilder painter supports a separate useful function. **Clicking** an *icon on the Power Panel* or **clicking** an *icon displayed on the Power Bar* starts a painter. Following is a brief introduction to each of the painters. In following chapters are more-detailed descriptions of each of the painters.

Opening a painter opens a new window. The title bar of the window indicates which type of painter is open. More than one painter can be open at the same time. More than one copy of the same painter can also be open at the same time. Be careful, though. If you open too many painters at the same time, you may run out of memory.

Application Painter

The framework for anything you build in PowerBuilder is an application. The application you build may contain many objects—windows, menus, graphs or reports. All these objects are within an application.

Clicking the application *icon on the PowerPanel* or **clicking** the application *icon on the PowerBar*, opens the application painter window. The application painter window looks like this:

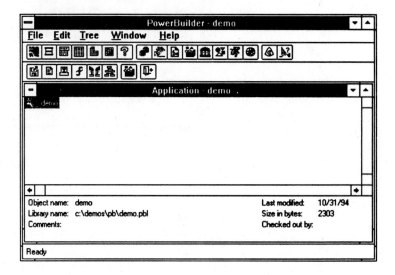

The application painter selects an existing PowerBuilder application or creates a new PowerBuilder application.

Look at the menus at the upper left hand corner of the application painter window. You can access the functions of the application painter through these menus.

A second bar of icons appears with the Application Painter. You may use these icons to access the facilities of the application painter.

Click and hold the *left mouse button* while the cursor rests on one of the icons. This displays at the bottom of the window a brief description of the command the icon executes. **Move** the cursor *away from the icon bar* and **release** to avoid an action. Application commands are also available from the keyboard. Consult your PowerBuilder manual for a list of keyboard commands.

Choose *File-Close* from the menus, or **type** *ctrl-F4* to close the application painter.

Preference Painter

The preference painter allows changing various settings that control the operation of PowerBuilder. You can change default values for a variety of system settings including

- ✓ the current application
- ✓ the database environment.
- ✓ default formats for windows
- ✓ default values for menus
- ✓ default values for data windows
- ✓ database settings
- ✓ PowerBuilder library
- ✓ debugging
- ✓ PowerBuilder environment

Here is the preference painter window:

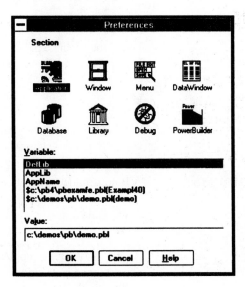

Database Painter

The database painter provides facilities for database maintenance including data definition and data access. With the database painter, you may create a new database or remove an existing database, add or delete tables in a database, or change the format of tables in the database. You can also change permissions and add indices. Finally, you can use the database painter to add to or change the data in the database.

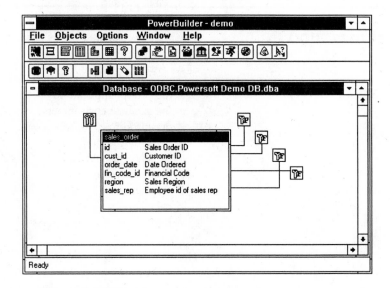

While the database painter is useful, some operations are not supported. The tools provided with certain database managers may allow you to change the format of a column in a table while the database painter will not. If there is some operation you would like to perform that is not available from the database painter, you should see if the facility exists within the tools native to the database manager.

Library Painter

A PowerBuilder application typically includes many objects. Objects like windows or controls reside in PowerBuilder libraries. A PowerBuilder library is a file that has a name with the suffix *.pbl* (called *pibble*).

All the objects for an application can reside in a single library. Or, the objects for an application can go into multiple libraries. The user decides to place a PowerBuilder object in one library or another.

The library painter provides all the facilities needed for managing libraries and the objects within the libraries. The library painter provides facilities for creating a new library or removing an old library. The library painter provides commands for copying or moving objects between libraries. This is how it looks:

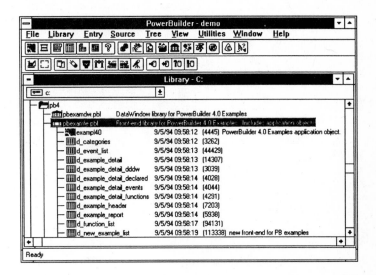

The library painter also provides two browsers. A browser is a tool used to search for objects. Selections under the Utilities menu select the class hierarchy browser or the object browser.

Window Painter

A later chapter describes various types of windows. With the window painter, you can construct any of these window types. Windows are the basic building blocks of an application. Other objects like controls, menus or graphs appear on a window. This illustration shows a sample window being developed:

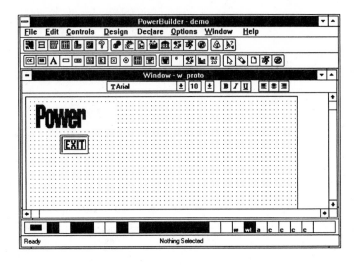

Data Window Painter

Data windows are "SQL smart" objects that you will only find in PowerBuilder. PowerBuilder when you build a data window object with the data window painter automatically provides the SQL for controlling the window. The data window also formats data for reports. No other client-server development tool provides the power of the PowerBuilder data window.

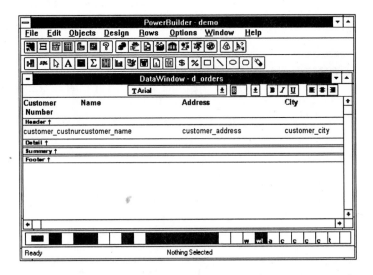

The data window painter creates a data window object. The window painter creates a data window control. The data window control on a window may then be associated with a specific data window object.

Please note this difference between a data window object and a data window control, as it produces confusion.

Menu Painter

A menu is an object that can be added to a window in a PowerBuilder application. The menus that you build with the menu painter resemble the familiar menus in any windows application. The following illustration shows the main window of the menu painter. Use the menu painter to create new menus or modify existing menu.

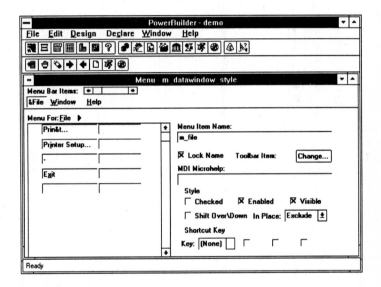

Structure Painter

PowerBuilder supports a wide variety of data types. Variables hold various kinds of data. Variables can contain many different types of data including, but not limited to, strings, dates, integers, and real numbers.

A structure is a group of variables held under a single name by which the structure can be referenced. You can reference any element of the structure by name.

The following illustration shows the structure painter. This painter creates a new structure or modifies an existing structure. The painter allows you to add new elements to a structure or change the elements already in a structure.

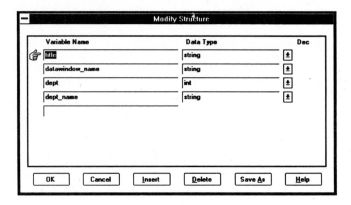

Query Painter

SQL (Structured Query Language) is an industry standard language for accessing or modifying data held in a database. Part Two describes SQL at length. SQL statements select or manipulate data in a database held on a server. In some cases, as when you build a data window, PowerBuilder creates the SQL for you. In other cases, you may want to write your own SQL statement.

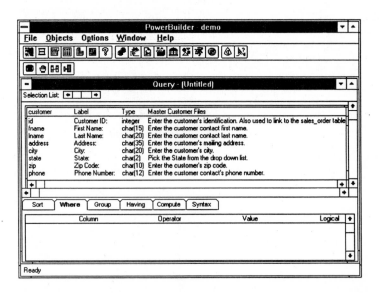

The 4.0 release of PowerBuilder also includes new English language wizards. You can define dictionaries that associate English words with database items. Using the English names can make it easier for a user to make queries.

User Object Painter

PowerBuilder provides a variety of built-in objects, such as windows, menus and controls. You can create your own custom objects with the user object painter. You can create your own object that contains a window, a data window, some controls and a menu. This illustration shows the user object painter:

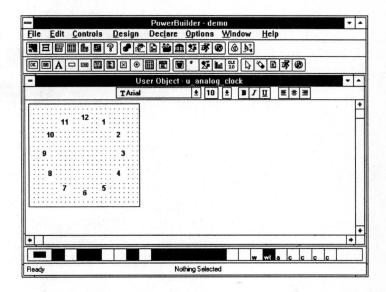

Script Painter

Most PowerBuilder objects have associated events. To illustrate, a PowerBuilder application has *open*, *close*, *system error*, and *idle* events associated with it. A PowerBuilder script— the program that executes when the event occurs— can fit any event. You use the script painter to write these scripts.

For example, you can create a script for the application *open* event. You can use the same script painter to create a different script for the application *close* event. A script executes when the corresponding event occurs.

The same script painter works throughout the PowerBuilder environment. For instance, you can call the same script painter from within the menu painter or the application painter to write event scripts for those objects.

In most applications, you write few, short scripts due to the power of the Powersoft model. Scripts attach to events, but they are usually unnecessary. Scripts that are written for events tend to be short because of the simplicity of the scripting language and the power of the built-in function library.

This illustrates the script painter:

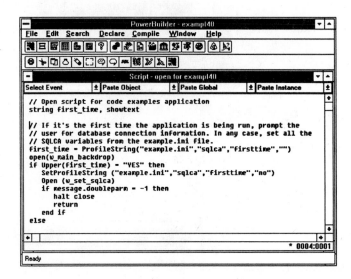

The script painter is called from within other painters rather than from the PowerBar or PowerPanel.

Debugger

PowerBuilder includes an interactive debugger. With the debugger, you may set break points, step through the execution of an application and examine variables as their values change. The PowerBuilder debugger provides all of the facilities you need for determining what problems a running program may have.

```
┌─────────────────────────────────────────────────────────────────┐
│ ─                    PowerBuilder - exampl40                  ▼ ▲ │
├───────────────────────────────────────────────────────────────────┤
│ File  Run  Debug  Window    Help                                  │
├───────────────────────────────────────────────────────────────────┤
│ [▦][☰][▦][▦][▦][▦][?]  [✦][▦][▦][▦][▦][▦][▦][⊕]  [△][✗]          │
├───────────────────────────────────────────────────────────────────┤
│ [▦][▦][▭][INT][▦][▦][▦][▦]                                        │
├───────────────────────────────────────────────────────────────────┤
│ ─              Debug - open for w_connect_db                 ▼ ▲ │
│ ├─────────────────────────────────────────────────────────────┤ ▲ │
│ │  0001: // Open script for w_connect_db                      │ ↑ │
│ │  0002:                                                       │   │
│ │  0003:                                                       │   │
│ │  0004:                                                       │   │
│ │  0005: //SetTrans is the default transaction type for this datawindow al│
│ │  0006: //From the user screen                               │   │
│ │  0007: //SetTrans sets the values in the internal transaction object for│
│ │  0008: //the values from transaction (for example, the database name). T│
│ │  0009: //will be run by "simulating" a clicked event on the radio button│
│ │  0010:                                                       │   │
│ │⊞ 0011: rb_settrans.triggerevent("clicked")                  │   │
│ │  0012:                                                       │   │
│ │  0013:                                                       │ ↓ │
│ │  0014:                                                       │   │
│ │ ◄                                                          ► │   │
│ ├─────────────────────────────────────────────────────────────┤   │
│ Ready                                                            │
└─────────────────────────────────────────────────────────────────┘
```

On-Line Help

PowerBuilder includes a complete on-line help facility. Press the *F1 key* from anywhere within PowerBuilder to access on-line help. You may also access help from the PowerBar and PowerPanel:

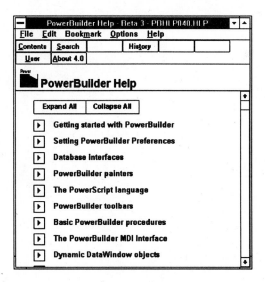

Help is available for all PowerBuilder features. You can search (in a hypertext format) for help on a particular topic or let the help facility take you from one topic to other related topics.

Summary

The preceding sections have introduced the tools in the PowerBuilder environment. Next: using these tools to build applications.

This is your first hands-on chapter. In this chapter, you learn how

✓ to build a new PowerBuilder application.

In following chapters, you learn how

✓ to add to that application

✓ to build windows, place controls, objects and menus on the windows

✓ to link to a data source like a relational database management system

✓ to write PowerScripts that control the processing of events

A PowerBuilder application is a collection of objects, such as windows, data windows, menus and controls. The objects, when used in a running application, provide services for some activity like order entry or inventory control. All the objects for an application are in one (or optionally several) PowerBuilder libraries.

demo.pbl

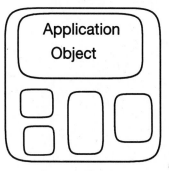

The foundation of any application is an application object. The application painter creates and modifies application objects. Application objects store in a PowerBuilder library.

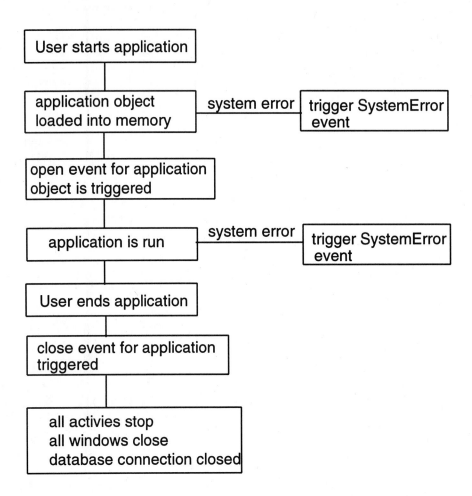

The application object contains the entry point for the application. When the application runs, the application object is loaded into memory and execution is started at its entry point.

The diagram above shows the sequence of events that occur when an application runs.

An application is not a visual object. The only part of the application that is ever seen is the icon associated with the application. Unlike some other PowerBuilder objects, such as windows or controls, you never see the application object on-screen. There are other PowerBuilder objects that are not visual objects, like data structures and functions.

Every PowerBuilder application object has the following attributes associated with it:

✓ the application name
✓ the application icon
✓ the library search path
✓ the default text font
✓ global variables
✓ global external functions

Each application object has values that associate with each of these attributes. The application painter changes these values.

There are also certain events associated with an application object. These events are

✓ open
✓ close
✓ idle
✓ systemError

The open event triggers when the user starts the application. The script associated with the open event starts all the activity that later occurs within the application. A typical opening script for an application object is in the next chapter on PowerScript programming.

The application closes when the close event triggers. The SystemError event triggers if a system error occurs when the application starts, or if a system error occurs while the application is running.

You can set the idle event to trigger after some number of seconds of user inactivity. (The following chapter on PowerScript programming describes functions.) A call to the idle function sets the time that an application waits until the idle event triggers. The idle function is one of the many functions supplied with PowerBuilder.

All the other objects that comprise an application—windows, menus, controls, etc.—exist within the context of the application object. You must start building an application by creating an application object.

USING THE APPLICATION PAINTER

To start the application painter, **single click** the application painter *icon* on the PowerPanel, **or single click** the application painter *icon* on the PowerBar. You may also start the application painter from the keyboard by typing *shift-F1*.

The following figure shows the running application painter.

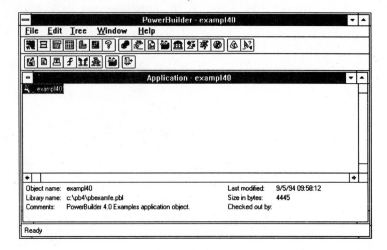

Only one copy of PowerBuilder can run at-a-time. When PowerBuilder is running, a single application is selected. The name of the application displays at the top of the application painter window.

There is *always* a current application. When PowerBuilder starts, the last application with which you were working is the selected application. If there were no prior application, you receive a prompt to select one.

After the application painter starts, you can change to a different existing application, or you can create a new application. If you create a new application, then it becomes the current application.

Notice the menu and row of icons along the top of the application painter window:

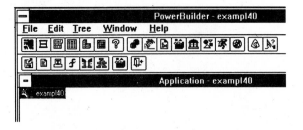

These icons, or corresponding menu choices, control the running application painter. Click once an icon to start the desired activity. Click and hold an icon to display a brief description of the function of the icon at the bottom of the screen.

From left to right, the icons can

- ✓ select an application
- ✓ write a script for an application event
- ✓ change the icon associated with the application
- ✓ change the default font
- ✓ set library list
- ✓ set default global variable type
- ✓ create an executable module
- ✓ close the application painter

Many menu commands are also available directly from the keyboard. You can access menu items with the accelerator keys shown on the menu items. You can also use the following application painter shortcut keys:

Menu Item	Shortcut key
Close	Ctrl+F4
Collapse Branch	Ctrl+-
Debug	Ctrl+D
File Editor	Shift+F6
Expand Branch	Ctrl++
Go to Painter	Enter
PowerPanel	Ctrl+P
Run	Ctrl+R
Script	Ctrl+S
Update	Ctrl+T

SELECTING AN EXISTING APPLICATION

To open an existing application, **pull down** the file menu and choose *open*, or use the application *icon* at the left end of the icon bar. The following figure shows the menu choice for opening a new application.

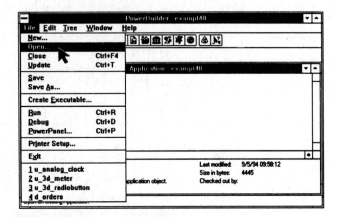

Opening an existing application presents the window shown below.
This window displays a file hierarchy in the lower right corner.
Double-click the hierarchy box to select any directory of your choice.

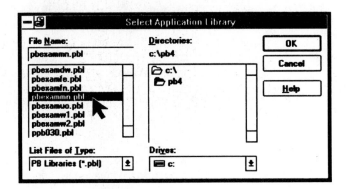

As you change from directory to directory, the box in the left may
display a list of library names. This is the list of libraries in the directory
you have selected.

A PowerBuilder application object always stores in a PowerBuilder
library. You may select one of the library names displayed in the lower
left corner by clicking it. Clicking a library name selects the library. If
the library contains a PowerBuilder application object, the name is
displayed in the upper left corner of the window—as shown above.

Click the *OK* button to select the named application. This causes the
selection window to disappear. The application painter window
reappears, and the name of the application you selected shows at the top
of the window.

CREATING A NEW APPLICATION

A new application is created by building a new application object. The new application object must reside in a PowerBuilder library. When you create a new application, you may need to create a new library to hold the application object. You can perform both of these steps from within the application painter, as shown below.

While you read through this section, you should follow along and create a new application of your own. You need an application with which to work in succeeding chapters.

If you have not done so already, make a directory to hold the sample application you are about to build. For example, on my system the files are held in the directory c:\demos\book.

There are a number of files that you need that you will find on the sample diskette that came with this book. The files you need are found in the diskette directory named examples. Copy all the files from the examples diskette directory to the directory you created on your hard drive.

While the application painter is running, create a new application object by **selecting** the new choice from the file menu. You can also **click** the selection *icon* for the application painter. In either case, the following window appears:

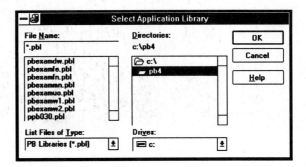

You need to select the directory where the application will be saved. If the directory does not yet exist, use the Windows file manager to create this directory before proceeding.

To select the directory, **double click** in the directories and drives areas in the lower right corner. Select a directory in which to store the application. Create any needed new directory with the Windows file manager, outside of PowerBuilder, before creating the new application.

Please note that I run Central Point Tools for Windows on my computer. Central Point Tools has added the file drawer icon you see at the upper-left corner of the window. This additional icon will not appear on your window if you are not using Central Point Tools. This icon provides common file-manipulation commands, such as creating a new directory. If you program with PowerBuilder, I highly recommend Central Point Tools for Windows, a product which includes many useful tools.

Select a directory by **double-clicking** directory names in the file hierarchy until you have selected the desired directory. The directory you select will contain the new library containing the new application object you are about to create. This example selects the directory I use:

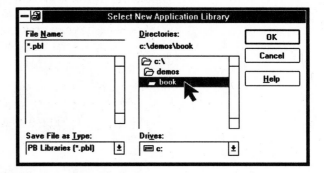

Second, **enter** the name (up to forty characters long) of the library in the upper-left portion of the form. For this example, use the name "demo." Optionally, you may also enter any comments about the application in the comments box:

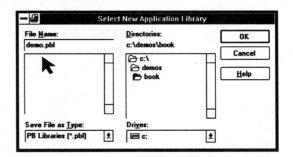

Click on the *OK button*. The following window appears.

Third, **type** a library name for the application. **Click** the *OK* button to create the new library and save the new application. With the application successfully saved, PowerBuilder returns to the application painter. The name of the new application, "demo," displays at the top of the application painter screen:

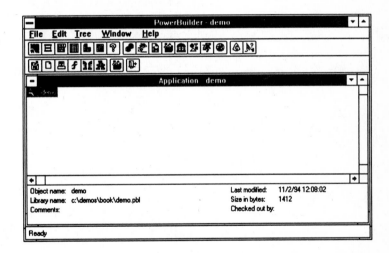

BROWSING THE APPLICATION'S STRUCTURE

Selection of an application causes the icon and name for the application to display in the application painter window.

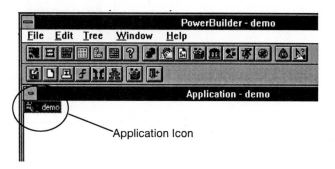

Application Icon

Later, when you have added objects to your application, **double clicking** the application icon lets you browse the application structure. Use the tree commands from the menu, or continue to double-click displayed selections to expand and contract the displayed hierarchy.

If you want to try this now, do it with an existing demonstration application already in a library. For example, the demonstration application shipped with PowerBuilder 4.0:

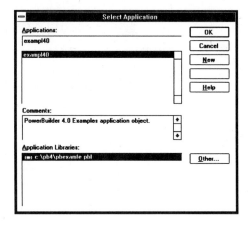

If you try it with your brand-new application nothing happens because there are no objects in the library yet besides the application object. The following display shows the hierarchy for the PowerBuilder 4.0 sample application:

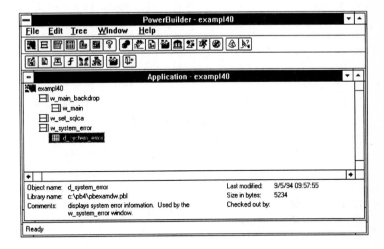

Clicking the right mouse button when the cursor is on an object in the hierarchy shows a pop-up window:

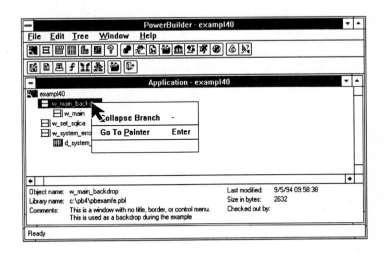

You may use this window to expand and contract the hierarchy display:

Expand Branch	**+**
Collapse Branch	**-**
Go To Painter	**Enter**
Object Hierarchy...	

Consult the PowerBuilder *User's Guide* for further useful information about displaying the application hierarchy or about changing the attributes or icon associated with the application object.

1-3 Basic Script Writing

A PowerBuilder application is event driven. The user controls the running application by triggering events. For example, each action a user takes, like opening an application or clicking a control, triggers an event. Scripts define the processing that takes place when an event is triggered. Scripts are the way to create methods in PowerBuilder.

This chapter introduces script writing.

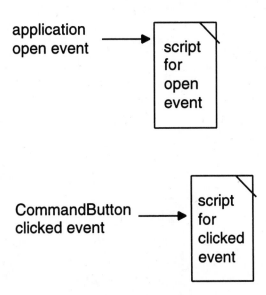

You use the PowerScript language to write scripts. It is simple and you should find it easy to learn. Scripts can include statements, commands and functions. Following sections describe each of these. For more detailed information on writing scripts, consult the Powerbuilder *PowerScript Language* reference manual.

THE POWERSCRIPT PAINTER

The script painter is always called from within another painter. For example, the script painter is available from the application painter or the window painter. The following illustration shows the running application painter and highlights the icon that starts the script painter:

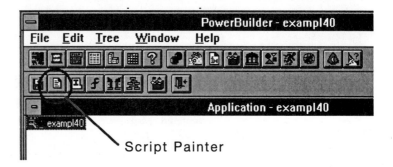

Script Painter

NOTE: In Chapter 1-2, you created an application. Make sure to have the application painter running with your application selected.

To start the script painter from the application painter, **click** the script painter *icon* found on the application painter icon bar (see the illustration above). You may also start the painter from the application painter with the keyboard (ctrl+s,) or with a script selection in the edit menu. Every painter that has access to the script painter provides the same commands to access the script painter. The next illustration shows the running script painter as called from the application painter:

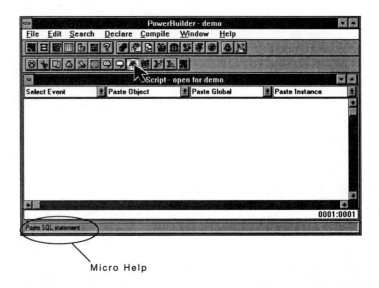

Micro Help

Note the icon bar that runs across the top of the window. The cursor points at an icon on this bar. This is the painter bar for the script painter. This bar presents icons that provide direct access to various script painter commands. As elsewhere in PowerBuilder, commands are available from an icon bar, menu selections, or keyboard commands.

Note the cursor shown in the illustration. The user has **clicked** and **held** the *left mouse button* while the cursor is pointing at an icon on the painter bar. While the mouse button is pressed, a description of the icon's function appears in the lower-left corner of the window. Take a moment to explore the menu choices.

The short help description shown at the bottom of the screen is *micro-help*. Micro-help appears in MDI (multiple document interface) style applications. Many serious windows applications, such as PowerBuilder, Microsoft Word and others, are MDI applications. A later chapter describes MDI applications and demonstrates how to build them.

SCRIPTS AND EVENTS

A script always associates with an event. You select an event from within the script painter. The script you write associates with the event you selected. The following illustration shows the script painter running from within the application painter and the pull-down menu of events for an application object:

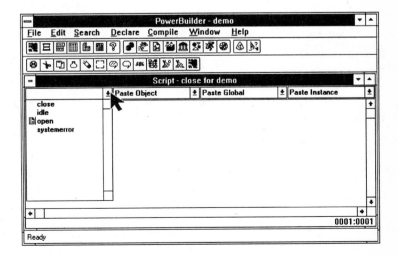

Note the small script icon shown next to the open event name. This indicates that a script has been written for this event. Any event that has an associated script similarly has a tag. No script appears on your application because you have not yet written one.

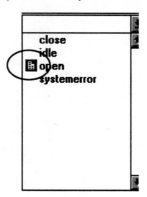

Since the script painter in the above illustration is running from the application painter, only four events are available, *open*, *idle*, *close* and *systemError*. These are the only events associated with an application object. Other objects like windows have more events associated with them than does an application object.

You do not write a script for your application here. You write it in a later chapter. For now, close the script painter and the application painter.

POWERSCRIPT BASICS

PowerScripts can contain a variety of different elements. These include

Script Element	Example
variable declaration	integer i_last
assignment statements	i_last = i_last + 1
flow of control	if i_last > 0 then . . .

embedded SQL	select emp_name
	    into :emp_name
	      from employee
	        where . . .

function calls	result = sle_emp.Clear( )

A sample script for the open event of an application follows. This script would be run each time the application opens. This particular script connects the application to the PowerBuilder demo database. The next chapter completely describes how a PowerBuilder application or the PowerBuilder development environment connects to a database.

```
/* Script to establish a database connection
   This script runs when the application is opened */
SQLCA.DBMS="ODBC"
SQLCA.DBParm = &
"Connectstring='DSN=PowerBuilder Demo&
DB;UID=DBA;PWD=SQL'"
Connect Using SQLCA;
if SQLCA.SQLCODE <> 0 and SQLCA.SQLDBCode <> 0 Then
  messagebox("connect","Unable to connect to database");
  Halt Close
end if
open(w_main)
```

Comments

The first two lines of the script are a comment. Note that /* starts the comment and */ ends the comment. You may also use two slashes to mark the remainder of a single line as a comment, thus,

```
a = a + 1      // This is a comment
```

Continuing Statements

Statements may continue over more than one line. Note the ampersand that ends line six in the foregoing script.

```
SQLCA.DBParm = &
"Connectstring='DSN=PowerBuilder Demo&
   DB;UID=DBA;PWD=SQL'"
```

The ampersand indicates that the statement continues on the next line. Statements do not automatically continue across line boundaries. You must explicitly continue a statement by placing an ampersand at the end of each line of a multiple line statement.

Note: you can use the ampersand to continue a quoted string over a line break. You cannot, however, split a variable name over two lines with the ampersand. So the following **would not work**.

```
SQLCA.DBP&
arm = &
"Connectstring='DSN=PowerBuilder Demo&
 DB;UID=DBA;PWD=SQL'"
```

Also, an ampersand within a comment is taken as part of the comment and will not continue the comment to the next line.

Finally, you do not have to continue SQL statements that are embedded in a script. If you are not yet familiar with SQL, consult the appropriate chapters in Part Two of this book or the user's manuals supplied with your database management system.

Here is an example of a SQL statement that might occur in a script. Note that the statement continues across several lines, but does not employ any continuation characters.

```
select emp_id, emp_lname, emp_sal
into :id, :name, :salary
from employee
where emp_id = :id
using mytrans;
```

White Space And Tabs

Blanks, tabs, form-feeds and comments all signify white space. The script compiler ignores whitespace, except as part of a string literal. For example, the result of the following statement differs from the previous statement. The additional white space in this statement actually binds the connect string. When the connect string is used at run time, the extra space is present in the string.

```
SQLCA.DBP&
arm = &
"Connectstring='DSN=PowerBuilder          Demo&
    DB;   UID=DBA;    PWD=SQL'"
```

The next chapter describes the connect string and its use.

You should use tabs in scripts to indent statements so that they are easier to read. In the later sections on control statements like the DO . . . LOOP and IF . . . THEN statements, tab characters indent the statements, making them easier to read.

DATA TYPES & DECLARATIONS

The following sections describe how data is manipulated from within a PowerBuilder script. These sections describe data types used in a PowerScript, means of data declaration, and means of data assignment or manipulation.

Identifiers

Identifiers within a PowerScript identify objects including *variables*, *labels*, *functions*, *windows*, *controls*, and *menus*. An identifier must start with a letter and use forty characters or fewer: it

- ✓ must not contain white space
- ✓ can include some non-alphabetic characters, including

  - Dash

  _ Underscore

  $ Dollar Sign

  # Number Sign

  % Percent Sign

Note that identifiers are not case sensitive. The identifier *Subtotal* is equivalent to the identifiers *subtotal* and *subTotal*.

While you can use special non-alphabetic characters like a dash or underline in an identifier, this is not the best technique. Instead, use upper and lower cases to distinguish identifiers. For example, use *SampleVariableName* instead of *Sample_variable_name*.

You should use the underscore character in identifiers as a prefix that indicates the type of object. Identifiers that associate with windows should start with *w_*, for example *w_Main*.

You should adhere to a naming convention when writing PowerBuilder applications. If you use a consistent naming convention, your applications will be much easier to read and maintain. Appendix C provides a list of naming conventions for PowerBuilder objects, controls and variables.

Reserved Words

You may not use certain words as identifiers because PowerBuilder reserves them for its own purposes. Directions for using of some of these reserved words are in later sections. Here are some PowerBuilder-reserved words:

and	enumerated	library	select
call	event	loop	selectblob
case	execute	next	shared
choose	exit	not	step
close	external	of	subroutine
commit	false	on	super
connect	fetch	open	system
continue	first	or	then
create	for	parent	this

cursor	forward	prepare	to
declare	from	prior	true
delete	function	private	type
describe	global	procedure	until
descriptor	goto	protected	update
destroy	halt	prototypes	updateable
disconnect	if	public	using
do	immediate	readonly	variables
dynamic	insert	ref	while
else	into	return	with
elseif	is	rollback	within
end	last		

Standard Data Types

Certain data types are intrinsic to the PowerScript language. These include data types found in other programming languages including character strings and numbers. This table lists the standard data types:

DATA TYPE	DESCRIPTION
Blob	Binary Large Object. Unformatted data, for example a picture or block of text.
Boolean	TRUE or FALSE.
Char or Character	A single character
Date	Calendar date displayed in yyyy--mm-dd format yyyy year 0000 to 3000 mm month 01 to 12 dd day 01 to 31 Hyphens (-) are required, no blanks allowed. For example 1990-02-19 is February 19, 1990.
DateTime	Date and time combined into a single data type; only used to read and write to a database. Time portion of DateTime is in microseconds.

Decimal	Signed decimal numbers up to 18 digits long. The decimal point is not a digit.
Double	Signed floating point number. Has 15 digits of precision and ranges from 2.23E-308 to 1.79E+308
DragObject	Can contain any dragged object type including all controls, but not a drawing object.
Integer, Int	16-bit signed integers. Ranging from -32768 to +32767
Long	32-bit signed integers. Ranging from -2,147,483,648 to +2,147,483,647
Object	Contains an enumerated type for a PowerBuilder object. Values can include all windows and controls.
PowerObject	Holds any PowerBuilder object including structures.
Real	Signed floating point number with up to 6 digits of precision ranging from 1.18E-38 to 3.40E+38
String	Contains from 0 to 60,000 ASCII characters.

Time	Time in 24 hour format: hh:mm:ss:ms where: hh is a number 00 to 23 mm is a number 00 to 59 ss is a number 00 to 59 ms is a number 00 to 999999 The colons (:) are required and blanks are not allowed. Example 23:59:59:999999 is 1 second before midnight. Note, the time includes microseconds.
UnsignedInteger	16-bit unsigned integers.
UnsignedInt	Ranging from 0 to 65535 Abbreviated forms: unsignedint or uint
UnsignedLong	32-bit unsigned integers.
Ulong	ranging from 0 to 4,294,967,295

Enumerated Data Types

PowerBuilder provides many enumerated data types. These data types specify the attributes of an object. Enumerated data types are built-in, thus you never declare them.

For example, a window object has an attribute named *pointer*. The value of this attribute determines the shape of the pointer when the pointer is somewhere over the window. The pointer can assume a variety of shapes. Here is the list of enumerated types for the pointer attribute showing the possible shapes that a pointer can assume. Note that the enumerated data types always have a trailing exclamation point. The exclamation point ending the name of an enumerated data type notifies the script compiler that this is an enumerated type:

```
Arrow!
Beam!
Cross!
HourGlass!
SizeNESW!
SizeNS!
SizeNWSE!
SizeWE!
UpArrow!
```

The compiler checks enumerated data types when a script compiles. This means that an incorrect enumerated data type will be caught for you when you compile a script. This reduces the likelihood of a run-time error in a script.

You have three ways to see a list of enumerated types.

(1) You can **open** the *PowerScript Painter* and **click** the *Browse* icon. You can also use the Browse Objects selection found on the Edit menu.

(2) You can **open** the *Library painter* and **use** the *Browse Objects* choice found on the Utilities menu.

(3) You can consult the PowerBuilder documentation or the on-line help topic "Enumerated Data Types."

Declaring Variables

Assigning a name and referencing a type declares a variable is declared in a PowerScript, for example,

```
int Subtotal
```

This PowerScript statement defines a variable named *Subtotal*. This variable can hold an integer value. You may, of course, declare a variable to hold any of the basic data types supported by PowerBuilder, such as strings and real numbers.

You may declare more than one variable on a single line of a PowerScript. An example is

int SubTotal, GrandTotal, RunningTotal

Initializing Variables, Literals

You may set a variable to an initial value when you declare the variable. An example is

```
int GrandTotal = 3, SubTotal = 0
string method = "A34"
date today = 1994-08-07
```

Each of the values used in the above expression to initialize a variable is a *literal*—a single value of one of the basic data types.

Arrays

An *array* is a series of values with a single name. You specify its size when it is declared. An example is

```
int A[5] = {1, 2, 3, 4, 5}
```

The values held in this array are accessed by using an index into the array.

```
int A[5] = {1, 2, 3, 4, 5], B = 0
B = A[3]
```

The above assigns the value found in the third array element to the variable named B.

In that example, you determined the size of the array when you wrote the script. When the script compiles and the application runs, five spaces are reserved in memory, one for each of the array items.

You may also declare an array where the memory for the array allocates when the program is run, rather than when the program compiles. This example declares a variable length array of integers:

```
int MyArray[ ]
```

Here are script statements that assign values to this array:

```
MyArray[200] = 50
MyArray[100] = 25
MyArray[250] = 75
```

The first statement sizes the array to two hundred elements. The element numbered two hundred then gets the value of fifty.

The second statement assigns the value of fifty to the array element number one hundred. This does not cause the array to grow in size as two hundred elements have already been assigned.

The last statement expands the size of the array to two-hundred-fifty elements. The last element, number two-hundred-fifty, gets the value of seventy-five.

Please note that an attempt to access an array element beyond the size of a fixed array will cause an error at run-time.

Multi-Dimensional Arrays

Arrays may have multiple dimensions. For example, an array can have two dimensions. You may think of such an array as holding rows and columns. The following example declares a two dimensional array:

```
int MyScore[3,2]
```

This statement declares an array with two dimensions. You *cannot* initialize an array when it is declared. Multi-dimensional arrays can have fixed length.

A final example of arrays declares a three-dimensional array:

```
int AllScores[3,2,5]
```

SCOPE OF VARIABLES

The scope of a variable determines where the variable can be accessed from a PowerBuilder application. All variables have scope. The way you declare the variable determines the scope of a variable. The scope of a variable can be

✓ global
✓ instance
✓ shared
✓ local

Global Variables

A global variable is available anywhere in a PowerBuilder application. You can access a global variable from any script, anywhere in an application. You can declare a global variable by selecting the Global Variables menu item from within the Window, User Object, Menu, or PowerScript painters. This illustrates the global variable window:

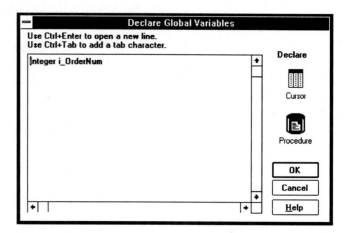

Please note that a correctly-written application will have a minimum of global variables, if any.

Instance Variables

Instance variables always correspond to an instance of an object. Instance variable define new attributes for an object. You might want to associate a variable with a window object. You could create an instance variable for the window to access a part number or an order number.

Instance variables can exist for the following objects

✓ window
✓ application
✓ user object
✓ menu

Selecting the instance variable choice from the Declare menu in the application, window, user object, or menu painter declares application level variables. The instance variable declaration window resembles the global variable declaration window.

Scope Of Instance Variables

Instance variables can have one of three access levels, *public*, *private* and *protected*. The following table describes each of each of these access levels:

Public	Any script in an application can access a public instance variable.
Private	Instance variables are defined for an object. Only from a script written for the same object can you access private instance variables.
Protected	You can access a protected instance variable from any script written for an object or from any script written for a descendant of the object.

Declaring Instance Variables

The declaration of the instance variable determines the access level of an instance variable. Here is a declaration of each type:

```
private int x,y,z
public int Count, Total
protected int RecNum
```

Note that declarations can group. This shows grouped declarations:

```
private:
    int x, y, z
    string a, b, c
public:
    real f, g, h
    int q, r, s
```

Local Variables

You can declare a variable in any script. Only in that script can you reference local variables. Local variables hold temporary values.

Search Order For Variables

You can qualify a variable used in a script. For an object named x, the following script selects the attribute a for the object x:

```
x.a = x.a + 100
```

You can reference variable names without their being qualified. It is acceptable to use variables in a script without qualification. This script would also work:

```
a = a + 100
```

If an unqualified variable occurs in a script, PowerBuilder must resolve that variable. The script compiler must discover which variable to use. PowerBuilder resolves variables in the following order, searching each type of variable for the named variable:

✓ local variables

✓ shared variables

✓ global variables

✓ instance variables

If a script references an unqualified variable name, PowerBuilder first searches any local variables to find the named variable. If the variable is not among the local variables, PowerBuilder then searches, in order, through shared variables, global variables and instance variables, looking for the named variable. If the named variable is not in any of these locations, an error occurs.

THIS, PARENT, SUPER,

Any object in a PowerBuilder application must have a name. For example, a window can be called *w_main* or a menu could be called *m_main*. These names are nouns (a label that identifies an object).

When using a language like English, you can refer to a friend as *Sally*, her unique name (a proper noun), or use the pronouns *she* or *her*. If you are in a room and there is only one Sally, the noun will uniquely identify Sally. The pronouns *she* or *her* can allude to any woman in the room.

The four reserved words *This*, *Parent*, *Super* and *ParentWindow* are pronouns. A pronoun can be used in place of a noun. Instead of referring to a PowerBuilder object by its unique name, you can refer to it with a pronoun. A pronoun gives you a more general facility for identifying an object in a PowerScript.

This

The pronoun *This* in a script refers to the window, user object, MenuItem, application or control with which the script associates. You might write a script for a menu itemin which the pronoun *This* refers to that menu item. If you are writing a script for a window, the pronoun *This* refers to the window with which the script associates. To illustrate, the following statement can be in a script for the selected event of a menu item. Triggering the selected event causes the script to run, executing this statement and placing a check mark next to the menu item:

```
This.Check()
```

The following script changes the value of the attribute *x* of a command button. (Detailed description of command buttons are in a later chapter.) The attribute *x* determines the horizontal position of the CommandButton. The following script changes the value of the *x* attribute for the command button:

```
This.x = This.x + 40
```

In many cases, you can refer to an object without qualification. This script would also modify the *x* attribute for a command button:

```
x = x + 50
```

Reading scripts is easier through the use of a qualifier.

Parent

The pronoun *Parent* refers to the parent object to the object for which the script is written. The pronoun *Parent* can work in the script for a window, user object, or menu item.

A window might have a command button on it. The following statement, when used in the script for the clicked event for the command button, closes the window that contains the command button:

```
close(Parent)
```

When used in a script for a custom user object, the pronoun *Parent* refers to the custom object. In a script for menu item, "This" refers to the menu item a level up in the menu hierarchy.

ParentWindow

The pronoun *ParentWindow* can only serve in a script associated with a menu. *ParentWindow* refers to the window that contains the menu.

```
Close(ParentWindow)
```

closes the window the menu is on.

Super

You can create PowerBuilder objects through inheritance. A script written for an object can call scripts for any ancestor of that object. The Super keyword can reference the immediate ancestor; for example,

call Super::Clicked

executes the script for the clicked event of the parent object:

EXPRESSIONS AND OPERATORS

The previous sections have described data kinds available to a PowerBuilder application. These sections have shown how to declare and initialize your own variables and arrays.

The following sections demonstrate how variables are used in PowerScript expressions.

Operators perform various arithmetic calculations, such as addition, subtraction and exponentiation. Logical operators perform operations on Boolean values, that is, values true or false. Other operators permit the manipulation of strings.

Here is a list of the arithmetic and logical operators:

( ) Grouping. Enclose expressions in parentheses to identify groups. Parentheses can also determine the calculation order for expressions. Evaluation of nested groups is from the inside out. For example, *a+b* would calculate first in this expression: (w+(z*(a+b))).

NOT Negation. Turns a TRUE value into a FALSE or a FALSE into a TRUE.

^ Exponentiation. The following example results in two squared.

2 ^ 2

* / Multiplication and division numeric operators, such as

2 * @
4*3
4/2
a / b

+ - Addition and subtraction operators, such as

a + b
4 - 3

< > Logical operation with numbers, not equal to. For example, *a* is not equal to *b*.

```
a <> b
```

<=   Logical operation with numbers less than, or
       equal to. For example, a is less than or equal
       to b.

```
a <= b
```

>=   Logical operation with numbers, greater than or
       equal to. For example, a is greater than or
       equal to b.

```
a >= b
```

=   equal to

< >   Logical operation for numbers and text.

NOT   Logical operation.

AND   Logical operation.

OR   Logical operation.

PowerBuilder uses these rules in order of precedence to evaluate
expressions. This means that operators shown higher on the list evaluate
before elements lower on the list. Operators higher on the list have
precedence over operators lower on the list.

For example, the multiplication operator is higher on the list than the
addition operator. When the evaluation of

```
a = b * c + 3
```

occurs at run time, the value of b will be multiplied by the value of c.
Then the result increases by 3. Parenthesis can change the order of
evaluation. The following statement adds 3 to c. The result is then
multiplied by the value of b:

The expression

```
a = b * (c + 3)
```

adds 3 to c and multiplies the result by the value of b.

The plus (+) operator concatenates two strings, as in

```
string Sample
sample = "Part one" + " " + "Part Two
```

ASSIGNMENT STATEMENTS

An assignment statement assigns a value to a variable. The equal sign indicates assignment. Hence,

```
String1 = "This is a string."
```

assigns a string value to the variable String1. And

```
Rate = .05
```

assigns the value of *.05* to the variable named *Rate*.

Multiple Assignment

As shown on the list in the previous section on operators, the equal sign is also a logical operator. For this reason, PowerScript does not support multiple assignment. So,

```
A = B = C
```

is not a legal statement.

Array Values In Assignment Statements

Assigning multiple array values is possible with a single assignment statement. In

```
int ArrayA[ ]  // variable length array
ArrayA = [ 1, 2, 3, 4 ]
```

the array A can have several values.

Additional Operators

PowerScripts provide several other operators useful as shortcuts. Anyone who has programmed in C will find these operators familiar.

Assignment Operator	Example	Equivalent To
++	i++	i = i + 1
--	i--	i = i - 1
+=	i+= 2	i = i + 2
-=	i-=2	i = i - 2
*=	i*=2	i = i * 2
/=	i/=2	i = i / 2

If you have adopted the practice of using minus signs in variable names, you will need to leave a space before the -- and -= operators. For more information about using minus signs in variable names, see the previous section in this chapter on variable names.

Dot Notation

PowerScripts use dot notation to select an attribute of an object, as in

```
object.attribute
```

Object is the name of some PowerBuilder object and *attribute* is an attribute of the named object. The following exemplify fully-qualified variables in assignment statements:

```
/* assign a value of false to the Visible attribute
   of a check box named ChkboxOn*/
ChkboxOn.Visible = False
/* if the text attribute of the single line edit
   is the single character "N" then open the window
   named win1   */
If sle_emp.Text="N" then   &
   open (win1)
/* Assign the contents of the single line edit
   text attribute to the variable named Text_sample.
   Append the string "DAT" to the contents of the
   variable Text_sample. */
string Text_sample
Text_sample = sle_emp.Text + "DAT"
```

FLOW OF CONTROL

The following statements affect the control flow of an executing script. That is, these statements can control the order of executing script statements.

Call

Inheritance can create PowerBuilder objects. Each object in the chain of inherited objects can have its own scripts.

The call statement executes a script for an ancestor object. A call statement in a script for an object executes a script for an ancestor of that object; take for example,

call AncestorObject {`controlname}::event

Parameter	Description
AncestorObject	The name of an object that is an ancestor of the object containing the script.
controlname	An optional name of a control found in the ancestor object.
event	An event associated with the ancestor object.

The statement

```
call w_emp::Open
```

used in a script for an object executes the script for the *Open* event for the ancestor object named *w_emp*:

Choose Case

The Choose Case control structure uses the value of an expression or variable to select from a series of choices. The value of the expression determines selection of the choices:

```
CHOOSE CASE testexpression
   CASE expressionlist
     statementblock
   {CASE expressionlist
     statementblock
     . . .
   CASE expressionlist
```

```
     statementblock}
   {CASE ELSE
     statementblock}
END CHOOSE
```

Parameter	description
testexpression	evaluation of testexpression determining the matching expressionlist
expressionlist	expression defining one of the selections for the case
statementblock	statements executed when the testexpression is matched

The testexpression is an expression consisting of constants, variables and operators. Entering the case statement causes evaluation of the test expression. The evaluation of the test expression results in a value. The value selects from the choices in various expression lists.

For example:

```
choose case 3
case is 1
   statement block one. . .
case is 2
   statement block two. . .
case is 3
   statement block three. . .
end choose
```

In this trivial case, the test expression is an integer, 3. The value of 3 matches the value of the third expressionlist, "case is 3." This match executes the statements in statement block three. The *choose case* statement has selected one of the statement blocks for execution based on the test expression matching one of the expression lists.

Any *choose case* statement must have at least one CASE clause. There must always be an END CHOOSE at the end of the case statement.

A match of the testexpression and one of the expression lists executes the statement blocks for that expression list. After execution of the statements, control passes out of the choose case statement, and execution of the next statement after the END CHOOSE ensues.

If there are multiple expression lists, evaluation of each occurs until a match. If no match is found, execution of any statements in the optional *case else* block ensues. If there is no *case else* block and no expression lists match, control passes from the *choose case* statement, and no execution of statement blocks occurs.

The test expression can be more complex and include variables and relational operators. In this more useful example

```
int i_block
i_block = 3
choose case i_block
case is 1
   statement block one. . .
case is 2
   statement block two. . .
case is 3
   statement block three. . .
end choose
```

the test expression still evaluates to 3. This selects the third block of statements for execution. This is because the test expression *i_block* matches the third expression list, *case is 3*. The test expression can be any valid statement that evaluates to a value corresponding to one of the expression lists. The expression list can include

✓ a single value
✓ a list of values separated by commas. for example, 1, 2, 3
✓ a TO clause. For example 1 to 20
✓ IS followed by a relational operator and a value. For example, is > 5
✓ Any combination of the above where there is an OR implied between expressions. For example, 1, 2, 3, 4, 5 to 10, is > 100.

Here are two more examples:

```
choose case Weight
   case is < 16
      Postage = Weight * 0.30
      Method = "USPS"
   case 16 to 48
      Postage = 4.50
```

```
      Method = "UPS"
   case else
      Postage = 25.00
      Method = "FedEx"
end choose

real select_case
select_case = Real(sle_real.Text)
choose case selector
case is < 11
   sle_message.Text = "Less than 11"
case 11 to 20
   sle_message.text = "eleven to twenty"
case is < 200
   sle_message.text = "less than two hundred
case else
   sle_message.text = "other cases"
end choose
```

Do Loop

There are four variants of the DO ... LOOP statement. Each of the DO ... LOOP statements executes a statement block until achievement of an end condition.

1. Do While The Condition Is True:

```
DO WHILE condition
   statementblock
LOOP
```

2 Do Until The Condition Becomes True:

```
DO UNTIL condition
   statementblock
LOOP
```

3. Repeat While The Condition Is True:

```
DO
   statementblock
LOOP WHILE condition
```

4. Repeat Until The Condition Is True:

```
DO
    statementblock
LOOP UNTIL condition
```

Parameter	Description
condition	determinant of timing for statement block's execution
statementblock	statements executed with the testexpression

The first two variants of the loop statement test the condition at the beginning of the loop. With these two loops, skipping the statement block occurs if the condition is not met in the first execution of the loop.

The second two loop statements test the condition at the end of the loop. Using either of the two variants when the test is performed at the end of the loop guarantees execution of the statement block at least one time. Use the LOOP WHILE or LOOP UNTIL variants to enforce the statement block's always being executed at least once.

The following statement executes the statement block until A is greater than *20*:

```
Int  A = 1
DO UNTIL A > 20
   A = A + 1
LOOP
```

In the example

```
Int  A = 1
DO WHILE A <= 15
   A = A + 1
LOOP
```

less than or equal to 15 causes execution of the statement block.

In this sample,

```
Int  A = 1
DO
   A = A + 1
LOOP UNTIL A > 15
```

the statement block is executed until the value of A becomes greater than 15.

In this example,

```
Int  A = 1
DO
   A = A + 1
LOOP WHILE A <= 15
```

the statement block executes as long as the value of A remains less than or equal to 15.

Exit

An *EXIT* statement can serve anywhere within the statement block. The *EXIT* statement causes execution of the statement block and the loop to end. Control then passes to the first statement following the LOOP keyword.

In this example,

```
Int A = 1, count = 0
DO WHILE A < 20
   If count > 15 then EXIT
   count = count + 1
   A = A + 1
LOOP
   // The exit statement passes control here
   A = 0
```

the loop statement continues execution of the statement block as long as the value of *A* remains less than *20*. The *If* statement found in the statement block executes an *EXIT* statement when the value of *count* grows larger than *15*. This exits the loop statement and passes control to the next statement following the loop.

Continue

When a CONTINUE statement occurs in a DO . . . LOOP, control passes to the next LOOP statement; the statements between the CONTINUE statement and the LOOP statement are skipped in the current DO . . . LOOP. In a nested DO . . . LOOP structure, a CONTINUE statement bypasses statements in the current DO . . . LOOP structure.

This Beep function begins upon on the first 3 iterations of the loop:

```
Int  A=1, B=1
DO WHILE A < 11
   A = A + 1
   B = B + 1
   If B > 3 then CONTINUE
   Beep(2)
LOOP
```

For Next

The FOR . . . NEXT statement executes a block of statements for a specified number of times. Arguments you specify in the FOR . . . NEXT statement determine the number of block executions. The FOR . . . NEXT statement executes the statement block the specified number of times:

```
FOR varname = start TO end { STEP increment }
   statementblock
NEXT
```

Parameter	Description
varname	the variable that counts each iteration of the loop
start	the starting value for the iterations of the loop
end	the ending value for the loop iteration
increment (optional)	the value added to varname for each loop; defaults to one
statementblock	the block of statements excuted for each loop

Note that specifying an increment for the loop instead of using the default increment of one requires the keyword STEP. Also note that FOR . . . NEXT statements can nest. Each FOR statement requires a NEXT statement.

This example,

```
FOR n = 5 TO 25
   A = A + 10
NEXT
```

executes a statement block that only has one statement, *a = a + 10*. This statement adds *5* to the variable *A* during each loop. The loop executes the first time with *n* equal to five. The value of *n* increases by one after each execution of the statement block. Execution of the statement block continues until *n* reaches a value of *25*. The statement block executes the last time when *n* assumes a value of *25*. That is, the statement block executes as long as *n* is >= *5* and <= *25*.

In this example,

```
FOR n = 5 TO 25 STEP 5
   A = A + 10
NEXT
```

the loop variable *n* increments by *5* instead of the default value of one. The statement block recurs five times. The loop variable *n* assumes the values *5*, *10*, *15*, *20* and *25*. The statement block recurs once for each of these values of the loop variable.

The example

```
INT  TestArray[120,50,200]
FOR x = 1 to 120
   FOR y = 1 to 50
      FOR z = 1 to 200
         TestArray[x,y,z]
      NEXT
   NEXT
NEXT
```

uses a FOR . . . NEXT to populate an array. This example also demonstrates that FOR . . . NEXT statements can nest:

Exit

An *EXIT* statement can serve anywhere within the statement block. The *EXIT* statement causes execution of the statement block and cessation of the loop. Control then passes to the first statement following the NEXT keyword.

In the following example,

```
Int   A = 1, count = 0
FOR count = 1 TO 25
   A = A + 10
   if A > 15 then EXIT
NEXT
```

the loop statement continues execution of the statement block as long as the value of *count* remains less than *25*. The *If* statement in the statement block executes an *EXIT* statement when the value of *A* grows larger than *15*. This exits the loop statement and passes control to the statement following the *NEXT* keyword:

Continue

When a *CONTINUE* statement happens in a *FOR . . . NEXT*, control passes to the beginning of the statement. Any statements between *CONTINUE* and *NEXT* have no effect.

When a *CONTINUE* statement happens within a loop, statements have no effect in the current *FOR . . . NEXT*. In a nested *FOR . . . NEXT* structure, a *CONTINUE* statement only skips statements in the current *FOR . . . NEXT*.

In this example,

```
Int   A=1, B=1
DO WHILE A < 11
   A = A + 1
   B = B + 1
   If B > 4 then CONTINUE
   Beep(3)
LOOP
```

the *Beep* function only occurs on the first 4 iterations of the loop.

In this example,

```
FOR n = 5 TO 25
   A = A + 10
NEXT
```

the statement adds *10* to *A* as long as *n* is >= *5* and <= *25*. The statement block occurs for each of the values *5, 6, 7, 8, . . . 25*.

The example

```
FOR n = 5 TO 25 STEP 5
   A = A + 10
NEXT
```

adds 10 to A and increments *n* by *5* as long as *n* >= *5* and <=*25*. The increment of *5* causes *5* to be added to *n* each time through the loop. Thus, this loop recurs five times, once for each of the values of *n* of *5, 10, 15, 20* and *25*.

The example

```
INT   SampleArray[120,50,200]
FOR x = 1 to 120
   FOR y = 1 to 50
      FOR z = 1 to 200
           SampleArray[x,y,z]
      NEXT
   NEXT
NEXT
```

populates the elements of an array.

Continue

A *CONTINUE* statement in a *FOR . . . NEXT* statement block passes control to the following *NEXT* statement. This causes any statements in the statement block between the *CONTINUE* statement and the *NEXT* statement to be skipped, as in

```
int  a = 0, b = 0
FOR Count = 1 to 100
   a = a + 1
   IF Count > 15 then CONTINUE
   b = b + 1
NEXT
// Upon completion, a = 100 and b = 15
```

Goto

A label uniquely identifies a statement in a PowerScript. In the example,

```
Here: if Count>15 then CONTINUE
```

the identifier *Here* labels this statement.

In the example,

```
GOTO label
```

the *GOTO* statement transfers control from one part of a PowerScript script to another. Control passes from the *GOTO* statement to the label specified within the *GOTO* statement.

In the example,

```
goto Here
statements...
Here:
```

the statement transfers control to the statement associated with the label *Here*. Note in this example that the labeled statement is blank.

Avoid *GOTO* statements. Hardly ever would a correctly-written script require a GOTO statement. Well structured scripts use other statements like *loop* and *if* to control the flow of a program. These other statements clarify the structure of a script.

Halt

The *HALT* statement immediately terminates a running application. Use:

```
Syntax
HALT {CLOSE}
```

A *HALT* statement causes the running application to close immediately. The Halt statement with the optional *CLOSE* keyword triggers the Close event for the application. The *HALT CLOSE* statement runs the script for the application's close event. If there is no script, the application ends immediately.

The statement

if sle_password <> MyPassword then HALT

halts the running program if the variable named *sle_password* matches the variable named *MyPassword*.

The script

```
if sle_password <> MyPassword then HALT close
```

triggers the close event for the application if the user enters the wrong password.

If Then Else

There are two types of *IF . . . THEN* statements, single line and multiple line. A single line *IF . . . THEN* statement allows a single choice. Multiple line *IF . . . THEN* statements allow a choice between multiple conditions.

Single Line If Statement

The single line statement executes a statement block when the stated condition evaluates to true. It optionally executes another statement block if the condition evaluates to FALSE, as in

```
IF condition THEN statementblock1
{ ELSE statementblock2 }
```

Parameter	Description
condition	a statement that evaluates to a logical true or false
statementblock1	statement executed when the condition evaluates to true
statementblock2	statement executed when the condition evaluates to false

In the simple example,

```
IF X + 1 = Y THEN X=0   ELSE X = -1
```

sets X to *0* if X plus *1* equals Y. If $X + 1$ is not equal to Y, then the variable X takes a value of *-1*.

In the example,

```
IF X+1=Y+2 THEN halt
```

if X plus *1* is equal to Y plus *one*, the application halts.

In the example,

```
int x=1, y=2
if x = 1 then
   x = x + 1
   y = y + 1
end if
```

the statements in the first statement block execute if the condition *x=1* evaluates to true; the first statement block contains several statements.

You can separate statements in a statement block by semicolons or place them on separate lines.

This equivalent example

```
int x=1, y=2
if x = 1 then
   x = x + 1 ; y = y + 1
end if
```

demonstrates the use of the semicolon to separate statements in a statement block:

Multiple Line If . . . Then Statement

The multiple line *IF . . . THEN* statement allows a selection among successive conditions. The selected condition determines the block of statements.

```
IF condition1 THEN
   statementblock1
{
ELSEIF condition2 THEN
   statementblock2
. . .
}
{ELSE
   statementblock3
}
END IF
```

Parameter	Description
condition1, condition2, condition3	statement that evaluates to a logical true or false
statementblock1	statement executed when condition1 evaluates to true
statementblock2	statements executed when the condition2 evaluates to true
statementblock3	statement executed when condition2 evaluates false

Note that multiple *ELSEIF . . . THEN* clauses are allowable in an *IF . . . THEN* statement.

The example

```
IF WINDOW6.X > WINDOW7.X THEN
   WINDOW6.X=0
END IF
```

compares the horizontal positions of WINDOW6 and WINDOW7. If WINDOW6 is to the right of WINDOW7, the X attribute of WINDOW6 will be greater than the X attribute of WINDOW7. If WINDOW6 is to the right of WINDOW7, the statement moves WINDOW6 to the left side of the screen by setting the X attribute to zero.

This example,

```
IF X = Y THEN
   BEEP(2)
ELSEIF X=Z THEN
   Show (Parts); SetState(Parts,5,TRUE)
ELSEIF X=" " THEN
   Show (Choose)
ELSE
   HIDE (BUTTON1)
   SHOW(BUTTON2)
END IF
```

✓ Causes a Beep if *X* equals *Y*
✓ Displays the Edit ListBox and highlights item 5 if *X* equals *Z*
✓ Displays the Choose ListBox if *X* is blank
✓ Hides button1 and stops the script if neither condition is TRUE.

The multiple-line if statement can cause the same kind of selections as a *CHOOSE . . . CASE* statement. The *CHOOSE . . . CASE* statement is more efficient at selecting from a set of fixed choices. If you are making a selection where the choices are naturally grouped, use the *CHOOSE . . . CASE* statement. For example, if you are selecting from ranges of test scores, use a *CHOOSE . . . CASE* statement.

Parameter	Description
label	An identifier that labels a PowerScript statement

Return

A *RETURN* statement in a script stops execution of the script and waits for the next event. A *RETURN* statement can also serve in a function to stop execution of the function. The next section and a later chapter describe at length functions. The later chapter also describes the use of the return statement in functions.

In the example,

```
beep(1)
Return
beep(3)
```

the second beep statement does not execute.

EMBEDDED SQL STATEMENTS

You may include SQL statements in scripts. These statements can be standard SQL statements that the script uses to request database services. Embedded SqL statements also provide extensions to standard SQL that accompany transaction objects. The next chapter describes transaction objects. Finally, some embedded SQL extensions provide support for stored procedures.

All SQL statements must

✓ begin with an SQL verb (like *connect* or *select*)
✓ end with a semicolon
✓ not include a continuation character (*&*)

If a variable is referenced in an embedded SQL statement, a colon must prefix the variable name, as in

```
select inv_no
into :inv_no
from invoices
where inv_no = 12343
```

FUNCTIONS

A function is a pre-defined group of statements identified by a unique name that performs a specific task. Functions are useful because they allow creating a method that different scripts can then reuse.

You can create your own function and assign it a name with the function painter. You then write the script for the function with the script painter. After saving the function, you can call it by name from within a script. For example, you could write the function

```
f_postage()
```

You can then call the function by name from within a script.

PowerBuilder supplies many built-in functions for a variety of purposes. You may also use the function painter to write your own functions. A later chapter shows you how to write your own functions. This section shows how to use the functions that come with PowerBuilder.

PowerBuilder also supports external functions. External functions are functions written outside of PowerBuilder that are called from a running PowerBuilder application. To wit, you can write a function in C or Pascal and call that function from a PowerBuilder application. You should consult documentation accompanying PowerBuilder for information about external functions. This book does not describe external functions.

A function takes arguments. These arguments pass values to the running function. The function can use these values to perform calculations. Here,

```
functionName({arg1, arg2, arg3, ..., argn})
```

is the syntax for a function call.

When a PowerBuilder function runs, it must return a value to the calling script. All PowerBuilder functions return a value, usually an integer or string.

Often PowerBuilder functions return a value of *1* if they are successful in their computations and a value of *-1* if unsuccessful.

For instance, the function *f_postage* can return the amount of postage with a value of *-1* if it fails and a positive value if it succeeds. You can use the return value in the calling script to perform the appropriate action. The script

```
if f_postage(10) < 0 then
   . . .code for fail condition
   return -1
else
   . . .code for successful return
   return Postage
end if
```

calls the postage function with a package weight. The function computes the weight and returns the amount of the postage. If the function failed for some reason, it returns a -1:

PowerScript Functions can supply information about an object, string, or number. The function can return this information to the calling program. You can also use functions to change the appearance or behavior of an object by modifying its attributes. You can alter the appearance or behavior of an object as well as change or manipulate data with functions.

Types Of Functions

Use categorizes PowerScript functions:

Function type	Use
Date Function	returns information about a date or a comparison of two dates
DDE Function	provides DDE (Dynamic Data Exchange) support
Numeric Function	returns the result of a number transformation (for example, the absolute value of a number)
Object Function	changes the appearance or behavior of an object or obtains information about an object
Print Function	controls the printing of lists and reports
Special Functions	perform specific tasks like sounding a beep or filling an array with a specific value

String Functions	string manipulations including insertions, deletions and comparisons.
Text File Functions	support for reading, writing and manipulating files.
Time Functions	provides information about a time or the comparison of two times
Type Conversion Functions	converts an argument into another data type or another format.

A running PowerBuilder application can establish a connection to a database. You must write a script for this connection. This script is often placed in the open event for the application.

You can also can also connect to a database from within the PowerBuilder development environment. The connection occurs when you create a DataWindow object, as shown in a later chapter, or use the database painter, also described in a later chapter.

CONNECTING FROM THE DEVELOPMENT ENVIRONMENT

To connect to a database from the development environment, you must first set the preferences for that connection. There are three ways to change these preferences. First, you could edit the pb.ini file, the PowerBuilder profile file. This is not a good idea, as it requires stopping and starting PowerBuilder for the changes to take effect. Second, you can call the database profiles window as described below in the section on correcting connection problems. Third, you can change preferences with the preference painter.

Start the preference painter from the PowerBar or PowerPanel with the preferences icon.

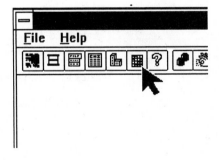

After starting the preference painter, the following window appears. This window provides a variety of selections for changing the PowerBuilder operating environment. **Click** the database icon to select the database connection preferences. **Click** any preference to see its current setting. The value of the preference appears in the Value field at the bottom of the window. If there is no value, the Values window is empty.

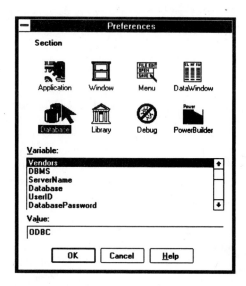

The settings for the database preferences are used when establishing a connection to a database. These settings are used whenever you connect to a database with the DataWindow painter or the database painter.

Clicking the *Help* button shows the on-line help entry for the selected preference. Upon selection of the database preferences in the above illustration, help appears for the database preferences.

Click the *OK* button to close the preferences painter.

Database preferences identify the default database connection within the development environment. The values of each of the preferences varies between database systems. The preferences for a connection to an Oracle database greatly differ from the preferences for a connection to a Sybase or DB2 database.

You should consult the official PowerBuilder manual for your particular database vendor. These individual manuals for each type of database provide detailed information about the connection between PowerBuilder and a specific database. You may also consult a database administrator or systems administrator for help in setting these preferences. The PowerBuilder CDROM may also have further information on connecting to the database of your choice.

Here is a listing of each of the preferences that you can set with the preference painter as taken from PowerBuilder on-line help. Do not worry right now about the details of these preferences. Description of database preferences follow later in this section.

Variable	Description
AutoCommit	FALSE to have normal recoverable transaction processing take place at CONNECT time. TRUE to turn off normal recoverable transaction processing. The default is FALSE.
AutoQuote	Specifies whether single quotation marks are automatically placed around a string specified in the Expression 2 box in the Where Criteria window in the Query or Select painter. When the option is 1 (the default), quotes are automatically applied to a string in the Expression 2 box (if you didn't enter quotes yourself). When the option is 0, quotes are not applied.
Columns	The number of table or view columns that display when you expand a table. If the number of columns in the table exceeds the specified number, a vertical scrollbar displays so you can scroll to display all the columns.
Database	The name of the default database.
DatabasePassword	The database password you use.
DBMS	The name of your default database management system vendor (one of the vendors specified in Vendors).

`DbParm`	Database dependent.
`ForeignKeyLineColor`	The RGB value of the color you want to use for the line between the foreign key symbol and the table. The default is blue.
`IndexKeyLineColor`	The RGB value of the color you want to use for the line between the index symbol and the table. The default is red.
`PrimaryKeyLineColor`	The RGB value of the color you want to use for the line between the primary key symbol and the table. The default is green.
`Prompt`	1 to prompt for database information when you connect to a database, 0 (the default) to turn off the prompt. This option is typically set in the Database Profile Setup window.
`Lock`	The isolation level. Database dependent.
`LogId`	Your logon id.
`LogPassword`	Your password.
`NoCatalog`	Catalog access. No to create the repository tables automatically the first time a user connects to the database using PowerBuilder. Yes to allow DDL and DML (CREATE, INSERT, or DELETE) statements. If the repository tables do not exist, PowerBuilder does not create the repository tables. If the tables exist, PowerBuilder will not reference the tables. The default values will always be used. The default is No.

ReadOnly
Database access. When this variable is set to 0, PowerBuilder will create the repository tables automatically the first time a user connects to the database using PowerBuilder. When this variable is set to 1 and the repository tables do not exist, PowerBuilder does not create them; the default values are used. If the tables exist, PowerBuilder will use the tables but will not allow users to modify information in the tables.

ServerName
The name of the server.

ShowIndexKeys
0 to not display the index keys and 1 to display them.

ShowReflnt
When this option is 0 referential integrity is not painted in the Database Painter (that is, foreign keys, primary keys and the lines associated with them). When the option is 1 (the default), referential integrity is painted.

StayConnected
Option to start the database transaction the first time a painter requests it and close the transaction only when you exit PowerBuilder. The default is 1 stay connected, 0 is close the transaction when you leave the painter.

TableDir
Option to suppress display of the table list. When TableDir is 1 (the default), PowerBuilder

automatically lists the tables in the current database when you open the Database Painter. When TableDir is 0, PowerBuilder does not display the table list when you open the painter. To open a database table when TableDir is 0, click the Tables icon . A dialog box displays, select the name of the database table you want to open and click Open.

TableSpace	Database dependent. See the appropriate database interface manual for more information.
TerminatorCharacter	The character used to terminate a SQL statement.
UserID	Your user ID.
Vendors	The name of your DBMS vendor (for example, Gupta, Oracle, or Sybase). Specify each DBMS to which you have access; enter the default vendor first and separate vendors with commas.

The settings you set with the Preference Painter reside in the PowerBuilder profile file, *pb.ini*. The profile file is in the directory in which you have installed PowerBuilder.

Profile files divide into various sections. The preferences you alter with the Preference Painter reside in the corresponding area of the profile file. The following lists the database section of the *pb.ini* file. This section shows the correct connection settings to the demonstration database that comes with PowerBuilder. If you are having trouble connecting to the sample database, these settings should assist. You can use these settings to set preferences with the Preference Painter. Each of the preferences you see in the Preference Painter has a corresponding setting in the following profile.

```
[database]
Vendors=ODBC
DBMS=ODBC
LogId=
LogPassword=
ServerName=
Database=PowerBuilder Demo DB
UserId=dba
DatabasePassword=
TableDir=1
StayConnected=1
AutoCommit=0
TerminatorCharacter=;
; Columns defines how many columns are displayed
; when a table is expanded
Columns=8
ShowRefInt=1
ShowIndexKeys=1
IndexKeyLineColor=255 0 0
PrimaryKeyLineColor=0 128 0
ForeignKeyLineColor=0 0 255
DbParm=ConnectString='DSN=PowerBuilder Demo
DB;UID=dba;PWD=sql'
; DBParm=DelimitIdentifier can be added to DbParm
; to control whether quotes are placed around
; table and column names in SQL
; DbParm=DelimitIdentifier='YES'
Lock=
Prompt=0
```

Correcting Connection Problems

Database preference settings must be absolutely correct when connecting to a database. You must consult the PowerBuilder-supplied documentation to determine setting preferences for a connection to your particular type of database.

Preference settings vary greatly between RDBMS products. You may also need to consult the systems administrator for your database. Your systems administrator may have to establish a login id or password for you at the database.

If you do not have the preferences set correctly, the a message box similar to the following may display when you try to connect to the database. An attempt to connect occurs if you open the database painter or the data window painter. Do not attempt to do so now.

NOTE: in severe cases, the PowerBuilder development environment may halt entirely if the preferences are incorrect during an attempt to connect to a database. Because of this danger, save any other work you may be doing before changing database preferences! For example, you may get an error message similar to the following:

Clicking the *OK* button may cause a series of message boxes to appear. The error messages might include one similar to:

Click the OK button in this message box. This causes a database profiles window to appear on screen.

This window is also available at any time from within the database painter. **Do not** start the database painter now, just read the example. With the database painter running, **selecting** the *Connect Setup* menu choice from the File menu allows you to edit a the profile for a database connection.

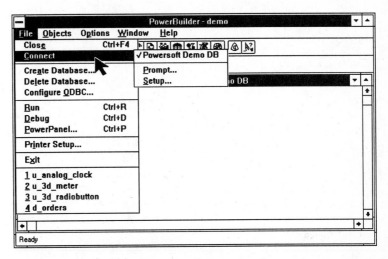

Refer again to the Database Profiles window in the illustration before last. Any installed databases show in the Profiles window. Clicking the *OK* button causes an attempt to connect to the highlighted database. **Click** the *New* button to set up a new database connection. **Click** the *Edit* button to change the preferences for the highlighted database selection. This presents a database profile setup window. In this window, you can edit the database preferences, as shown here.

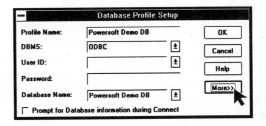

Clicking the *More>>* button enlarges the window and display more database preferences:

```
┌─────────────────────────────────────────────────────┐
│ ▬          Database Profile Setup                     │
├─────────────────────────────────────────────────────┤
│ Profile Name:    ┌─────────────────────┐   ┌────────┐ │
│                  │Powersoft Demo DB    │   │   OK   │ │
│ DBMS:            │ODBC            │▲│       └────────┘ │
│                  └────────────────┴─┘    ┌────────┐   │
│ User ID:         ┌────────────────┬─┐    │ Cancel │   │
│                  │                │▲│    └────────┘   │
│ Password:        └────────────────┴─┘    ┌────────┐   │
│                  ┌─────────────────┐     │  Help  │   │
│ Database Name:   │Powersoft Demo DB│▲│   └────────┘   │
│                  └─────────────────┴─┘                │
│ □ Prompt for Database information during Connect      │
│                                                       │
│   CONNECT OPTIONS                                     │
│   Server Name:     ┌────────────────┬─┐               │
│                    │                │▲│               │
│   Login ID:        ┌────────────────┬─┐               │
│                    │                │▲│               │
│   Login Password:  ┌────────────────┐                 │
│                    │                │                 │
│   DBPARM:          ┌────────────────┬─┐               │
│                    │ConnectString="DSN=Po│▲│           │
└─────────────────────────────────────────────────────┘
```

This screen presents an opportunity to modify database connection preferences. You can use this screen in addition to the database preference painter screen to change database connection preferences.

When you have completed the preferences to your satisfaction, **click** the *OK* button. The database profiles screen appears yet again. Make sure to highlight the database of interest and **click** *OK*.

Practice now by making sure that you can connect to the sample database provided with PowerBuilder by opening, and then closing, the Database Painter. If presented with a dialog box requesting a selection from a list of tables, just **click** on the *cancel button* to continue. When you are done, exit the Database Painter. If you are unable to connect to the sample database provided with PowerBuilder 4.0, consult the PowerBuilder documentation or seek assitance.

TRANSACTIONS

As described in Chapter 2-6, a relational database management system is responsible for supporting data integrity. One mechanism provided for supporting data integrity is the transaction or logical unit of work.

Transactions are supported with the PowerScript language. Scripts can use transactions to allow recovery from an incomplete or incorrect transaction. Scripts can use transactions to support concurrency control. Scripts can maximize performance by using transactions to minimize the number of connects and disconnects. Scripts can also enhance performance by using COMMIT statements to free resources no longer needed.

TRANSACTION OBJECT

PowerBuilder supports many types of objects including windows, data windows and controls. One of these built-in data types is the transaction object. PowerBuilder applications use a transaction object to manage the connection to a database.

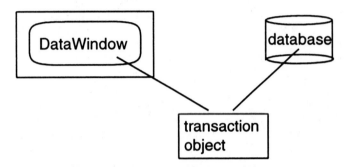

A transaction object species database information including the database name and user id. The transaction object also returns status information from the database management system to the running application. The following statements can accept the name of a transaction object

✓ connect
✓ commit
✓ delete
✓ disconnect
✓ insert
✓ rollback
✓ update

The example,

```
connect using SQLCA;
. . .statement block
disconnect using SQLCA;
```

connects to the database using the default transaction object, executes various statements, then disconnects from the database.

Note that embedded SQL statements end with a semi-colon.

A transaction object is a non-visual object. An application can create and use multiple application objects, although one may be enough. A single transaction object makes a single connection to a database. Multiple connections require multiple transaction objects.

Every PowerBuilder application can access a default transaction object named SQLCA. Creation of an application object automatically creates this transaction object.

Transaction Object Attributes

Every PowerBuilder object has attributes. The attributes of the transaction object specify the values needed to establish and maintain a database connection. The values of some of the attributes serve when connecting to the database. For example, the database name connects to a specific database.

A connection to a database from a running application or from the PowerBuilder development environment requires certain elements of information. For example, the name of the database must be available. A user ID or user password might also be necessary. With a running application, this information resides in a transaction object.

Some of the transaction object attributes return values that describe the result of recent database activity. For instance, there is an SQLCode attribute that returns the status of the last database operation.

Some of these attributes, like the database name, are necessary in almost every database connection supported by PowerBuilder. Some attributes, like the server name, are only necessary in a few database management systems. Some attributes, like Autocommit, may serve some database management systems, but are not vital to those database management systems. PowerBuilder interface manuals are available for every database vendor. You should consult the PowerBuilder documentation or the PowerBuilder CDROM for more-detailed information. The information required to connect to a database differs from RDBMS to RDBMS. The information on the CDROM should be particularly helpful.

Here is a complete list of the attributes of a transaction object as taken from PowerBuilder on-line help. For a detailed explanation of these attributes, you should consult the PowerBuilder connection manual for your database.

Attribute	Data Type	Description
DBMS	String	The name of the database vendor (for example, ODBC, Informix, ORACLE, or Sybase).
Database	String	The name of the database to which you are connecting.
UserId	String	The name or ID of the user who will connect to the database.

`DBParm`	String	DBMS specific.
`DBPass`	String	The password that will be used when connecting to the database.
`Lock`	String	The isolation level.
`LogId`	String	The name or ID of the user who will log on to the server.
`LogPass`	String	The password used to log on to the server.
`ServerName`	String	The name of the server on which the database resides.
`AutoCommit`	Boolean	The automatic commit indicator: TRUE - Commit automatically after every database activity. FALSE - (default) Do not commit automatically . Tip AutoCommit must be TRUE to create temporary tables.
`SQLCode`	Long	The success or failure code of the most recent operation: 0 - Success 100 - No result set returned. -1 - Error (use SQLDBCode or SQLErrText to obtain the details)
`SQLNRows`	Long	The number of rows affected. The database vendor supplies this number; therefore, the meaning may not be the same in every DBMS.
`SQLDBCode`	Long	Database vendor's error code.
`SQLErrText`	String	The database vendor's error message.
`SQLReturnData`	String	The database-vendor specific.

All database management systems return the following attributes, except SQLReturnData. Only some database management systems use SQLReturnData.

These attributes are used to return status information about the results of the most recent database operation. The remaining attributes in the list above preserve information used to establish the database connection.

SQLCode

SQLNRows

SQLDBCode

SQLErrText

SQLReturnData

Creating A Transaction Object

Every PowerBuilder application automatically instantiates (that is creates an instance of) a transaction object. This instance is named SQLCA. Unless a specification of a different transaction object is specified, all database operations use this object by default. Use the SQLCA transaction object if there is only one database connection in an application.

An application can create and use multiple transaction objects. Multiple transaction objects can maintain multiple database connections or maintain multiple transactions with a single database.

Opening an application creates the default transaction object SQLCA. Closing an application destroys the default transaction object SQLCA.

Setting Transaction Object Attributes

Initializing a transaction object precedes its availability. Placing statements in a script, prompting the user for input, or retrieving the values from a profile file can initialize a transaction object.

Coding Attributes Into A Script

Assignment statements in a script assign values to the attributes of a transaction object. The format of the assignment statement

```
object_name.attribute_name = value
```

assigns a value to an attribute of an object.

Therefore, the format

```
transaction_object.variable = value
```

assigns to the attributes of the transaction object.

The scripted assignment statements

```
sqlca.DBMS = "Sybase"
sqlca.Database = "PBDemo"
sqlca.LogId = "PBUs01"
sqlca.LogPass = "ixlfrap"
sqlca.ServerName = "rotorooter"
sqlca.AutoCommit = FALSE
```

assign values for a connection to a Sybase database.

Setting Attributes From A Profile File

In the previous example, the script had encoded values for the attributes of the transaction object. You can get the values from a profile file instead of writing values directly into an application.

A profile file is a file with a suffix of *.ini,* such as *myapp.ini.* Windows provides built-in facilities for manipulating *.ini* files. Windows uses *.ini* files to maintain its own attributes.

Profile files are ASCII files. They are divided into sections. Each section contains one or more entries. PowerBuilder provides several functions for manipulating the contents of *.ini* files, including

ProfileString()	retrieves *.ini* string values
ProfileInt()	retrieves *.ini* integer values
SetProfileString()	Set .ini string value entries
SetProfileInt()	sets *.ini* integer value entries

The format of the function that retrieves profile information is

```
ProfileString(filename,section_name,keyname,default_
value)
```

The *filename* is the name of the profile file. The *section_name* is the section of the searchable file for values. The *keyname* gives the useable item. The *default value* serves if no value is in the profile file. Take a file named *app.ini,* which has a database section like this:

```
[database]
```

```
LogId = "PbUs01"
Database = "Pbdemo"
ServerName = "rotorooter"
```

The script example

```
sqlca.DBMS = "Sybase"
sqlca.database = ProfileString("c:\a\app.ini","database","Database",
"" )
sqlca.LogId = ProfileString("c:\a\app.ini","database", "logid", "")
sqlca.ServerName = ProfileString("c:\a\app.ini","database",
SeverName, "")
sqlca.AutoCommit = FALSE
```

sets the attributes of the SQLCA transaction object to the values found in the profile file. The script takes the appropriate value from the database section of the profile file. The set attributes of the SQLCA transaction object reflect these values.

A SAMPLE CONNECTION SCRIPT

Here is the connection script for the sample application shipped with PowerBuilder, Sample40.

```
// Open script for code examples application
string first_time, showtext
// If it's the first time the application is being run, prompt
the
// user for database connection information. In any case, set
all the
// SQLCA variables from the example.ini file.
first_time =
ProfileString("example.ini","sqlca","firsttime","")
open(w_main_backdrop)
if Upper(first_time) = "YES" then
  SetProfileString ("example.ini","sqlca","firsttime","no")
  Open (w_set_sqlca)
  if message.doubleparm = -1 then
    halt close
    return
  end if
else
  SetPointer (HourGlass!)
```

```
  sqlca.DBMS       =
ProfileString("example.ini","sqlca","dbms","")
  sqlca.database   =
ProfileString("example.ini","sqlca","database","")
  sqlca.userid     =
ProfileString("example.ini","sqlca","userid","")
  sqlca.dbpass     =
ProfileString("example.ini","sqlca","dbpass","")
  sqlca.logid      =
ProfileString("example.ini","sqlca","logid","")
  sqlca.logpass    =
ProfileString("example.ini","sqlca","logpass","")
  sqlca.servername =
ProfileString("example.ini","sqlca","servername","")
  sqlca.dbparm     =
ProfileString("example.ini","sqlca","dbparm","")
    connect;
  if sqlca.sqlcode <> 0 then
    MessageBox ("Sorry! Cannot Connect to Database",
sqlca.sqlerrtext)
    halt close
    return
  end if
end if
// set the application attribute that determines whether any
toolbars
// in the application show with large buttons with text or
small
// buttons without text.
showtext = ProfileString ("example.ini", "application", &
 "showtext","yes")
toolbartext =  (showtext = "yes")
// hide the message that was shown while we were connecting to
the database
w_main_backdrop.wf_openmain(. . .
```

You should spend some time working your way through the demonstration programs provided with the 4.0 release. They will serve you as an excellent example of a working PowerBuilder application. The programs also show how many operations are scripted. If you are having a problem writing something in a script, look through the sample applications. They may well have a script sample that demonstrates the functionality you need.

In Chapter 1-2 you created an application of your own. Now you will write a script that connects your application to the sample database supplied with the PowerBuilder demo.

Have PowerBuilder running with your application selected as the current application. If your application is not the current applicaiton, use the application painter as shown in Chapter 1-2 to select your demo application.

If the application painter is not open, open it now. From the running application painter, **open** the script painter. **Select** the script for the open event from the pulldown events window on the script painter.

You should have copied the files from the exercise directory on the samples diskette to the directory holding the demonstration application you are building. Look for the sample script file named *ap-open.scr*. This file contains a script that you can use to connect your application to the PowerBuilder supplied demonstration database.

Hint: use *Import* from the File menu of the script painter to copy the application *open script*. Be sure you have all files displayed in the file selection window, not just script files. Here is the script from the diskette:

```
// Open Script for Demonstration Application
SQLCA.DBMS="ODBC"
SQLCA.DBParm = &
"ConnectString='DSN=Powersoft Demo
DB;UID=dba;PWD=sql'"
Connect Using SQLCA;
if SQLCA.SQLCODE <> 0 and SQLCA.SQLDBCode <> 0 Then
        messagebox("connect","Unable to connect to
database");
        Halt Close
end if

// open(w_main)
```

Note that the last line of the sample script is commented out. This line would attempt to open a window you have not yet built. You will build this window in a later chapter.

From the script painter compile the script with ctrl-l or from the menu. Close the script painter and the application painter when you have completed the working script. If the script is correctly compiled, the painter will close. On closing, any remaining errors will be shown and will prevent you from closing the painter.

Click on the *icon* that runs the application as shown here:

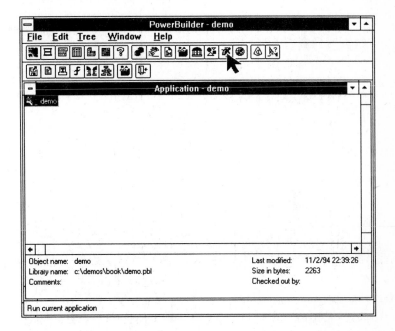

A promt requests you to save the changes you have made. **Click** on the *Yes button.*

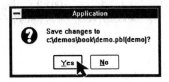

This runs the application. Nothing will appear as the application runs, though. This is because the application contains no windows yet. The PowerBuilder screen will dissapear, the disk will work and the screen will clear. After a delay, the PowerBuilder screen returns. If any error messages appear, there is a problem in your script for the application open event. Return and correct the errors before trying again.

You have run the application. The application started, connected to the database and then ended. After the application ends, control is passed back to the PowerBuilder development environment. Congratulations! You now have written an application, even if it does not yet do much.

USING USER DEFINED TRANSACTION

An application requires a separate transaction object for every database connection. To use multiple database connections from an application you will have to instantiate a transaction object for every connection. Here is how to create and use a user-defined transaction object.

Define A Transaction Object

A variable declaration defines a transaction object; for example,

```
transaction SYBTrans
```

Note that since a transaction object is a variable, the variable, like any other variable, will have scope. Be sure to create the variable with a scope wide enough that it can be used wherever it is needed.

Instantiate A Transaction Object

A create statement, like

```
SYBTrans = create transaction
```

instantiates a transaction.

Initialize A Transaction Object

Initializing a transaction object, once instantiated, is necessary:

```
SYBTrans.DBMS = "Sybase"
SYBTrans.Database = "PBDemo"
SYBTrans.LogId = "PBUs01"
SYBTrans.LogPass = "ixlfrap"
SYBTrans.ServerName = "rotorooter"
SYBTrans.AutoCommit = FALSE
```

Destroy a transaction object that is no longer needed. This frees the resources used by the transaction object. This exemplifies the destroy statement:

```
destroy SYBTrans
```

Connect To A Database

One a transaction object has been instatiated and initialized, it can establish a connection to a database. The connect statement opens the connection:

```
connect {using transaction object};
```

Note that the connect statement is an embedded SQL statement. Embedded SQL statements must end with a semicolon. The statement

```
connect;
```

connects with the default SQLCA transaction object.

The statement

```
connect using SYBtrans;
```

uses the SYBTrans transaction object to connect to a database.

Check The Connection

The script

```
if sqlca.SQLCode < 0 then   // Didn't connect!
   . . .statement block
     halt close
end if
```

determines if the connection succeeded or failed. Checking the attributes of the transaction object determines the success or failure of the connection.

In this example, the *halt close* statement stops the application and immediately closes it.

Using The Connection

As long as the connection is open, you can use embedded SQL statements to query or modify the database. For example, you could embed a *select* or *delete* statement in a script to select rows from the database or to delete rows from the database. Later, a *close* statement can close the connection to the database.

The connection can also serve with a data window object. The later chapter on data window objects describes this use.

Breaking the Connection

The connection to the database ends with a disconnect statement, as in

```
disconnect using SQLCA;
if SQLCA.SQLCode < 0 then     // Error
   . . . statement block
else                          // No Error
   . . . statement block
end if
```

Note again that the disconnect statement, an embedded SQL statement, must end with a semicolon. Note, too, checking the SQLCA transaction object confirms the success of the disconnect.

The interface between a user and a PowerBuilder application is one or more windows. The user interacts with a running application through an active window. Windows can display information or respond to mouse or keyboard actions. The user can enter information into a window. During use of an application, windows open and close in response to requests from the user.

This chapter describes how to build and to use windows for personal applications. This chapter also describes the use of controls and objects on windows. One exception is that a separate, later chapter describes DataWindow objects and DataWindow controls.

STYLE

A window, like any other PowerBuilder object, has attributes and events. The attributes of the window control the appearance and behavior of the window. For example, a window has attributes controlling its size and shape or possibly its resizeability or visibility. Some of the attributes of a window are visual, such as the size of the window, the shape of the window, or the presence of a title bar.

The attributes of a window, taken together, determine the style of the window. The style of the window determines its appearance and its behavior.

CONTROLS

Anything that appears on a window is a control. Controls are objects. Controls are objects placed within a window. Controls display data, accept data, or validate data. Controls can respond to a user action like a mouse click.

Controls, like any other object, have their own attributes and events. Some controls are standard Windows objects, others are unique to PowerBuilder. More-over, you can also create your own custom controls.

BUILDING WINDOWS

Use the window painter to create new windows or modify existing windows. To create a new window, start the window painter, build a new window, and save the window object into a library. To **start** the window painter, use the window icon on the PowerPanel or PowerBar.

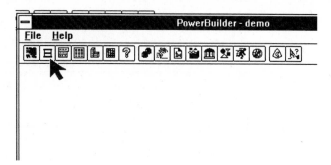

When you start the window painter, a window similar to the following window appears. The window that displays for your application lists none of the entries shown below. This is because your application includes no window objects yet.

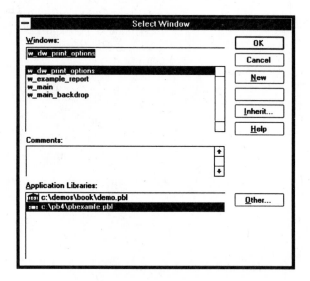

The illustration shows the window painter being opened with the PowerBuilder-supplied sample library. This demonstrates what the window looks like when there are a variety of existing windows from which to choose.

Before trying this yourself, if you have not already, **use** the application painter to **select** the application that you created in chapter 1-2.

Once you have selected your application, you can use the window painter to create the first window for your application. To create a new window, **click** the New button on the window shown above. This causes a window like the following to appear.

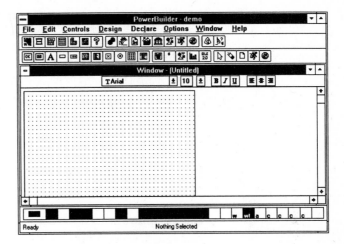

This is a new, blank window. The window you will create with this painter becomes a prototype for the application. You can then use the prototype window to create other windows through inheritance.

To save this window object into your PowerBuilder library, **select** the Save option from the file menu. Enter a file name as shown below. **Save** this window with the name *w_proto*. Notice that there is also a place to save a comment along with the new window object. Also, note that the path of the library appears. This should show the path to your application library.

Remember from Chapter 1-1 that with PowerBuilder you can create new classes through inheritance. The illustration below shows the browser with the PowerBuilder class hierarchy including the object type of window.

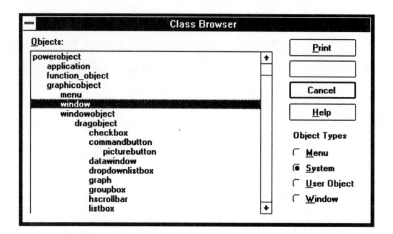

In this example, you have created a new class that descends from the PowerBuilder object window. As this example continues, you will add controls to the *w_proto* object.

This window, *w_proto*, will not be used directly in the application. Instead, you will create a second new window, *w_main*, which inherits the attributes of the *w_proto* object. This window, *w_main*, is the main window for the application you are building.

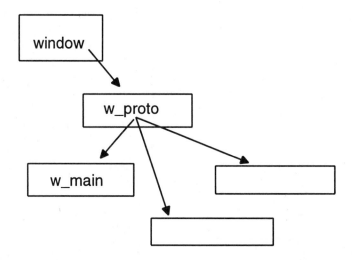

You have created a new class names w_proto and saved the w_proto object in the library for your application. Now, modify the window by increasing its size. **Place** the cursor on the lower right corner of the window. When the cursor turns into a double-headed arrow, **click,** and hold the left mouse button. While pressing the mouse button, **enlarge** the window. Note that you can drag the window to make it bigger than the workspace.

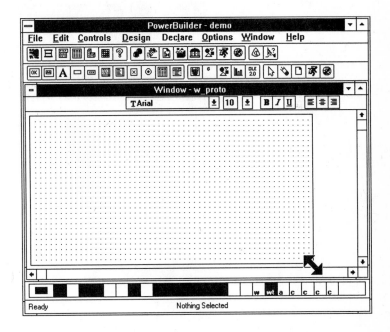

Next, place the cursor somewhere in the window you just enlarged and **double click.** This causes the Window-style window to display. **Click** the *Cancel* button to close this window.

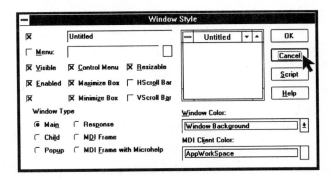

As an alternate way to display this window, **Place** the cursor on the window you are building and **click and hold** with the right mouse button. A response window appears with a list of attributes. A check mark indicates selected attributes. To select, or deselect the style attribute, **position** the cursor over the name style and **release** with the right mouse button.

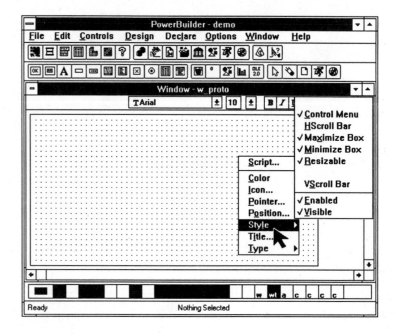

Release outside the response window to avoid a choice.

Shortcut Keys

Window Painter Shortcut Keys include:

Action	Shortcut Keys
Bold	Ctrl+B
Center Text	Ctrl+N
Close	Ctrl+F4
Copy	Ctrl+C
Cut	Ctrl+X
Debug	Ctrl+D
Delete	Del
File Editor	Shift+F6

Duplicate	Ctrl+T
Edit Text	Ctrl+E
Font Face	Ctrl+F
Italic	Ctrl+I
Left Justify Text	Ctrl+L
Next Window	Ctrl+F6
Paste	Ctrl+V
PowerPanel	Ctrl+P
Preview	Ctrl+Shift+W
Return Focus to the Control	Ctrl+O
Right Justify TextCtrl+G	
Run	Ctrl+R
Run Window	Ctrl+W
Script	Ctrl+S
Select All	Shift+A
Switch To	Ctrl+Esc or Alt+Esc
Tab Backwards	Shift+Tab
Underline	Ctrl+U
Undo	Ctrl+Z

Window Types

Note that six window types are window styles. They are

- ✓ main
- ✓ child
- ✓ popup
- ✓ response
- ✓ MDI Frame
- ✓ MDI frame with microhelp

Main Windows

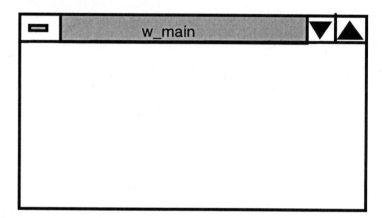

A main window is the first window that appears for an application. It is a standalone window, and it operates independently of other windows in the application.

The *w_proto* window is currently a main window. This is the correct selection for *w_proto*. Double-click in the window to display the style selections. Note that the window type selected is *Main*. Close the style window.

Child Windows

A child window shows the status of items on the parent window. A child window remains secondary to a parent window, able to exist only within the frame of its parent window. Hence, the child window automatically closes when the parent window closes. A child window is never the active window. Any user attempt to move the child window outside the parent window frame crops the child window. Finally, minimizing the child window reduces it to an icon. The icon appears within the parent window.

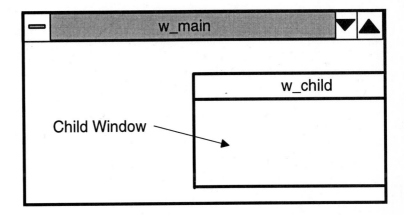

Popup Windows

Popup windows typically display information, such as on-line help. A popup window always displays in a parent window. The popup cannot be behind the parent window. Unlike a child window, it can display outside the parent window frame. Minimizing the popup window displays the icon outside the parent window near the bottom of the screen. Minimizing the parent window also minimizes the popup window.

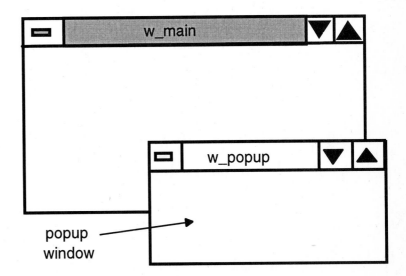

Response Window

A response window displays error or warning messages. A response window can request critical information from the user. A response window often prompts the user for needed information before work can proceed. See the select window in the window painter.

A response window is application modal; therefore, the user cannot minimize the window. Because the window is modal, the user cannot select other windows in the running application so long as the response window shows. The user can use windows in other running applications while a response window displays. The response window remains active until the user makes some response. That is, the response window stays visible until the user performs an activity specified by the response window.

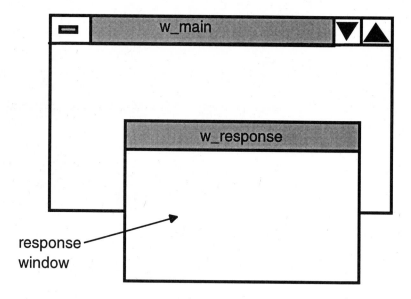

response window

MDI Windows

Descriptions of MDI (Multiple Document Interface) windows are in the later chapter devoted to MDI applications.

Selecting An Icon

A minimized window appears as an icon. You can select any icon to appear when the window is minimized.

If you have not done so already, **copy** the icon file, *demo.ic,* from the application diskette to the directory containing your application.

From the window painter, **click** the right mouse button: the window style response window appears.

Put the cursor on the item named *Icon* and **release** the *right mouse button*. The icon selection window appears:

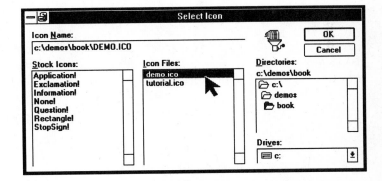

Use the cursor and mouse to move to the directory containing your application. If you have copied the icon file, *demo.ico,* from the diskette provided with this book to your application directory, the name *demo.ico* will appear in the Icons frame as shown above. **Click** the *demo.ico* selection. The displayed icon changes from the default PowerBuilder application icon to the icon shown above. **Click** *OK* to accept this as the icon for the window and to return to the window painter.

NOTE: You can use a similar technique to change the icon for the application. Take this opportunity to **start** the application painter again.

Minimize the window painter window. Use the *application painter icon* from the PowerBar or PowerPanel. When the application painter opens, **use** the *icon* selection from the painter bar or **take** the *Application Icon* selection from the Edit menu. The same icon selection window appears. Use this window to change the application icon to the icon, *demo.ico*. **Close** the Application painter. Save the change.

Selecting A Pointer

Maximize the window painter window labeled *w_proto*.

You can change the window pointer from the popup style menu. **Take** the *Pointer selection* from the menu. This screen *will* appears:

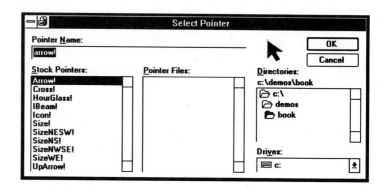

You can use this screen to change the pointer to any pointer shown in the Stock Pointers list. Do not change the application painter for your application. **Click** *Cancel* to close this window.

Size And Position

Select *Position* from the style popup menu and get the following window:

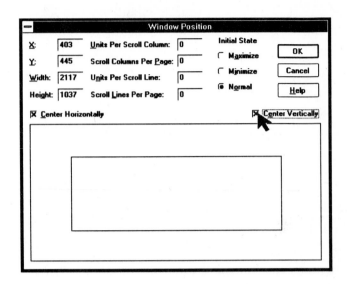

Check the *Center Horizontally* and *Center Vertically* boxes to have the window open in the center of the screen. You can set the size at which the window will open. You can drag the sample window by grabbing its corner. You can select the opening window state of *normal, maximized* or *minimized*. Click the *OK* button to save your changes.

PowerBuilder Units

PowerBuilder units (PBUs) measure objects. A single PBU is 1/32 of the size of the system font width for horizontal measurements and 1/64 of the system font height for vertical measurements. Measuring objects in PBUs makes easier the building of applications similarly sized on screens of different sizes or aspect ratios.

CONTROLS

You can add various standard Windows controls, specialized PowerBuilder controls, or user-defined to a window. Here are the objects and controls that you can add to a window:

Name	Description
CheckBox	a small square box used to select an option
CommandButton	a button with text; triggers an action when clicked
DataWindow	a data-window control is a place to put a datawindow object

DropDownListBox	uses a text box and an arrow to allow the user to display available options
EditMask	determines the format and validation for a line edit
Graph	a graph derived from program data
GroupBox	a rectangle with a title used to combine a group of related buttons
HScrollBar	a horizontal bar used to scroll information that will not fit into a window
Line	a straight line, solid line, or dashed line
ListBox	displays a list of items for a user selection
MenuItem	an item in a menu
MDI Client	the area within an MDI frame; name of this frame is MDI1
MultiLineEdit	a text box that allows multiple lines of data entry
Oval	a circular or oval figure
Picture	a graphical object like a bitmap
PictureButton	a button that has a graphical object like a bitmap showing on it
RadioButton	a button; commonly used in groups to select one of several choices
Rectangle	a rectangle
RoundRectangle	a rectangle with rounded corners
SingleLineEdit	a text box used to enter a single line of text
StaticText	a text string; the user cannot change a StaticText item

User Object	an object defined by the application developer, inheriting its attributes and events from a standard PowerBuilder object
VScrollBar	a vertical bar used to scroll information that will not fit completely on screen
OLE 2.0	object that supports Microsoft OLE version 2.0

The following table suggests uses for the various controls and objects in the table above:

Function	Object or Control
Initiate an Action	CommandButton PictureButton
Existential, Sets a State of Being	CheckBox RadioButton GroupBox
Display Data	DataWindow Control Graph Control
Enter Data	DataWindow Control SingleLineEdit EditMask MultiLineEdit
Headings or Labels	StaticText
List Items	ListBox DropDownListBox
Scrolling	HorizontalScrollBar VerticalScrollBar
Graphics	Picture, Rectangle, Rounded Rectangle, Oval, Line
Custom Control	UserObject Control

Placing An Object On A Window

From the window painter, you can select an object and place it on a window. You can also select a control name from the Controls menu to place a control on a window.

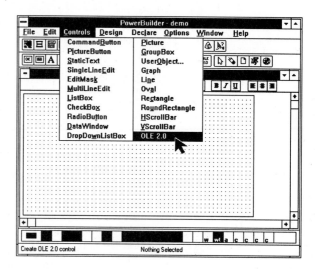

Start by adding a **Picture** object to the window. If you have not already done so, **Copy** the file named *pb-logo.bmp* from the diskette supplied with the book to the directory containing your application. This file is a standard Windows-format graphical object, a bit map.

You can tell that this file contains a Windows bit map because of the *.bmp* file suffix. If you wish, you can examine this bit map with the paint program that comes with Windows or almost any other paint program of your choice.

Add a Picture control to the *w_proto* window. **Pull down** on the Controls menu and **release** when the cursor is on the Picture menu item. You also can **click** on the *picture icon* on the icon bar.

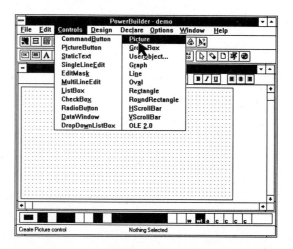

After **selecting** the *Picture object type* from the Controls Menu or Icon
Bar, **move** the *cursor* back onto the window you are designing. Note that
the cursor shape has changed to a cross.

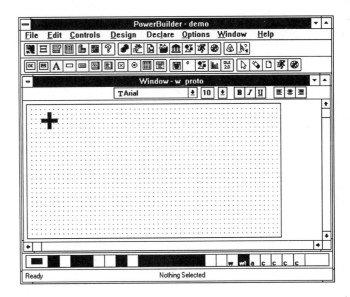

Move the *cursor* to where you want the picture to appear and **click** the
left mouse button. A box appears. This is the box in which the picture
will soon be placed.

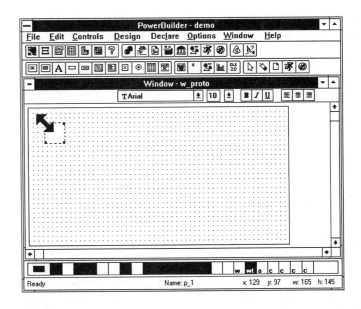

Move the *cursor* to a corner of the box. The cursor becomes an arrow, as pictured below. **Click and hold** the *left mouse button*. While holding the mouse button, **drag** the *cursor*. This enlarges the Picture control.

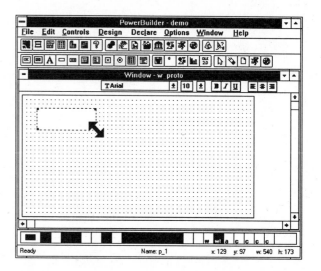

After you have enlarged the Picture control, **move** the *cursor* inside the now-larger control. **Click and hold** the *left mouse button*. While holding the mouse button, **drag** the cursor. This moves the picture control. When you have finished moving the control to a new location near the upper-left corner of your window, the result should somewhat resemble this:

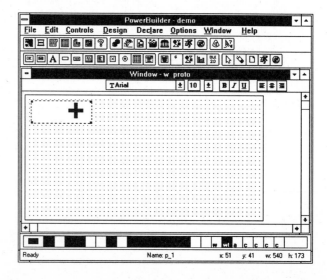

Now that you have sized the Picture control, you can attach the bit map graphic to it. **Place** the *cursor* in the middle of the Picture control and **double click** the *left mouse button*. The should appear:

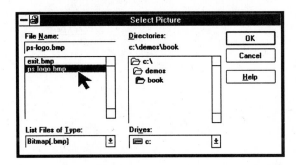

Use the Directories menu to select the directory holding the file named *ps-logo.bmp* moved from the samples diskette. To select this file, **move** the *cursor* to the name in the File name window and **click** the *left mouse button*. The file name highlights, and the name copies to the File Name area. **Click** the *OK* button to select the bit map. This screen appears:

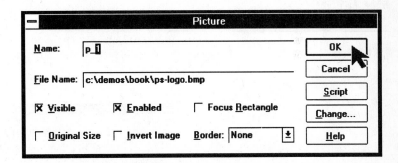

Note that the last character of the name, the numeral one, highlights. PowerBuilder has assigned a default name for the picture object. The prefix *p_* indicates the object is a picture. The number one indicates it is the first picture object placed on this window. **Type** the word *logo*. The name will now be *p_logo*. Click the *OK* button. The bitmap attaches to the Picture control. The end result appears:

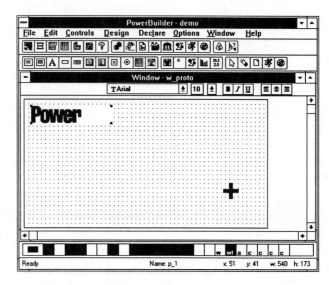

Congratulations! You have just placed your first control

ADD A PICTURE BUTTON

If you have not already done so, start by **copying** the file named *exit.bmp* from the diskette supplied with this book to the directory containing your application. This is another windows bit map.

From the Controls menu, **select** the *PictureButton* choice. **Move** the *cursor* to the window *w_proto*. **Click** once under the *PowerSoft logo Picture* object. A picture button appears at the cursor position. You see this here:

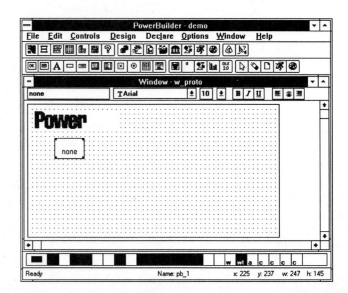

If the button is uncentered under the logo, you can move it. **Place** the *cursor* on the PictureButton. **Click** and **hold** with the *left mouse button*. **Drag** the *button* to the desired position, and **release** the *left mouse button*.

Note that the picture button has the label *none*. To get rid of the *none* and **put** the *picture* on the button, **move** the *cursor* to the button and **double-click** the *left mouse button*. This screen appears:

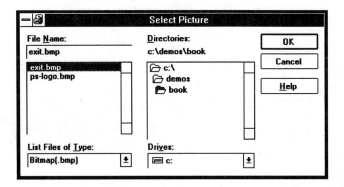

Use the directories window as needed to find the directory containing the *exit.bmp* file. **Click** the file name *exit.bmp*; this places its name in the File Name box. **Change** the *name* of the PictureButton from *pb_1* to *pb_exit*. **Select** the *text* in the Text box and **erase** it. The following window appears.

```
PictureButton
Name:          pb_1                                    OK
Text:                                                  Cancel
Enabled File:  c:\demos\book\exit.bmp                  Script
Disabled File:
[X] Visible  [X] Enabled  [ ] Original Size  [ ] Default  [ ] Cancel    Change Enabled...
Horizontal Alignment:  Center                          Change Disabled...
Vertical Alignment:    Bottom                          Help
```

Click the *OK* button. The PictureButton will now have the *exit bmp* in place of the text *none*. If the word *none* still appears, you forgot to erase it in the dialog box. This is the changed screen:

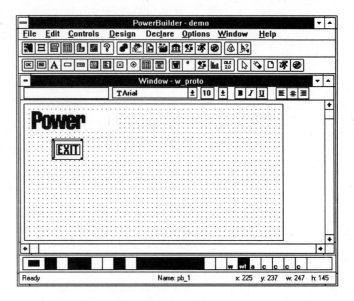

Now that you have placed an exit button on the *w_proto* window, you need to write a script for the button. **Place** the *cursor* on the *exit PictureButton*, and **click** your *right mouse button*.

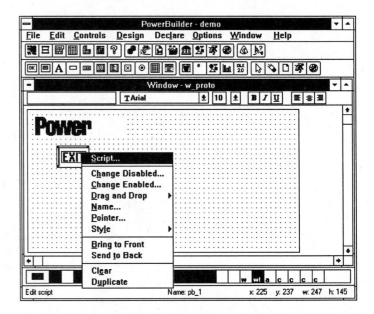

Select the choice *script*. Alternately, you could **left-double-click** the *PictureButton* then take the script choice in the window that appears. The script painter starts. **Enter** the following *script* for the Exit button. This script is also on the samples diskette as a file named *b_exit.scr*.

```
// Prompt the user to confirm exit and exit application.
If MessageBox('ExitApplication','Exit?',Question!,YesNo!) =
1 then
  DISCONNECT ;
  close (Parent)
End If
```

This script displays a MessageBox. The displayed button to select to exit the application. If the user chooses to exit the application, the script calls the close function. The function call *close (Parent)* triggers the close function in the parent object of the button. In this case, the parent object of the PictureButton is the window showing the PictureButton is on.

Compile the script by **typing** *control-L* or by **selecting** *Compile Script* from the compile menu of the window painter. When the script compiles successfully, **close** the script painter. Save your changes

You can preview the prototype window now, if you like. **Select** the *Preview* option from the Design menu, or **type** *control-shift-w*. The window appears as it would look in a running application.

You can **click** the *Exit PictureButton*. Despite the button click, the window does not close since this is preview mode. **Double-click** the *control box* in the upper-left corner of the window to close it or pull down on the menu and **select** *close*, or type *control-F4*.

Closing the WindowPainter prompts a message for you to save the changes you have made to the *w_proto* window. Save the changes by **clicking** the *Yes* button.

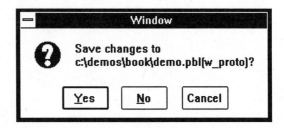

You have created a prototype window for your application, which you can use as the basis for other windows you build.

CREATE THE MAIN WINDOW

Now that you have created the prototype window for this application, you may use it to create the main window for the application. **Start** the window painter again. The Select Window will appear. This time **click** the *inherit button*. The following window appears:

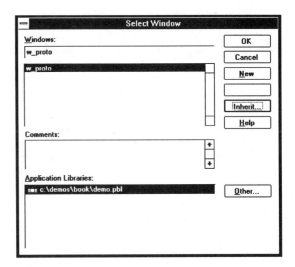

Select the *w_proto* window by clicking its name. **Click** the *OK* button. The Window Painter appears with the new, untitled window displayed. This window has inherited the attributes and controls of the *w_proto* window.

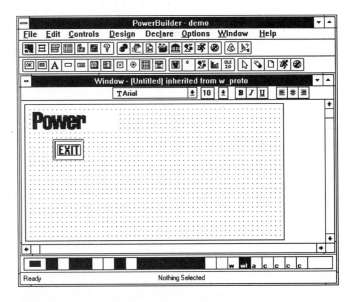

Start by saving this window with the name *w_main*. You can do this
with the **Save As** option of the file menu of the window painter.

If you have copied the *application open* script for your application from
the samples diskette, your application will not run correctly. You must
now go back to the application painter and edit the script for the
application open event.

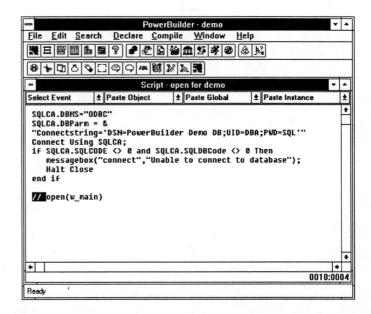

The last line of the script is a comment. The last statement opens the main window. Without this statement, the application runs then stops, and it looks as if nothing is happening. Remove the two slashes to make this a statement instead of a comment. Compile the script; save the application.

You may now run the application you have written. **Select** *Run* from the File menu, **use** the *application icon*, or **type** *control-r*. A short delay ensues as your application starts.

The application runs, and the main window displays. It looks like this on my system:

Click the *Exit* button to stop the running application. The message box appears. Close the application, and PowerBuilder reappears.

Congratulations again! You have just written your first PowerBuilder application.

You should note that you have had to do little development to get this far. Notice how little scripting was needed to connect the application to the database and to add functionality to the exit PictureButton. Although the application does not do much yet, it soon will. Building the application, building the window, and adding the controls was easy compared to any other system or language you may have used.

HINT: You may have noticed that upon opening the window for your application did not center on-screen. If you go back to the window painter and **right-click** in the *window*, you receive a list of choices about styles. **Select** *Position* from the list of styles. **Check** the *position vertically* and *position horizontally* boxes. The next opening, the window centers on-screen.

CONTROL STYLE

PowerBuilder objects have an associated style determined by their attributes. The style determines the appearance and behavior of the object. Here are the attributes of a PictureButton:

Option	Initial State or Value
Attribute	Data Type
BringToTop	Boolean
Cancel	Boolean
Default	Boolean
DisabledName	String
DragAuto	Boolean
DragIcon	String
Enabled	Boolean
FaceName	String
FontCharSet	FontCharSet (enumerated)
FontFamily	FontFamily (enumerated)
FontPitch	FontPitch (enumerated)
Height	Integer
HTextAlign	HTextAlign (enumerated)
Italic	Boolean
OriginalSize	Boolean
PictureName	String
Pointer	String
TabOrder	Integer
Tag	String
Text	String
TextSize	Intger
Underline	Boolean
Visible	Boolean
VTextAlign	VTextAlign (enumerated)

Weight	Integer
Width	Integer
X	Integer
Y	Integer

For a complete listing of the events and attributes of controls, see the PowerBuilder manual on objects and controls. You may also find this information within on-line help.

FOCUS

The *Focus* of a window determines where the next action occurs.

To establish focus, **move** the *cursor* to a control and **click**. **Press** the *Tab* key or the *Shift-Tab* key combination to change focus. When a CommandButton has focus, it may display a focus rectangle. When a SingleLineEdit has focus, it may display an I-Beam shaped cursor.

A control loses focus when the user changes focus to another control. Controls have a GetFocus and a LoseFocus event. You can write scripts for these events to control what happens when a control gains or loses focus.

TAB ORDER

The tab key changes the focus of a window from one control to another. The window painter can set the order of controls selection. Open the window painter with window *w_main*.

Select *Tab Order* from the Design menu. A value appears above each control. This number gives the tab order of the control. You may enter new numbers to change the tab order. Changing the tab order of an item to zero assures that the item will not be selectable.

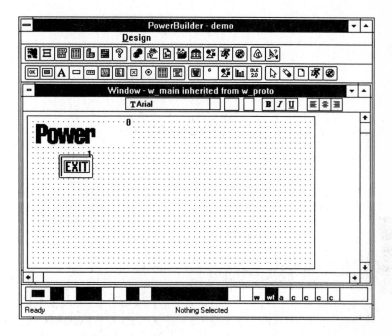

A value of zero indicates that the control cannot gain focus. That is, you cannot select it. Note that the picture object has a tab order of zero.

Do not change the tab orders for the objects on your *w_main* window. To change the tab order of controls, **put** the *cursor* over the tab order and **click** on it. **Type** a new tab order.

Go to the Design menu, and **click** the *Tab Order* selection again. This saves a new tab order incorporating any changes.

PRINTING A WINDOW

Select print from the file menu to print information about the current window. The printed report goes to the active printer selected in Windows. The information printed depends on the preferences you have set with the Preference painter.

1-6 Data Windows

DataWindows present, manipulate, update, and print reports of data. A DataWindow automates the interface to a data source like a relational database management system, a flat file, or another running application. A DataWindow also automates the interface between a running application and the user.

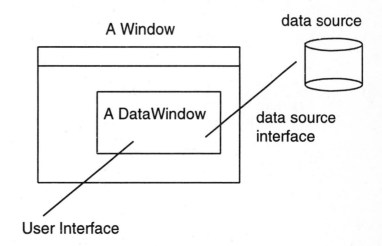

DataWindows provide many features useful for presenting data in an effective and pleasing manner. You can present data in a variety of formats including tabular presentations, free-form presentations, labels, graphs, and crosstabs. You can enhance each of these presentation formats. You can add graphical objects like lines, circles or boxes to a DataWindow object. You can format printed reports with headers, footers, or summary information. You can re-arrange data items or sort them in new orders. Any presentation style can apply to any data source.

This chapter and the next show how to create and use DataWindows in your applications. DataWindows are rich in their capabilities.

Beyond the scope of the introductory text is an in-depth presentation of DataWindows in depth. For further information, consult the PowerBuilder documentation. Another invaluable source of information is the several day long PowerBuilder course on Advanced DataWindows. There is no substitute for taking this highly-recommended course.

USING DATA WINDOWS

Please note the difference between a DataWindow control and a DataWindow object. This chapter introduces DataWindow objects.

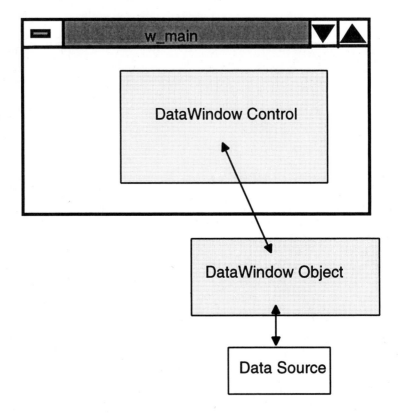

A DataWindow object manages the connection to a data source. The DataWindow painter creates a DataWindow object.

A DataWindow control is a PowerBuilder control that you place on a window. You use the Window Painter to create a DataWindow control.

You use the Window Painter to associate a DataWindow object with the DataWindow control. You can reuse a DataWindow object. The same DataWindow object can associate with several different windows in an application.

The DataWindow object manages the access to the source of data. The DataWindow control manages the presentation of the DataWindow object.

In this chapter, you learn how to add DataWindow objects and controls to an application.

DATA SOURCE

A DataWindow object can draw data from various sources. These sources include

- ✓ a relational database
- ✓ user input
- ✓ a text file
- ✓ a flat file manager, for example .DBF files.
- ✓ a DDE link to another application

When you create a DataWindow Object with the DataWindow painter, you select the data source. You also select what parts of that data are selected from the data source. For example, you can select information from more than one table in a relational database, or you can select only some of the columns from those tables. The examples in this chapter draw data from the demonstration database.

DATA SELECTION

Several possible ways select data from a data source:

- ✓ quick select
- ✓ SQL select
- ✓ query
- ✓ external
- ✓ database stored procedure.

Use the Quick Select option for retrieval of data from a single table; you only need to choose the columns, selection criteria, and sort order of the retrieved data. Do not use the quick select option if you need computed columns, grouping or other complex retrieval operations.

Use the SQL Select option for more control over data retrieval. This option allows joins between tables and more-complex retrieval options.

The Use the query option if the Query Painter created and saved a query.

Use the Database Stored Procedure option if the data retrieval operation resides in the database as a stored procedure. Note that not all DBMSs support stored procedures.

The External option applies when the data source is not a relational database management system.

PRESENTATION STYLE

The presentation style for a DataWindow object can be any of the following

- ✓ crosstab
- ✓ freeform
- ✓ graph
- ✓ grid
- ✓ group
- ✓ label
- ✓ N-Up
- ✓ tabular

Following are some examples of DataWindow presentation styles. Each example uses the same data drawn from the demonstration database.

Tabular Style

The tabular style presents data in columns across the page. Each column has a header. As many rows as can fit in the window display. Scroll bars can move all of the data into the display area.

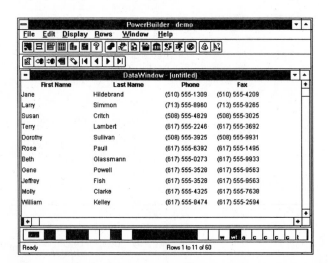

Freeform Style

The freeform style lists the columns down the page with a label for each column. The freeform style is useful for data-entry windows.

The tools provided within the DataWindow painter can move any of the objects displayed in the free-form data window. They can also change the text attributes or shapes of objects. Other tools make it easy to re-align objects or to add various graphical objects including lines, circles, or pictures. This allows presentation of your data in the most-pleasing format.

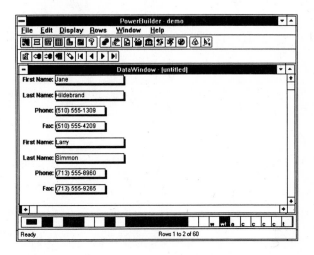

Grid Style

The grid style shows the data in a row-and-column presentation. Grid lines separate each of the rows and columns. Every data item must fit within one of the grid elements.

The DataWindow painter cannot move the columns and rows as does the freeform display. Selection of the data from the data source fixes this presentation.

The user can re-order the elements of the display at run-time, unlike with other presentation styles. The user can resize and reorder columns with the mouse while the application is running.

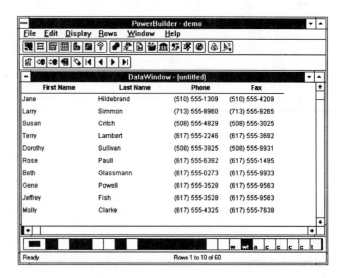

Label Style

The label style produces labels, such as mailing labels. Various common label formats have support.

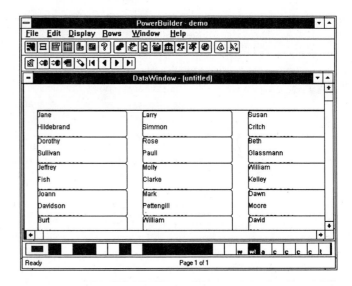

N-Up Style

The n-up style resembles the label style. It presents two or more rows of data, each of which is presented side by side. This allows presenting across the page several rows of information that form the database.

Group Style

The *group* style provides a tabular DataWindow object that has certain group properties pre-defined.

Graph And Crosstab Style

Graph and *Crosstab* styles both allow data presentation in a graphical format. Consult the PowerBuilder User's Guide for more information about these styles.

Composite

The composite type is new to version 4.0 and allows DataWindows to be held within other DataWindows.

PRIMARY BUFFER

A DataWindow control allows a user to retrieve, display, modify, and update information. This control presents data to the user for these operations. A buffer in memory holds data for the data window object; this is the Primary DataWindow buffer. The DataWindow object manages the connection to the database.

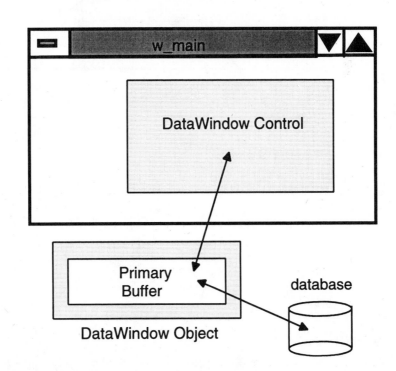

EDIT CONTROL

A DataWindow object divides into a set of cells. Each cell holds a single item of data retrieved from the database. The item has a defined type, like *integer*, *real*, or *string*.

Each DataWindow control has a single edit control. The edit control is a field that overlays a cell. The contents of the edit control is the *text* of the edit control.

As the user changes the focus from cell to cell to enter data, the edit control moves to the item with focus. Data entered by the user stays in the edit control until it can be validated. After data is validated, it moves to the buffer, as in the following figure:

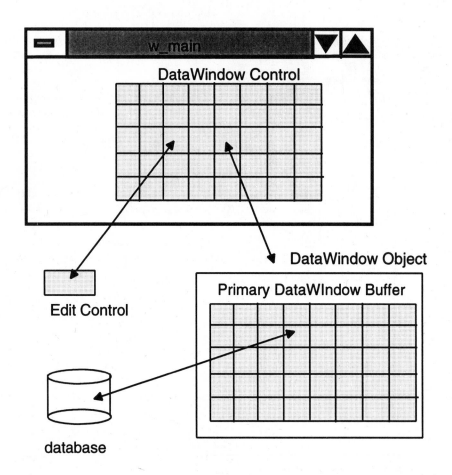

PROCESSING ENTRIES

When a user changes the data in a cell, and the focus then changes from that cell, PowerBuilder takes the following steps to process the entered data:

1. The text in the edit control converts to the data type of the cell in the primary buffer. For example, if the user enters the text 123 into the edit control, and the cell is of type integer, the text 123 converts into the integer value one-hundred twenty-three.

2. If the conversion of the text to the underlying data type is successful, PowerBuilder will attempt to validate the data. Validations can stay in the database or attach directly to a DataWindow.

3. A successful validation triggers the ItemChanged event for the DataWindow control.

4. After the triggered ItemChanged event, the ItemFocusChanged event triggers.

If there is an error—for example, if the data is not valid—or the text conversion is not successful, the ItemError event triggers.

If additional processing is necessary after validation of the entered text, you should write a script for the ItemChanged event.

For further information see the PowerSoft-supplied *Objects and Controls* manual or the *Function Reference*.

DATA VALIDATION

Data validation begins when the user has modified the contents of the edit control and any one of the following events happens:

- ✓ you press the ENTER key
- ✓ the focus changes to a different cell in the DataWindow control
- ✓ a script executes the AcceptText() function

When the user has entered something into the edit control, the contents of the edit control may differ from the contents of the cell in the buffer. The data entered by the user is held in the edit control until it is validated. The data in the cell in the buffer is unchanged until the data in the edit control receives validation. Once validated, the data in the edit control copies to the primary buffer. Then the contents of the edit control and the contents of the cell in the primary buffer are the same.

VALIDATION SEQUENCE

Four tests validate the data held in the edit mask. They occur in order. When the contents of the edit control have passed all the tests, the cell in the DataWindow buffer changes.

1. Did anything change?

2. Does the data type of the entered object agree with the data type of the cell?

3. Did the data meet the validation rules for the DataWindow object or the rules held in the database?

4. Has the ItemChanged event occurred?

ACCESSING THE TEXT FOR AN ITEM

Several functions are available for the current text in the edit control or a specific data item held in the primary buffer.

GetText()—returns the text in the edit control

SetText()—places text in the edit control

GetItemDate(), GetItemNumber(), GetItemDateTime(), GetItemDecimal(), GetItemString(), GetItemTime()—each returns the data from a cell in the PrimaryBuffer.

SetItem()—places an item in a cell of the PrimaryBuffer.

OTHER BUFFERS

A DataWindow object has three data buffers. The first buffer, as discussed above, is the primary data buffer. This buffer holds information returned from the database, or information that returned from the database then changed by the user.

Two other data buffers exist. It is possible to filter data from the data selected in the database. Only the data that passes the filter displays. That is, only the data that passes the filter copies to the primary buffer. The data that does not pass the filter stays in a filter buffer. Data deleted from the primary buffer stays in a deletion buffer. For example, if the user deletes a row from the DataWindow, that row copies to the delete buffer.

UPDATING THE DATABASE

Note that changes made to the primary DataWindow buffer do not automatically propagate to the database. To use the buffer changes to make database changes, you must call the Update() function from a PowerScript.

Other operations like deleting rows from the buffer, adding rows to the buffer, or sorting the rows in the buffer do not change the database, either. For example, deleting rows from the primary buffer just moves those rows to the delete buffer. For the results of any of these operations to be committed to the database, you must call the Update() function.

MANIPULATING THE CONTENTS OF THE EDIT CONTROL

The edit control for the primary buffer is similar in action to the window MultiLineEdit control. Several functions are available to change the contents of the edit control:

CanUndo()	Scroll()
Clear()	SelectedLength()
Copy()	SelectedLine()
Cut()	SelectedStart()
LineCount()	SelectedText()
Paste()	SelectText()
Position()	TextLine()
ReplaceText()	Undo()

FUNCTIONS

Several useful functions come with PowerBuilder for manipulating DataWindow controls. Some of the more-commonly-used functions are in the following table:

Function	Purpose
AcceptText()	starts processing of the text in the edit control
dwShareData()	lets two DataWindows share the same data
GetRow()	returns the number of the current row in the primary buffer
DeleteRow()	moves the current row to the delete buffer

Functions, Continued

Function	Purpose
Filter()	restricts the display of rows to those that pass the filter specification
InsertRow()	inserts a new row in the primary buffer
Reset()	clears the primary buffer
Retrieve()	retrieves the rows specified by the select from the database
ScrollToRow()	scrolls the data so the specified row is displayed
SelectRow()	highlights selected row
Update()	commits any changes to the database

1-7 Building Data Window Objects

In this chapter, you add a DataWindow object to the application.

When you created an application named "demo," you created a new PowerBuilder library named "demo.pbl" to hold the application object. You added an application object to the library and wrote a script for the open event. This script connects the application to a database.

You saved a window object named "w_proto" in the library. You put a logo and a picture button (to exit the application) on this window, and wrote a script for the PictureButton. Then you created the main window for the application by inheriting the prototype window.

These objects are all in the directory you selected in the library "demo.pbl" as shown in the following figure:

demo.pbl

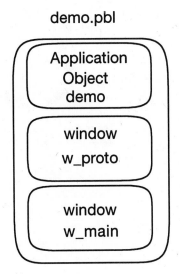

Finally, you ran the application.

BUILDING A DATAWINDOW

Adding a data window to your application is a three-step process. First, you build a DataWindow object with the DataWindow painter. Then you add a DataWindow control to an application window. Last, you attach the DataWindow object to the DataWindow control. This chapter describes how to build a DataWindow object. The next chapter describes how to associate a DataWindow object with a DataWindow control.

The steps in creating a DataWindow object are

- ✓ Choose a data source
- ✓ Choose a presentation style
- ✓ choose design options
- ✓ Select tables
- ✓ Select columns from tables
- ✓ Select retrieval arguments (optional)
- ✓ Speciry update options
- ✓ Save the DataWindow object

Note that the following sections assume that you have set the PowerBuilder database preferences with the Preference Painter to select the demonstration database shipped with PowerBuilder. When the DataWindow painter starts, a connection automatically occurs to the most-recently-used database. The information needed to connect to the last database used stays in the *pb.ini* file.

Start The Datawindow Painter

From the PowerBar or PowerPanel, **start** the DataWindow painter.

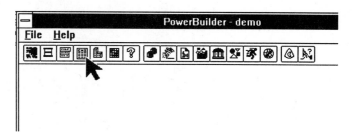

A short delay may follow as PowerBuilder connects to the demonstration database. During this pause, you should see the message *Connecting to database* in the lower-left corner of the screen.

Create A New DataWindow Object

When the DataWindow painter connects to the database, the Select DataWindow window appears:

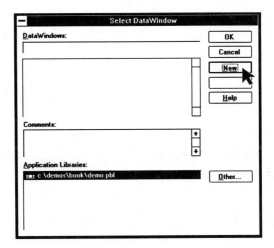

Note that no data windows appear in the list. You have not yet created any data windows for your application. If there were DataWindow objects for this application, they would appear on the list in the Select DataWindows control.

You could edit an existing DataWindow object by clicking its name to select it then clicking the *OK* button. As with other selection windows, you can move between directories looking for objects with the file tree shown in the Directories box.

Click the *New* button, and the New DataWindow window appears:

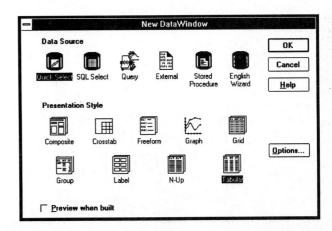

With this window you select the data source, the presentation style, and attributes for the DataWindow object.

Preview When Built

For this example, do not check the "Preview when built" button. Checking the *Preview When Built* box causes the DataWindow preview immediately to appear from the DataWindow painter. Later, you can use the preview icon from the DataWindow painter to preview the DataWindow object.

The Data Source And DataWindow Style

The data source and DataWindow object style selected are grey in the selection window. If they are not already selected, **click** *SQL Select* in the top section and *Tabular* in the lower section.

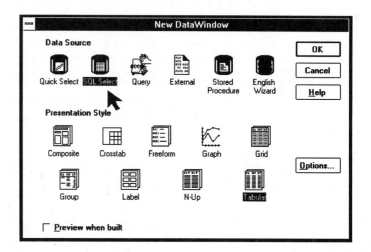

Options Button

To change the defaults used for some of the attributes of a DataWindow object, **click** the Options button to get this window:

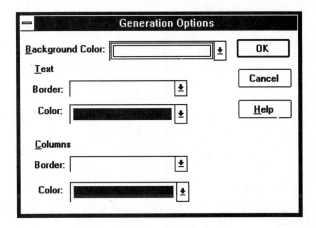

NOTE: Do not change any options.

You can change any of the options listed for the DataWindow object and click the OK button. To close the window without changing any of the options, **click** the *Cancel* button. *Help* starts on-line help and provides a description of each of the items listed on the window. For this example, **click** *Cancel* without changing any of the options.

Close The New Datawindow Window

The New DataWindow window is now on-screen. **click** *OK* to continue.

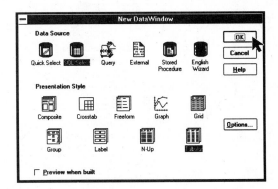

Select Tables And Columns

After a pause, the Select Tables window appears:

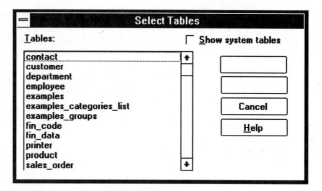

If the list of tables that appears differs from the list shown in the illustration above, you have connected to the wrong database. If an error message is presented instead of the Select Tables window, the system preferences are not set correctly, or the demonstration database was not installed properly.

If so, stop the selection process by **clicking** the *Cancel* button. Go back to the Preferences Painter and connect to the demonstration database as explained in the preceding chapter about connecting to a database.

Click on the *customer* and *sales_order* names in the list of tables.

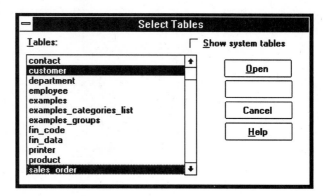

Click *Open* to continue.

The DataWindow Painter should now be on-screen:

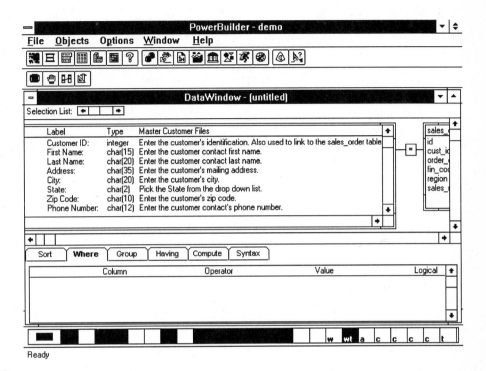

The remaining discussion in this chapter assumes that you are familiar with relational database technology including tables, columns and joins. If these concepts are unfamiliar, consult appropriate chapters in Part Two of this book.

The display shows the two tables you selected and the columns in those tables. In this case, *customer.ccust_id* is a foreign key into *sales_orders*.

In this example, you select data based on an equi-join of the customer andsales_orders tables. You will select the columns that appear in the join by clicking on their names in each of the tables as displayed in the DataWindow Painter. By pointing and clicking the names, you build an SQL select statement.

You select columns for the join by **clicking** on their *names* in the Columns list. You will have to use the scroll bars to bring some of the names to the display area. Note that clicking a name a second time removes the name from the selection.

Click on the names in this order:

    √ customer.id
    √ customer.company_name

✓ sales_order.id
✓ sales_order.sales_rep
✓ sales_order.order_date

Note that each column name appears at the top of the window as you select the column from the table. The order of clicking the names is important. The order determines the order that columns will display on the finished DataWindow object.

You can change the order in which columns appear in the DataWindow by dragging a name in the top bar. To change the position of a column, **Click and hold** on a name in the top bar. **Drag** the name to the desired new position. **Release** the mouse button. The name remains in the new position.:

If you have moved a column, **return** it to its *original position* before proceeding. Following is a picture of the window as appears at the end of the selection process. Note that the name of each selected field appears in the list of field names at the top of the DataWindow Painter window.

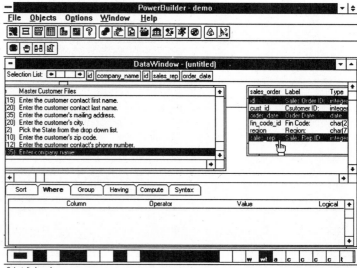

Now that all the desired columns are selected, **click** on the *design icon*:

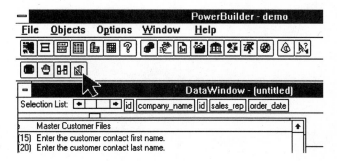

After a short pause. the DataWindow Painter appears on-screen as follows:

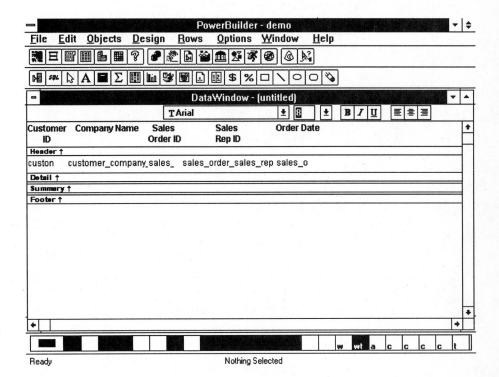

If your preferences dictate previewing the window, a list of data appears as shown following instead of the DataWindow Painter as shown above. If the window appears in preview mode with rows of data, close that window by **Clicking** the *Design icon* as shown here:

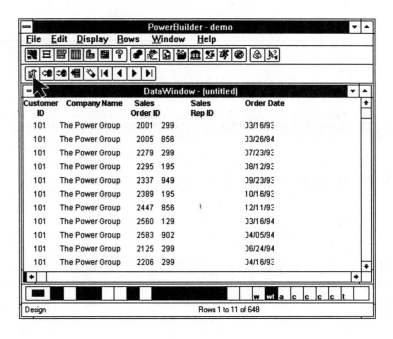

Save The DataWindow Object

Take this opportunity to save the DataWindow you have created. **Choose** the *Save As* option from the File menu. The following window appears:

The name *demo.pbl library* should appear in the Libraries box. **Enter** the name *d_orders* in the DataWindows box (see above). **Click** the *OK* button. This saves the new DataWindow object into the *demo.pbl* library and names it d_orders. The DataWindow painter appears again. Note how the DataWindow painter divides the display into header, detail, summary and footer bands.

SELECTING, SORTING, GROUPING

The select statement associated with the DataWindow object can restrict or group the data returned by the select statement. You can also restrict or group data within the application after its return by the select statement. This section describes modifications to the select statement that restricts, groups or sorts data at the database server. Consult the PowerBuilder *User's Guide* chapter on filtering, sorting, and grouping rows to get information on filtering returned data at the DataWindow object.

The select statement associated with a DataWindow object can have the following

✓ a *where* clause to restrict the selected data
✓ an *order by* clause to sort the data returned by the selection
✓ a *group by* clause to group the selected data
✓ a *having* clause to restrict the group by clause

In the following figure, the cursor shows a seledction within the SQL toolbox. This toolbox is used to modify the SQL select for the DataWindow object. Do not use the SQL tool box now with your application, just follow along with the illustrations.

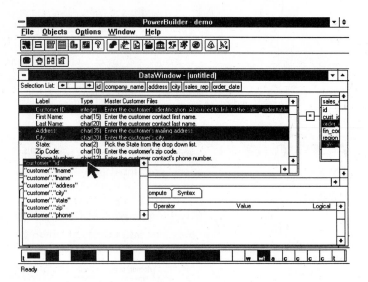

The window below shows criteria for restricting selections to orders with order numbers greater than 100. Do not add such a *where* clause to your selection.

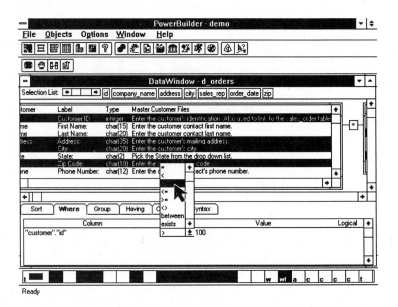

You can use this SQL Toolkit to build any *where* clause into the selection for the DataWindow object.

For further information on constructing clauses for select statements, consult the PowerBuilder *User's Guide*. For further information on SQL or select statements refer to Section Two.

MORE ABOUT THE DATAWINDOW PAINTER

The DataWindow painter should still appear on-screen:

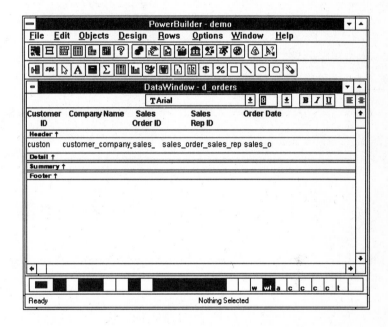

Changing The Display

The first section of the DataWindow display is the header bar. This shows the information appearing at the top of every screen or printed page. This information can include running headers or other information like a date.

The second area is the detail bar. This shows the data retrieved from the data source.

The third area is a summary bar. This bar displays summary information that appears after all other data or at the end of a printout. This area can add information like a total or count to the DataWindow object.

The last footer area adds information at the bottom of every screen or page. This area typically adds a page number or page count to the display.

You can change the position of any column, or any column heading, by clicking, **holding** and **dragging** the *item*:

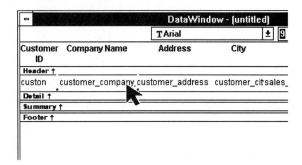

If you changed any fields, **Drag** *them* back to their original location.

You can change the size of any field by clicking on the field to select it. Then use thecursor to re-size the field. If you change the size of a field, be sure to restore it to the original size.

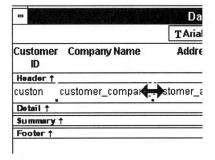

If you changed any fields, **Change** *them* back to their original size.

Preview The DataWindow

Preview the DataWindow object by **typing** *Control-W* or by **selecting** *Preview* from the Design menu. After a short delay, the DataWindow painter connects to the database, and the data window previews, thus:

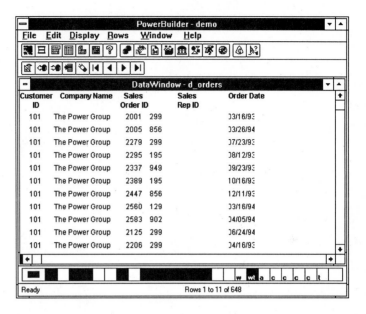

The data displayed in the preview comes from the demonstration database. The DataWindow object connects to the database, as it will later in the running application. Note that the total number of retrieved rows displays at the bottom of the window.

The next figure shows how the controls along the top of the window operate the DataWindow preview display:

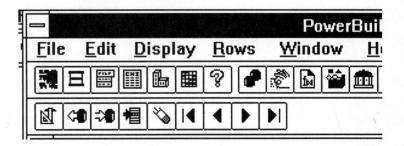

From left to right, the DataWindow icon closes the preview and returns you to the DataWindow painter. The second icon reselects rows from the database. Each time you click this icon, the select statement associated with the DataWindow object runs. Your design of the DataWindow object determined the selection.

The third icon updates the database with changes that you make to selected rows. You cannot change any rows right now but can soon.

The fourth icon inserts a row into the display. If you click this icon, a beep sounds but no row inserts. The reason is that the DataWindow yet lacks configuration for updating.

The fifth icon deletes the current row on the DataWindow. Since you have not yet enabled the DataWindow for updating, no row highlights as the current row.

The remaining icons scroll the display of data within the DataWindow. The icons move the display to the first data row, the previous window of data, the next window, and the last window, respectively. Try these, if you wish.

Nothe that the sales_order.id is not aligned properly under the column heading. **Click** on the *Design Icon* to return to the DataWindow Painter. Use the DataWindow Painter to re-align the columns under the headings. Hint: this will be easier if you start with the rightmost column name, the order_date:

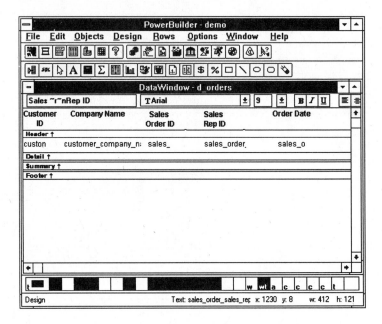

When you have completed the changes, save the DataWindow object with the Save item from the File menu.

Update Characteristics

The update characteristics of a DataWindow object are initially determined when the DataWindow object is created. This section demonstrates changing the update characteristics for a DataWindow object.

Single Table Select

If the selected columns all derive from a single table and you select the key column for the table, all the selected columns are updateable. The DataWindow object assigns a tab-order for each column. This allows the user to select any column for updating. The example above does not provide for updating, since data came from multiple tables.

Join

If the data selection for a DataWindow includes data from more than one table (that is, it uses a join to retrieve the data), the update characteristics prevent updating. The DataWindow you built does not yet allow updating. The reason is that the select statement for the DataWindow object includes a join.

Each DataWindow object can update a single table from the database. PowerBuilder does not directly support updating through a join, even if a view hides the join.

To manage updating multiple tables with a DataWindow object, you must write scripts for the DataWindow control that select each table in turn then update each table individually. The Advanced DataWindows course teaches the techniques for doing this updating. The scope of this introductory text does not include these techniques.

In the next section, you learn how to change the update characteristics of the DataWindow object to allow updating the *cust_orders* table. This lets the user modify information about orders with this DataWindow object.

Set The Update Characteristics For Updating

From the DataWindow painter, **select** Update from the Rows menu. The following window appears.

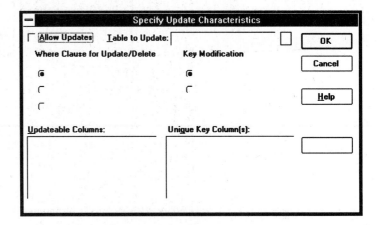

The Allow Updates selection in the upper-left corner shows as unchecked because the selection for the DataWindow object joins multiple tables. **Click** the *Allow Updates* check box. This enables the DataWindow object for updating. Field which were greyed-out will now appear in full color.

Select the sales_order table as the table to update:

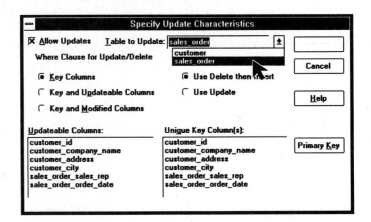

Next, select the two columns sales_rep and order_date from the Updateable Columns list.:

```
┌──────────────────────────────────────────────────────────────┐
│ ─        Specify Update Characteristics                        │
├──────────────────────────────────────────────────────────────┤
│ X Allow Updates    Table to Update: sales_order      [↓]       │
│   Where Clause for Update/Delete      Key Modification          │
│                                                      ┌────────┐ │
│   ⦿ Key Columns                ⦿ Use Delete then Insert│ Cancel │ │
│                                                      └────────┘ │
│   ○ Key and Updateable Columns   ○ Use Update                   │
│                                                      ┌────────┐ │
│   ○ Key and Modified Columns                         │  Help  │ │
│                                                      └────────┘ │
│   Updateable Columns:          Unique Key Column(s):            │
│   ┌─────────────────────┐      ┌─────────────────────┐┌────────┐│
│   │ customer_id         │      │ customer_id         ││Primary ││
│   │ customer_company_name│     │ customer_company_name││  Key   ││
│   │ customer_address    │      │ customer_address    │└────────┘│
│   │ customer_city       │      │ customer_city       │          │
│   │ sales_order_sales_rep│     │ sales_order_sales_rep│         │
│   │ sales_order_order_date│    │ sales_order_order_date│        │
│   └─────────────────────┘      └─────────────────────┘          │
└──────────────────────────────────────────────────────────────┘
```

Next, **click** the Primary Key button. Notice that after a short delay this enables the *OK* button and that the *OK* button no longer appears grey. Clicking the *Primary Key* button cancels any changes you may have made in the *Unique Key Columns* box. This also highlights and selects the default primary keys.

```
┌──────────────────────────────────────────────────────────────┐
│ ─        Specify Update Characteristics                        │
├──────────────────────────────────────────────────────────────┤
│                                                      ┌────────┐ │
│ X Allow Updates    Table to Update: customer   [↓]   │   OK   │ │
│   Where Clause for Update/Delete      Key Modification└────────┘ │
│                                                      ┌────────┐ │
│   ⦿ Key Columns                ⦿ Use Delete then Insert│ Cancel │ │
│                                                      └────────┘ │
│   ○ Key and Updateable Columns   ○ Use Update                   │
│                                                      ┌────────┐ │
│   ○ Key and Modified Columns                         │  Help  │ │
│                                                      └────────┘ │
│   Updateable Columns:          Unique Key Column(s):            │
│   ┌─────────────────────┐      ┌─────────────────────┐┌────────┐│
│   │ customer_id         │      │ customer_id         ││Primary ││
│   │ customer_company_name│     │ customer_company_name││  Key   ││
│   │ customer_address    │      │ customer_address    │└────────┘│
│   │ customer_city       │      │ customer_city       │          │
│   │ sales_order_sales_rep│     │ sales_order_sales_rep│         │
│   │ sales_order_order_date│    │ sales_order_order_date│        │
│   └─────────────────────┘      └─────────────────────┘          │
└──────────────────────────────────────────────────────────────┘
```

The OK button can now be selected. **Click** *OK*.

This has enabled the select statement of the DataWindow object for updating the *sales_order* table. Once you change the tab order, as shown in the next section, you can use the DataWindow preview to update the database.

The user can employ the DataWindow object to change information about sales orders, but not to change information aboutcustomers.

Insert Or Update?

The DataWindow object creates an SQL statement upon modification of the data for a DataWindow object and upon a request to commit the modifications to the DataBase. The Key Modification selection shown on the update window determines what kind of SQL statement generates when a key column changes. A key column is a column specified in the Key Columns box. These two options are

✓ INSERT and DELETE
✓ UPDATE

The *insert and delete* selection deletes the original rows from the database and then inserts new rows into the database. The second option updates existing rows. Use the update option to modify a single row; it is faster.

If the update changes multiple rows, a delete and insert always works; whereas, a series of updates may not. Imagine that an update changes the value of the key in the first of two rows. Then the update attempts to change the value of the key for the second row to the original value of the key for the first row. In some database management systems, an update sequence like this fails.

Where Clause For Updates And Deletions

When the data for a DataWindow object has changed and a request commits the modifications to the DataBase, the DataWindow object creates an SQL statement. The *where* clause generated for the DataWindow object determines updates or deletions. The selected *where* clause includes one of the following:

✓ Key columns only
✓ All key columns and all updateable columns
✓ All key columns and all modified columns

When multiple users might access a table simultaneously, you must select an update strategy. If you allow the application to update the database under any circumstances, users may conflict with each other, resulting in bad concurrency control. If you are unfamiliar with the issues surrounding concurrency control, see Section Two of this book.

You can control the update strategy. Specify which columns to include in the *where* clause in the update or delete statement generated by the DataWindow object:

```
delete
from table
where
   col1= value1
   and col2 = value 2
```

If you select the Key Columns Only option, the *where* clause includes the key columns only. The key columns are the columns selected in the Key Columns box of the Update Characteristics window. This causes a comparison of the values for the key items as originally retrieved against the key columns in the database. If they match, the update succeeds.

If you select Key and Updateable Columns, the *where* clause includes both. The values for the original key values and for the original retrieved updateable columns compare to the values in the database. The values must match the values found in the database for the update to succeed. If some other user has changed values in the database, the update fails.

If you select Key and Modified Columns, all key and modified columns appear in the *where* clause. The values originally retrieved for key and modified columns compared to the values in the database. If any values have changed since retrieval of the rows, the update fails.

Consider this example. A DataWindow object updates an employee table. There are three columns in the table—*EmpId*, *salary* and *name*. The employee table has a key of *EmpId*. All the columns in the employee are updateable. The user retrieves the row for employee number 1001. The user then changes the salary for this employee from $50,000 to $55,000. Here are the results for each of the three update options.

(1) If the option selected is *Key Columns*, the following update statement results:

```
update Employee
set salary = 55000
where EmId = 1001
```

In this example, the update succeeds even if another user has changed the row in the database. Any updating of the salary loses the change.

(2) If the option selected is *Key and Modified columns*, the following update statement results:

```
update Employee
set salary = 55000
where EmpId = 1001 and Salary = 50000
```

Here, the update fails if another user has changed the employee's salary.

(3) If the option selected is *Key and Updateable columns*, the following statement results:

```
update Employee
set Salary = 55000
where EmpId = 1001 and Salary = 50000
   and Name = original_value
```

In this example, the statement fails if another user has changed any of the updateable columns in the table since the record came from the database.

Set The Tab Order

While the update characteristics of the table have changed to allow updates to the *sales_order* table, the DataWindow object still cannot update. The reason is the tab order of each of the objects shown in the detail band is zero. The tab order of each object is zero because the DataWindow object originated from a join and a join by default disallows updates. **Select** *Tab Order* from the Design menu:

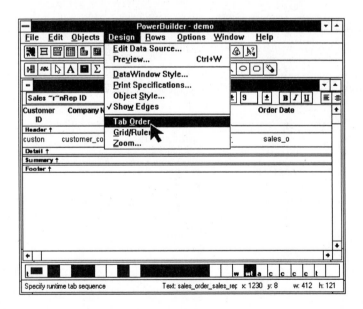

Click the tab order field shown above the sales_rep_id. **Type** a tab order of 1. **Click** on the *tab order* for the *order_date* field. Type in a tab order of 2.

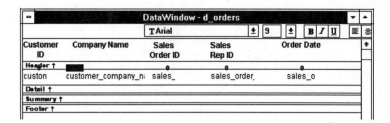

Click the *Tab Order* menu item in the Design menu. The tab order display disappears and the display returns to the DataWindow painter.

Type *Ctrl+W* or **select** *Preview* from the Design menu to preview the DataWindow object:

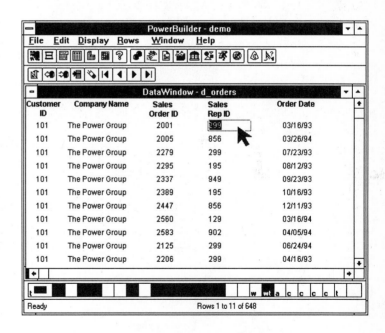

Note that you can now change sales order information. The Tab key moves the edit control from field to field.

All icons are now operational. You may enter new dates or amounts. You can update the database to reflect changes you have made. You can add new rows or delete existing rows.

Remember from the preceding chapter that any changes you make—additions, deletions or modifications—occur in the DataWindow buffers. The changes do not update in the database until you click the update icon or select *Save Changes to Database* from the File menu.

Click the *Design* icon to return to the DataWindow painter display. **Select** *Save* from the File menu to save any changes you have made to the DataWindow object. **Close** the DataWindow painter.

Congratulations, you have built your first DataWindow object! The next chapter explains how you can add this DataWindow object to a window in your application.

Shortcut Keys

The DataWindow painter supports the following shortcut keys:

Action	Shortcut Keys
Bold	Ctrl+B
Center Text	Ctrl+N
Close	Ctrl+F4
Debug	Ctrl+D
Delete	Del
DOS File Editor	Shift+F6
Edit Text	Ctrl+E
Font Face	Ctrl+F
Font Size	Ctrl+Z
Italic	Ctrl+I
Left Justify Text	Ctrl+L
Power Panel	Ctrl+P
Preview	Ctrl+W
Return Focus to the Object	Ctrl+O
Right Justify TextCtrl+G	
Run	Ctrl+R
Select Above	Ctrl+Up Arrow
Select All	Ctrl+A

Select Below	Ctrl+Down Arrow
Select Left	Ctrl+Left Arrow
Select Right	Ctrl+Right Arrow
Switch To	Ctrl+Esc or Alt+Esc
Tab Backwards	Shift+Tab
Underline	Ctrl+U

1-8 Data Window Controls

In the preceding chapter, you created a DataWindow control. In this chapter, you add the control to your application. You have already created the main window for your application, window *w_main*. Now you add a DataWindow control to the w_main window. Then, you associate this DataWindow control with the DataWindow object *d_orders*.

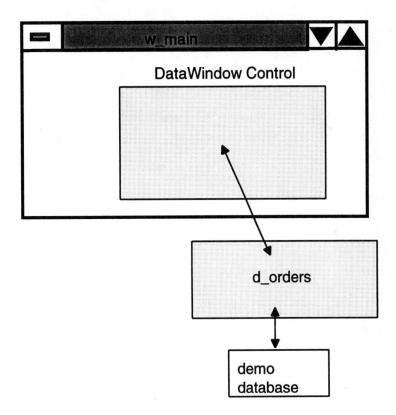

The script you wrote for the application open event and the tables and columns you selected for the DataWindow object determined the association to the data source. The application open script opens the demo database provided with PowerBuilder. You selected the tables for the DataWindow object and the rows from the tables when you created the DataWindow object.

THE DATAWINDOW CONTROL

From the PowerBar or PowerPanel, **start** the Window Painter.

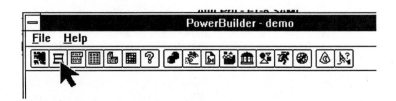

The following selection window appears:

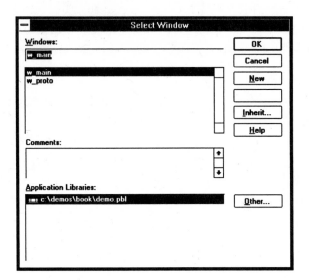

The window *w_main* highlights by default. **Click** the *OK* button to proceed to the Window Painter and the main window.

Select *DataWindow* from the Controls menu, or **select** the *DataWindow icon* on the Window Painter icon bar:

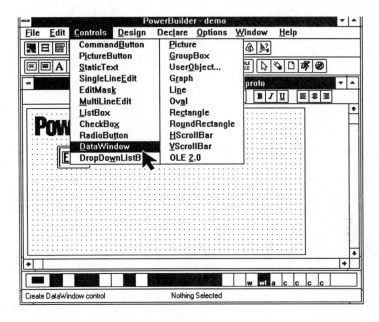

Selection of the DataWindow icon displays a cross-shaped cursor. **Move** the cursor to your preferred position for the upper-left corner of the DataWindow control. **Click** the left mouse button. A small DataWindow control appears:

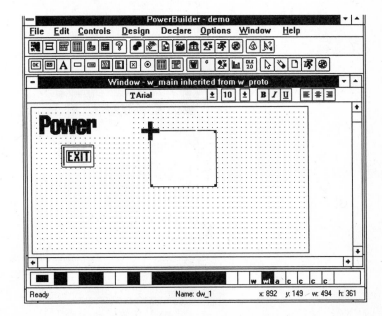

Move the control up and left to place it by the PowerSoft logo. To move the control, place the cursor within the control. **Click and hold** the left mouse button. While holding the left mouse button, **drag** the control to the new position.

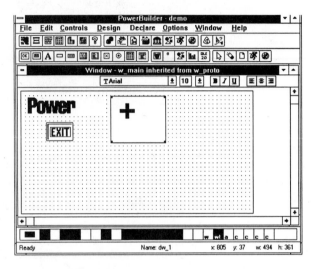

Now enlarge the control. **Move** the cursor to the lower-right hand corner of the control. The cursor becomes a double-headed arrow as shown below.

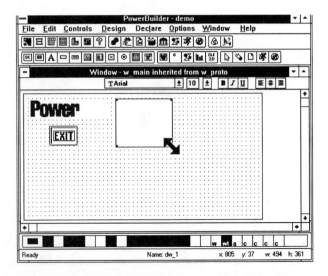

While holding the mouse button, move the cursor down and right. A shadow of the control enlarges to the size you determine. **Release** the mouse button when you have enlarged the control.

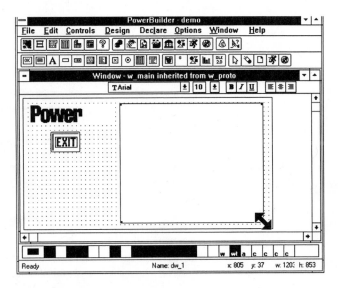

Place the cursor inside the DataWindow control and **double left-click** the mouse. This Select DataWindow appears; the *d_orders* DataWindow object already highlights.

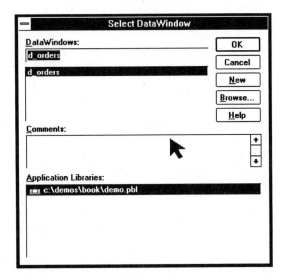

Click the *OK* button to attach the DataWindow object *d_orders* to the DataWindow control. The following window appears:

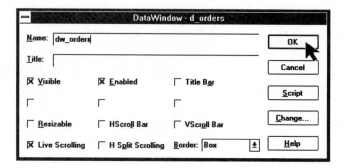

Click the Name box to change the name of the control to *dw_orders*.

Click the title bar button. Type the name *Orders* into the Title box. Click the *OK* button to accept the name. This screen appears:

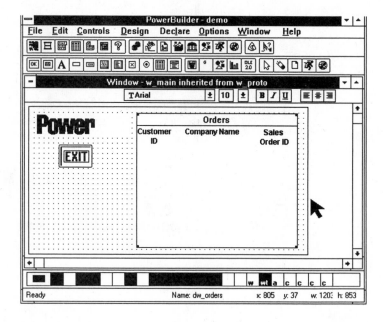

Place the cursor within the boundaries of the DataWindow control. Right-click the mouse. A menu of selections appears:

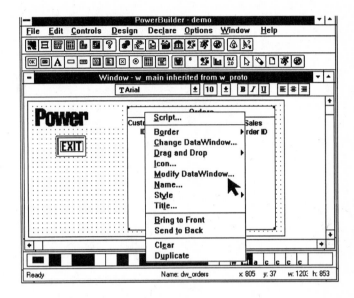

Right-click the Style selection. The style menu appears. Right-release
on the Horizontal Scroll Bar item. This adds a horizontal scroll bar to
the DataWindow control. Repeating this adds a vertical scroll bar to the
DataWindow control.

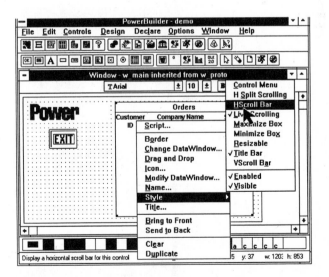

Below appears the DataWindow control with the newly-added
horizontal scroll bar. The vertical scroll bar does not show until the
application is running and needs to display additional information.

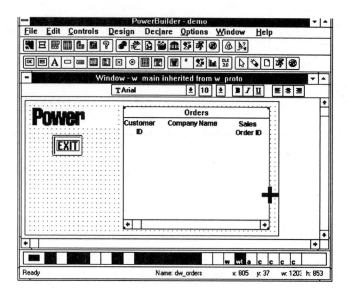

The horizontal and vertical scroll bars allow the user to move the tablular display of the DataWindow object back and forth within the control. This allows the user to move all the rows and columns in and out of the DataWindow control.

Note that this method of selecting scroll bars from the Style menu is an alternative to selecting scroll bars with the DataWindow style window shown above. Both methods assign the scroll bars to the DataWindow control.

Try previewing the Window. **Type** *control-w*. The following window appears, asking to confirm a save of changes made to the window object. Left-click Yes.

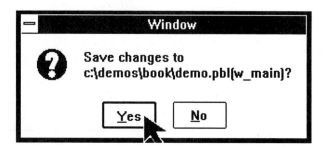

The following window appears, asking for a selection of the window to preview. To select the window *w_main*, **right-click** the Start button, or type *Alt-S*.

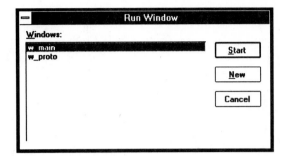

The preview window appears:

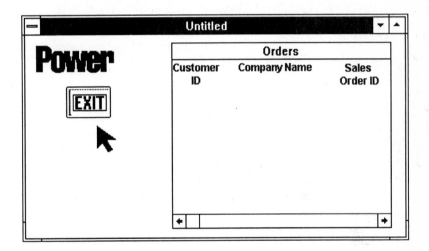

Note that the horizontal scroll bar is operational, but that no data appears in the DataWindow control. No data appears because the application has not yet called for it. The next section describes data retrieval.

Left-click the *Exit* button to close the preview and to return to the Window Painter. A confirmation response window appears. **Click** *Yes* to return to the Window Painter.

You can more quickly see the window as it appears in the running application, without actually running the window by **selecting** *Preview* from the Design menu, or type **ctrl-shift-w**.

The Window Painter reappears..

AN ASIDE ABOUT INHERITANCE

Double-click the *Exit* control you earlier added to the main window. The following window appears. **Click** the Script button.

The script painter appears. Verify selection of the clicked event for the button. The event name is in the title bar of the Script Painter window.

Pull down on the SelectEventmenu. Note that the clicked event is listed as having an associated script. The script window is empty, though. This is because the script was written for the button on the ancestor object, *w_proto*. **Pull down** on the menu item Compile item as shown in the following figure.

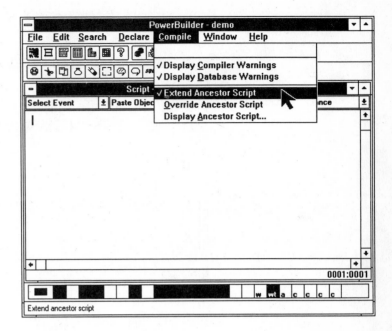

Look at the choices on this menu. The selection *Extend Ancestor Script* adds any statements written here to the script for the ancestor object. The other choice, *Override Ancestor Script*, causes a script written here to run instead of the script for the ancestor object. You may also select to display the ancestor script.

Do not add any additional script for this event. **Close** the script writer and return the the Window Painter.

MORE CONTROLS

If you preview the window, or run the application, no data appears in the DataWindow control. The reason is that there is no script to retrieve data from the database and place it in the DataWindow object.

Click the *CommandButton icon*, or select the *Command Button* from the Controls menu:

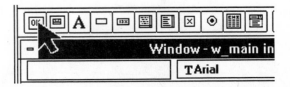

The cursor assumes a cross shape. **Move** the cursor below the Exit button and **left-click**. A command button appears.

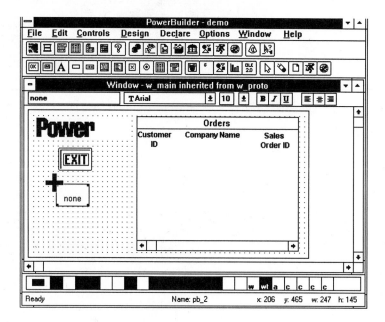

Center the cursor on the new command button. **Left-click** and hold. **Drag** the button to a position directly below the exit button.

Center the cursor on the command button and **double-left click**. The following window appears:

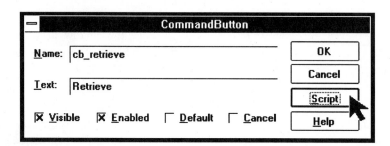

The number 1 already highlights in the Name box. **Type** in *retrieve* to rename the button *cb_retrieve*. **Click** in the text box and change the text from *none* to *Retrieve*. This text is the label that appears on the command button.

Click the Script button. The script painter appears. **Enter** the following script:

```
dw_orders.SetTransObject(SQLCA)
dw_orders.Retrieve()
```

From the Script Painter, **type** *control-L* or **select** *Script* from the Compile menu. This script should sucessfully compile.

The first line of the script associates the default transaction object *SQLCA* with the DataWindow object *dw_orders*. Although the application actually can run without this line, it is here to show you the use of the SetTransObject function. This line is not needed because the default transaction object SQLCL is being used.

The script then sends the retrieve message to the DataWindow object by calling the Retrieve function. This retrieves data from the data source into the DataWindow object's buffers.

Exit the script painter and **save** the changes to the script. **Close** the Window Painter, and **save** the changes to the window.

Return to the *Application Painter*. **Start** the *Script Painter* for the Application object. **Select** the *Open* event for the application. **Make sure** that the last line in the script, *the statement* that opens the window w_main, *is not a comment*. If you must, **remove** the *two slashes* that make the statement a comment. **Close** the *Script Painter*, **Close** the *Application Painter*.

Run the application by **clicking** the *icon* on the PowerBar or PowerPanel, or by selecting *Run* from the File menu, or by typing *ctrl-r*.

The application begins after a short pause. **Left-click** the *Retrieve* button. After a short delay, data appears in the DataWindow control. A vertical scroll bar also appears. Use the horizontal scroll bar to **move** the display to the first data entry field. The following illustration shows the running application after the horizontal scroll:

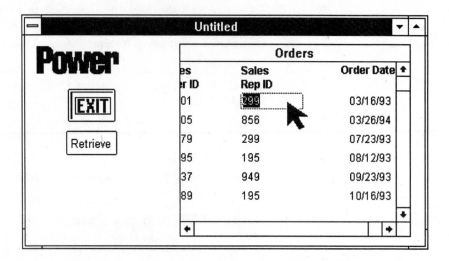

An edit control is on the first entry field, the Sales Rep ID. You can change the Sales Rep ID or the Order Date for any order shown on screen. You can move the focus from item to item with the Tab key or Shift-Tab key, or by clicking in the desired field. You can move the displayed data up and down in the DataWindow control with the vertical scroll bar.

Note that there is no way to apply the changes you have made in the DataWindow control back into the database. You need an update button which you will add shortly.

To stop the running application, **left-click** the *Exit* button.

Start the Window Painter and open the window *w_main*. **Add** another CommandButton. **Set** the text for the CommandButton to Update. Name the CommandButton object *cb_update*. **Edit** the script for the clicked event for the button. Include the following statement in the script:

```
dw_orders.Update()
```

Close the script painter. **Save** the script. Save the CommandButton.

Run the application again. **Save** the changes to the window when prompted. **Use** the *Retrieve* CommandButton to retrieve data from the database.

Scroll horizontally to the Balance column. **Click** in the edit control and change the Order Date for the first order to 3/17/93. **Left-click** the *Update* CommandButton to save the change you have made back to the database.

Click the *Retreive* CommandButton again to retrieve data from the database again. The screen does not change. The reason is that the data in the database now includes the change you made. Note that the data retrieved from the database, including the change that you made, still displays on-screen.

Congratulations, you have a running application!

Close the running application. Open the Window Painter again with the *w_main* window.

ERROR HANDLING

The scripts for the *Retrieve* and *Update* command buttons do not process any errors. What happens if something goes wrong during an update or retrieve?

The *Retrieve* function returns a number greater than zero for a successful retrieval. The number returned is the number of rows retrieved. In a successful retrieval, the *Retrieve* function returns a value of *minus one*. If no rows are retrieved, the function returns a value of *zero*.

You can use this return value to effect the operation of the running application. Here is an upgraded script for the clicked event of the Update CommandButton:

```
if dw_orders.Update () > 0 then
   commit;
else
   rollback;
end if
```

This script commits the transaction of a successful update. A failed update rolls back the transaction. See Section Two of this book if you are unfamiliar with transactions.

PRINTING THE RESULTS

Add another CommandButton to the window. Name the button *cb_print*. Change the text for the CommandButton to *Print*. Add the following statements to the script for the clicked event for the CommandButton:

```
int job
```

```
job = PrintOpen("Orders Report")
printDataWindow(job, dw_orders)
PrintClose(job)
```

Save the script. Save the changes. **Run** the application again. **Left-click** the *Retrieve* CommandButton. **Left-click** the *Print* CommandButton to print the retrieved records. Closee the Window Painter.

The final state of the window is as follows:

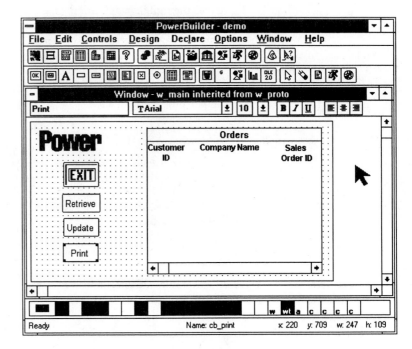

In this chapter, you add a menu to your application. You have used menus; they are everywhere in PowerBuilder and other Windows applications.

There are two steps to add a menu to your application. First, you create the menu with the Menu Painter. Then you associate the menu with a window. You make the association with the Window Painter.

Start by using the Window Painter to edit the window *w_main*, the main window for the application. **Remove** the *retrieve*, *update* and *print* buttons from the window. Menu items will replace them.

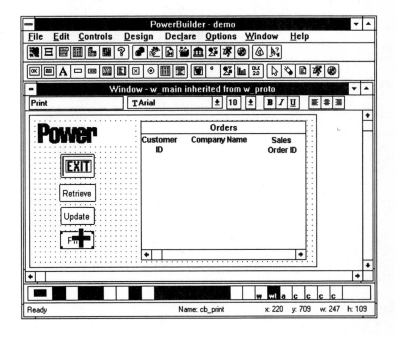

From within the Window Painter, **select** the *retrieve* button by placing the cursor on it and left-clicking. Or, to select all three buttons, **hold down** the *CTRL* key and **left click** on each of the *other two application buttons* on the window *w_main*.

You now have selected all three buttons on your application window.
Select *Delete* from the Edit menu, or **press** the *DEL* key. This removes
all three buttons.

Note that you cannot remove the *Exit* button from this window. That
button is inherited from the parent window *w_proto*.

Save the window with *Save* from the File menu. As you are using the
File menu, take a moment to look at the selections. This exemplifies the
type of menu you can add to your PowerBuilder application. **Close** the
Window Painter.

PARTS OF THE MENU

A Menu is a PowerBuilder visual object. A menu allows a user to select
options or actions from a list. The menu bar is an alternative to using
other controls like buttons.

When you have finished working with the Menu Painter, the menu is
saved in a PowerBuilder library. A menu has attributes. Attributes
govern the display of the menu or the allowability of shortcut keys or
accelerator keys.

The area of a window where the menu displays is the menu bar. The
menu bar lists commands or options. Each of these commands or
options is a MenuItem. A *command* MenuItem causes some action. An
option MenuItem displays a list of other options or items.

Take the Menu Painter as an example in the following figure. Each of
the MenuItems listed on the menu bar are options. That is, clicking on
any option shows a pulldown list of other options or commands, as
determined by the design of the Menu Painter. You can use your own
options or commands as MenuItems on a Menu Bar.

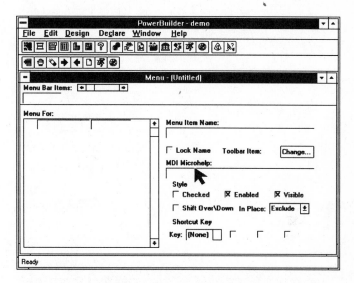

The MenuItems on the menu bar for the Menu Painter are *File*, *Edit*,
Design, *Declare*, *Window* and *Help*. Clicking on any of these MenuItems
produces a pulldown list of commands or options:

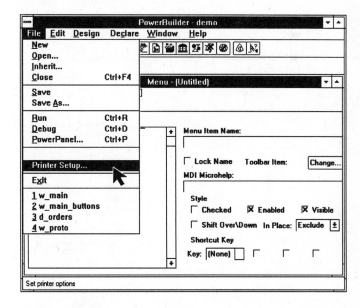

The choices for the File menu are *New, Open, Inherit, Close, Save, Save As, Run, Debug, PowerPanel, Print, Printer Setup* and *Exit*. Each of these MenuItems is a command. Clicking on any of these MenuItems starts an activity, as determined by the design of the Menu Painter. MenuItems at this level can also produce another list of options and commands.

All of the MenuItems under any option you create should relate to each other. For example, all the MenuItems under the File option are about file operations for the Menu object; *saving* the menu, *naming* the menu or *printing* the menu.

DISPLAYING MENUS

You can display menus several ways. *Dropdown* menus are lists produced under a MenuItem in a menu bar.

Selecting a dropdown MenuItem can display a cascading menu. The cascading menu shows further choices. Each of these choices should have something to do with the selected MenuItem.

A popup menu provides information related to a user request. A popup menu floats near the cursor position when the mouse clicks. Remember, this is like the popup menus in the DataWindow painter.

MENU OPTIONS

Various options allow you to make a menu easier to understand and use. As an example, look again at the File menu from the Menu Painter:

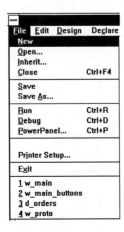

Separator lines indicate logically related groups of commands on the menu. Note the separator line under the Close MenuItem.

A check mark to the left of a MenuItem indicates selection of the MenuItem. The figure above does not show this.

Shortcut and accelerator keys allow you to access menu commands from the keyboard. A shortcut key executes a MenuItem with a single keyboard entry. Pressing *Ctrl+F4* closes the Menu Painter, as in the menu above.

Some MenuItems have an underline under one letter of the command name. The *F* in the *File* command for the Menu Painter has an underline, and the *O* in the *Open* command has an underline. These underlines show accelerator keys. Accelerator keys allow you to navigate menus from the keyboard. Pressing *Alt-F* opens the *File* menu. Pressing *Alt-N* selects the *New* MenuItem from the menu.

Note that three periods—punctuation known as an *ellipsis*—trails some of the MenuItems on the *File* menu. Any MenuItem marked with an ellipsis prompts the user for further information. If you select *Save As*, a window appears asking for information including the new name for the menu.

A greyed-out menu item marks an unavailable item. When the menu item becomes available the color returns to normal.

EVENTS

Each MenuItem has two events, *selected* and *clicked*.

Moving the cursor to a MenuItemA menu item selects and triggers the selected item. *Alt-F* pulls down the file menu. Moving the cursor keys up and down selects each MenuItem in turn. Selection of a MenuItem triggers the corresponding selected event. Clicking and holding the mouse allows the user at will to select MenuItems.

The clicked event occurs when the user left-clicks on a MenuItem or keyboards the MenuItem. Left-clicking and holding on the File MenuItem pulls down File menu. Holding the left mouse button down and moving the cursor selects each menu item to which the cursor points. Releasing the left mouse button during selection of a MenuItem completes the left-click and selects the highlighted MenuItem.

SCRIPTS

A PowerScript controls the processing for each of the clicked and selected events. A clicked-event script for a MenuItem can open a new window or spur some other activity.

Referring To Controls

A window can contain controls like control buttons or picture buttons. A menu associates with a particular window. Referring to a window control from the menu for the window is often necessary.

To refer to a window control in a script for a menu event, you must qualify fully the control name. That is you must specify the name of the window and the name of the control. The syntax is

```
window_name.control_name.attribute = value
```

You might take a menu associated with the window *w_main*. This window could have a command button named *cb_insert*. Setting the enabled attribute enables or disables the control button. To disable the *cb_insert* button, type:

```
w_main.cb_insert.enabled = FALSE
```

ParentWindow

A script for a menu event must use the pronoun *ParentWindow* to refer to the window with which the menu associates. Note that you must use the pronoun *ParentWindow* instead of the pronoun *Parent*.

The following statement in a menu script closes the window with which the menu associates:

```
Close(ParentWindow)
```

Note that you can only use the pronoun *ParentWindow* to refer to the attributes of the window. You cannot use the pronoun *ParentWindow* to refer to controls on that window.

Remember that the following statement enables the *cb_insert* button:

```
w_main.cb_insert.enabled = FALSE
```

The following statement WILL NOT WORK:

```
ParentWindow.cb_insert.enabled = FALSE
```

This

A script associates with an individual MenuItem. The pronoun *This* refers to the MenuItem for which the script is written.

USING THE MENU PAINTER

Start the Menu Painter with the Menu Painter *icon* from the PowerBar or PowerPanel:

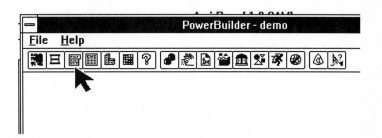

The Select Menu window appears.

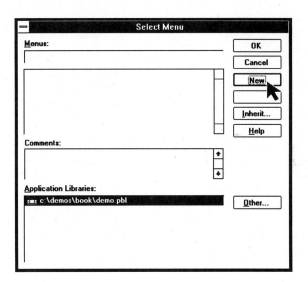

Left-Click on the *New* button and the Menu Painter starts.

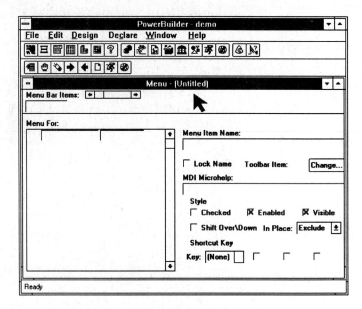

Note that Menus are one of the inheritable PowerBuilder objects. If you had other menus in your application, you could create the new menu by inheritance.

Notably, this is one of the easier painters with fewer choices of icons.

Set Menuitems

Start by entering the names of each of the MenuItems on the menu bar. The cursor should be in the first field on the menu bar in the Menu Painter. Type in the empty field the item name *&File*.

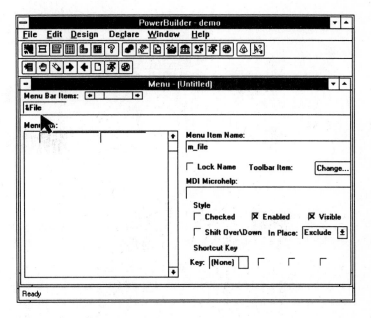

The ampersand indicates that the following character—*F* in this example—will be an accelerator key. You can put the ampersand anywhere in the MenuItem name.

Left-click on the menu bar just to the right of the File MenuItem that you just added. This creates a new empty slot for a second MenuItem.

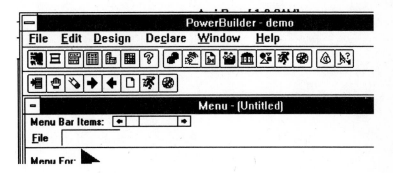

Enter the next MenuItem name, *&Help*. Remember if you want to make the accelerator key *e* instead of *h*, use *H&elp*:

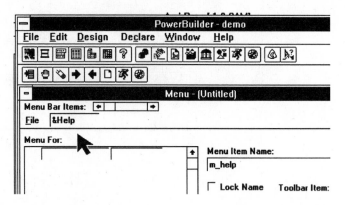

Note that the MenuItem is automatically assigned a name. This assigned name is based on the item you entered.

Position the cursor on the MenuItem named File and **left-click**. Below the File MenuItem is a list named *Menu For: File*.

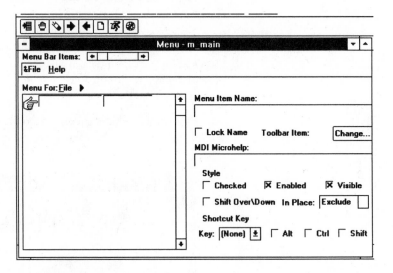

Position the cursor in this field and **left-click**. A hand indicating the active field appears, as shown below. You have selected the first MenuItem under the File MenuItem.

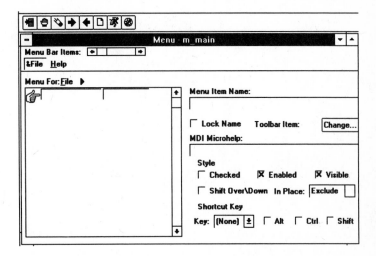

The selected field specifies the MenuItems under the File menu. **Type** in the name *&Retrieve* in the left field then **press** the *tab* key. Continue to enter item names. Use *&Save* and *&Print* for the next two items. For the fourth item, **enter** a single *dash* (—) in the left field. This puts a separator line on the menu. For the last item enter *&Exit*. The menu should look like this:

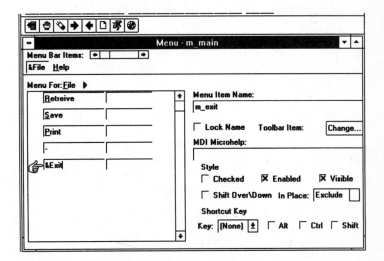

The cursor should still be on the last item in the menu, *&Exit*. **Pull down** on the *Shortcut Key* menu, as shown in the next illustration. **Scroll down** and **pick** *F10* as the function key. Now, the *F10* function key selects the Exit menu item when you run the application.

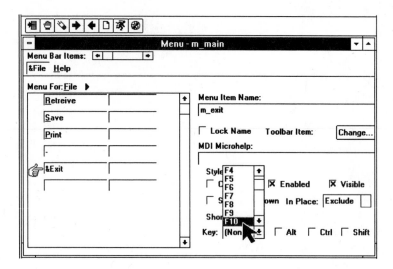

You can use *alt*, *control*, or *shift* key combinations for shortcut keys as well, Just select the check box to the right of the pulldown menu (see above).

Now is a good time to save the menu. Use the *File* menu for the Menu Painter to save the menu as *m_main*. This puts the menu in your *demo.pbl* library.

Each MenuItem must have a name. MenuItem names assign automatically. Look at the upper right corner of the Menu Painter. Note that the last entry you made for the exit key and the Exit MenuItem now has the name of *m_exit*. You can change the suggested name to anything you like. For now, leave the default name as is.

Every MenuItem has an enabled attribute. If the enabled attribute is assigned the logical value of FALSE, the user cannot use the MenuItem. The running application can toggle the value of the attribute between *enabled* and *not enabled*. Similarly, the visible attribute determines if the item is shown on the menu at all.

The remaining attribute available is the checked attribute. Setting the checked attribute to a logical value of TRUE puts a small check mark to the left of the MenuItem. This confirms selection of the menu item. You should recognize this usage from familiar Windows applications.

Now, preview your menu. **Press** the shortcut *ctrl-w* or select *preview* from the Menu Painter Design menu. Note that you now know how to assign short-cut keys like these in your own applications.

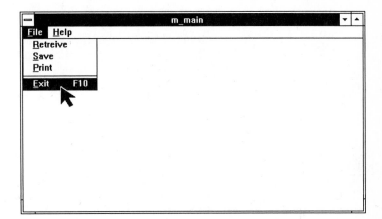

Pull down the File menu with a **left-click** on *File*. **Left-click** *Print* to select that MenuItem. Nothing happens as you select the MenuItems. The reason is that you are previewing the menu, not running the menu from a running application.

Press the *F10* key to select the exit menu item. Note that the File MenuItem is selected. **Press** the escape (*ESC*) key to unselect the File MenuItem. **Double-click** the *control box* in the upper left corner of the window, or **press** *F4* to exit the preview mode. The Menu Painter window returns to your screen.

Assigning The Menu To A Window

Minimize the Menu Painter window. **Open** the Window Painter. **Select** the main window for the demonstration application, *w_main*. **Select** *Window Style* from the Design menu, or **position** the *cursor* on the window (but outside of the DataWindow) and **double-left click**. The style window appears.

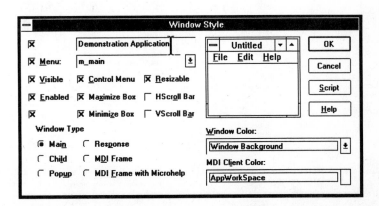

Left-click the Menu *check box*. The menu name *m_main* enters automatically. While here in the Style Window, **change** the title of the window to *Demonstration Application*. **Click** the *OK* button to close the Style window. You have associated the menu *m_main* with the window *w_main*.

Close the Window Painter, and **save** your changes. **Run** your application. It should begin and include a menu as well as the new title.

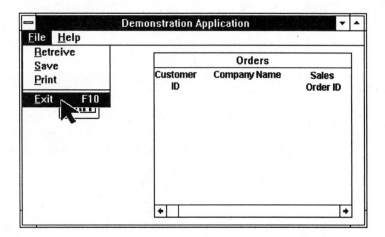

Close your running application, and **return** to the Menu Painter.

Writing Scripts

Maximize the menu painter window. The menu *m_main* displays. **Left-click** the *Retrieve* MenuItem. **Click** on the script *icon*, or **select** *Script* from the Edit menu, or **press** the *ctrl-s* accelerator key.

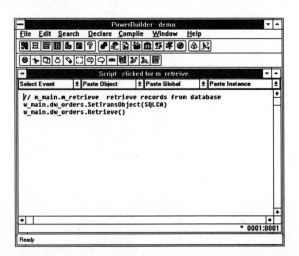

The script painter appears. Make sure that you have selected the clicked event for the *Retrieve* menu item. **Enter** the following with the script painter:

```
// m_main.m_retrieve  retrieve records from database
w_main.dw_orders.SetTransObject(SQLCA)
w_main.dw_orders.Retrieve()
```

Selecting the *Retrieve* MenuItem causes this script to retrieve records from the database. **Save** the script, and **run** the application. When you select *Retrieve* from the menu, records from the database display in the DataWindow.

Similarly, here is the script for the *Save* MenuItem. **Add** this script to the clicked event for the Save MenuItem

```
w_main.dw_orders.Update()
```

Here is a script for the Print MenuItem:

```
int job
job = PrintOpen("Orders Report")
printDataWindow(job, w_main.dw_orders)
PrintClose(job)
```

Here is the script for the MenuItem that exits the application:

```
close(ParentWindow)
```

Now, **add** another MenuItem before the Print MenuItem called "Printer Setup." Use the Insert MenuItem on the edit menu. Here is the script for calling the printer setup utility supplied with Windows.

```
//Clicked script for m_printsetup
if PrintSetup( ) = -1 then
   MessageBox("Error!","PrintSetup Failed")
end if
```

Close the Menu Painter. Save your changes. Run the application and try the new menu. Close the Menu Painter. Save your changes. Run the application and try the new menu.

As shown in chapter 1-3, a function is a script that has a name and performs a specific task. A function can contain any statement that is legal in a script. You can call a function by its name from a PowerScript. This causes the statements in the function to execute. Arguments pass the function data for the calculations.

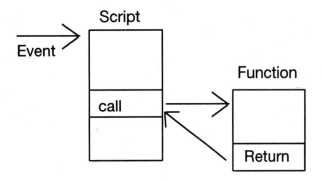

When the function has finished its computations, it can return a value. A returned value is often a string or an integer. Often a function returns an integer value of 1 if it succeeds in its calculations and a value of -1 if not. A function that does not return a value is a subroutine.

Functions allow you to create methods. You can reuse these methods thoughout an application. This ability to reuse code shortens your development time by reducing the required programming. Functions also make scripts more readable. Using a call to a function within a script makes the script easier to read than including a block of code. The reason is that scripts stay smaller.

SCOPE OF FUNCTIONS

The scope of a function determines its accessibility from the application. Functions can have one of three access levels. These access levels determine the scope of the function. The access levels are:

✓ public
✓ private
✓ protected

Functions with an access level of *public* are global functions. Calling a function with an access level of *public* is possible anywhere in an application from any script. If a function is general in purpose and potentially useful throughout an application, you can make the access level *public*.

You can write functions that associate directly with windows, menus or user objects. These functions are object-level functions. Obect-level functions can have an access level of *private* or *protected*.

You can call an object-level function with an access level of *private* from the scripts for a single object. You can call an object-level function with an access level of *protected* from the script for an object or from a script for any of its decendants.

Different object-level functions with the same name are allowed because PowerBuilder is polymorphic. There is not any ambiguity in referencing an object-level function because an object name is always used in a call to an object-level function.

As an example, take an application named *demo* that contains several objects including two windows, *w_data_entry* and *w_sales_oe*. Two different object-level functions have definitions, one for each of the two objects. Although the objects have the same name, they can do different things.

You can start the function painter from the PowerBar or PowerPanel. You can also start the function painter from the declare menu in the window, menu or user-object painters. Lastly, you can start the function painter from the declare menu in the script painter—when you have started the script painter from the window, menu, or user-object painter.

When you have started the function painter from the PowerBar or PowerPanel, the access level for the function you create will always be public. That is, you can only create global functions from the PowerBar or PowerPanel. When creating a script from an object painter or the script painter, you will be allowed to specify the access level as public, private or protected. You can create global or object-level functions from within these painters.

WRITING A GLOBAL USER

A global user function has an access level of public. To start the function painter, **click** the function icon on the PowerPanel or PoweBar.

After you select the function painter, the following window will appear.

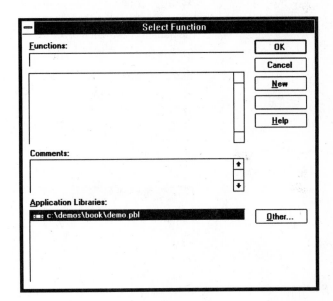

Existing functions are listed by name in the upper left hand window. You could select a function, if any were listed, by clicking on any function name and then clicking on the OK button to modify the selected function. The Other button allows you to search other libraries for functions.

To create a new function, **click** the New button. Clicking on the New button will cause the following window to display:

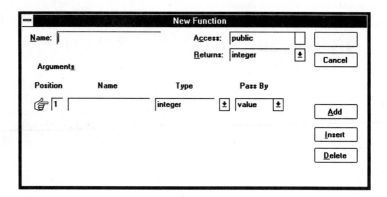

As this is a global function, the access level is set to public and cannot be changed. **Click** in the Name window on the form and then type in the name of your choice, for example, **f_postage**. Note that only lower-case letters are allowed.

Next, **specify** the type of the return value, such as string or integer. The type will default to integer. **Pull-down** on the return menu and select a type. You can write a function that does not have a return value. To write a function that does not have a return value, **select** *(None)* as the type of the return value. For this example, **leave** the *return value* type as an *integer*.

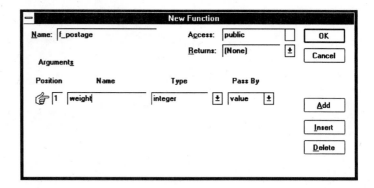

Next, you must specify any arguments. **Click** in the name box and type in the name of your choice, for example "weight." Note that while you may type in upper case letters for an argument identifier, they will all be converted to lower case when you save the function. Next, **pull-down** on the type menu to select the type of the argument, for example the default of integer.

The argument you have just specified, weight, is called a formal argument. It sets the pattern for the argument when the function is called in a running application. In this example, the formal argument is used to represent the weight transmitted to the running function.

Later, when the function is called from a running script, an actual argument is used. For example, you could call the function with the following statement:

```
if Postage(MyPackage) > 0 then
   . . .do this
else
   . . .error processing goes here
end if
```

This sample calls the Postage function with the actual argument MyPackage. The value of the actual argument MyPackage is sent to the called function via the formal argument.

The last choice in the window determines how the actual argument is passed to the running function. Actual arguments can be passed by reference or by value.

When an argument is passed by value, the function receives a copy of the value the argument contains. If the function changes the value of the formal argument, the value of the actual argument doesn't change.

When the argument is passed by reference, the identifier for the actual argument is passed instead of the value that the actual argument contains.Changing the value of the formal argument causes the value of the item passed to change. If a function changes a value passed by reference, when control is passed back to the calling script, the original item will contain the new value.

You can add additional formal arguments to the function definition by clicking on the new button or insert button. You can remove formal arguments with the delete button.

Once you have completed the definition of the function, **click** the OK button to make the script painter appear:

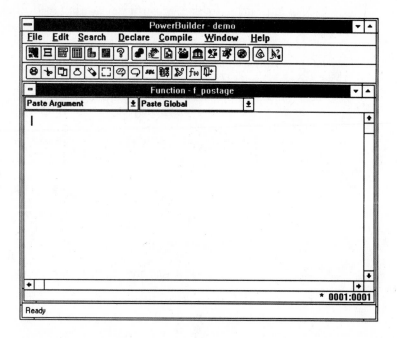

Now you can enter the script for the function. Here is a sample script for the postage function. Note that a variable named *Postage* is defined as a local variable at the top of the script. This variable is used to hold the return value for the function.

```
// compute postage given weight
real Postage
choose case Weight
   case is < 16
      Postage = Weight * 0.30
   case 16 to 48
      Postage = 4.50
   case else
      Postage = -1.0
end choose
return Postage
```

Note too, that there is no local variable defined for the weight. This is because the weight is already defined as a formal argument. The function painter, and the script for the function, know about the formal arguments.

When you are writing a function, you can see a list of arguments at any time by **pulling down** the paste argument window. Click any of the arguments listed to place the name in the script at the current cursor position.

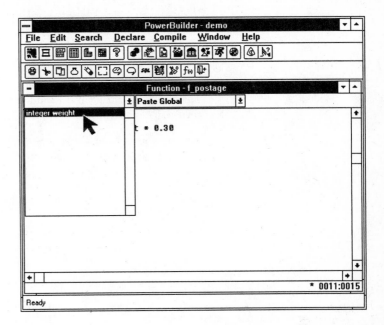

When you have typed in a script, **compile** it with the compile menu choice or by typing control-1. The compiler will indicate any errors. Correct any errors and save the script. You have created a function. If you attempt to save the function, the function will also be compiled. If there are any compile errors you will be given an opportunity to correct them.

Don't save this function! Close the Function Painter. If you have saved the function, use the Library Painter to remove it from the library.

You can save a script that does not compile correctly. When you close the function painter, the script is compiled automatically. You will be given a choice that allows you to save the script even though it contains errors.

AN EXAMPLE

Here is an example of a function and its use. The following is a line from a script written for the close event of a window named w_financial. This statement calls a function named f_close_sheet.

```
...
   f_close_sheet(w_financial,"financial")
   . . .
```

The function call uses two actual arguments, w_financial and "financial." W_financial is a window object. The second argument, "financial", is a string.

The function has two formal arguments, aw_selected and as_name. The argument aw_name is type window. The argument as_name is a type string.

Here is the script for the f_close sheet function. This function does not return a value.

```
string ls_key

// set the screen pointer to an hour glass shape.
SetPointer(HourGlass!)

if aw_selected.WindowState = Normal! then
  // Save the x and y position of the window
  ls_key = aw_name + "X"
  SetProfileString("carcost.ini","application",ls_key, &
    String(aw_selected.X,"####"))
  ls_key = aw_name + "Y"
  SetProfileString("carcost.ini","application",ls_key, &
    String(aw_selected.Y,"####"))

  // Save the width and heigth of the window
  ls_key = aw_name + "W"
  SetProfileString("carcost.ini","application",ls_key, &
    String(aw_selected.width,"####"))
  ls_key = aw_name + "H"
  SetProfileString("carcost.ini","application",ls_key, &
    String(aw_selected.height,"####"))
end if

SetPointer(Beam!)
return 0
```

The function is called with two actual arguments. The first argument is used to pass a window object to the function, w_financial. The second argument passes a string containing a name, "financial".

The first statement in the script defines a local string variable named ls_key. The second statement in the script calls a PowerBuilder supplied function named SetPointer. This function is used to change the type of pointer that is displayed. In this example, the call changes the pointer to an hour glass shape to indicate a delay to the user.

The if statement detects whether or not the window state is normal size rather than some other reduced state like iconized. If the window is in the normal size, the following statements save the size and position into the profile file for the application.

You can use the PowerBuilder on-line help to see the format of the SetProfileString function. This function saves information into the portion of the profile file pointed to by the arguments.

WRITING AN OBJECT-LEVEL FUNCTION

Functions can have an access level of public, private or protected. Global functions have an access level of public. Object-level functions can have an access level of private or protected. The procedure for writing object-level functions is the same as shown above for global functions. Call the function painter from the window, menu or user-object painter, or the script painter. When you have called the function painter from an object painter, you can specify an access level of private, protected or public. Specifying an access level of private or protected will create an object-level function.

MODIFYING USER-DEFINED

You can easily change an existing function. To change a functions' return type, arguments or access level, open the function painter. Select, by name, the function you wish to modify. The function painter workspace will display.

To change the function declaration, chosse the Function Declaration item from the Edit menu. The function declaration window will appear.

CALLING A FUNCTION

A user defined function is called by a reference to its name. The reference is followed by a list of arguments in parentheses. For example:

```
integer total
total = f_payment(12, 8.5)
```

This example references (calls) a function named f_payment. The function has two arguments, an integer amount and a real number.

The number of actual arguments that you use when the function is called must match the number of formal arguments you used when you defined the function. Each of the actual arguments must agree in type with the formal function. That is, if you defined the first argument of a function as a real number, you must call the function with a real number or a variable of type real.

Object-level functions must include the name of the object in the function call. Here is the syntax for a call to an object-level function:

```
object.function(arguments)
```

Here is an example of a call to an object-level function:

```
w_dentry.f_getNames(names,"~t")
```

1-11 Sealing Off an Application

Windows programs arrive as executable files. These files carry an *.exe* suffix. For example, PowerBuilder itself starts by having Windows load and run the file *pb040.exe*.

A running Windows application can reference various libraries. A library holds items including code and graphics objects. Windows libraries are files with a suffix of *.dll* (Dynamic Link Library). A running PowerBuilder application can also access a library. A PowerBuilder library is a *.pbd* file, a PowerBuilder Dynamic Library.

To deliver a PowerBuilder application, you must create an *.exe* file from the contents of the *.pbl* files that comprise the application. The user runs the resultant PowerBuilder *.exe* file by loading and running the *.exe* file from within Windows. In object-oriented terminology, creating the executable file from your PowerBuilder application is called "sealing off the application.

The *.exe* file contains a bootstrap routine that Windows can execute. The bootstrap is the code that Windows uses to interpret the sealed off application. The library also contains the compiled version of all objects that your application references in the libraries.

RUNNING THE APPLICATION

When an application starts, Windows runs the bootstrap routine found in the *.exe* file. The bootstrap routine uses the PowerBuilder Database Development and Deployment Kit. The DDDK includes various programs that allows Windows and the sealed off application to access the compiled objects in the executable file.

To deliver a PowerBuilder application, you must seal off the application to make an *.exe* file. The user needs the .exe file and the DDDK. The user does not need the full PowerBuilder development environment to run the application but does need the DDDK, which is a series of Windows programs and libraries. If your application uses PowerBuilder libraries, you need to give users these libraries with the application as well.

SEALING THE APPLICATION

Use the Application Painter to seal off the application and create the *.exe* file. For a simple application like the demonstration program you have built, just **select** the Create Executable MenuItem from the File menu of the Application Painter.

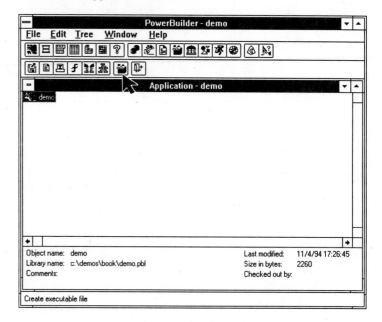

This window appears:

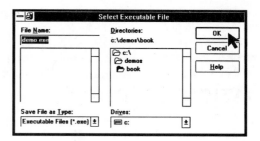

The name of the proposed *.exe* file has a default name, in this case *demo.exe*. You may change this name, but the suffix *must* be *.exe*. **Left-click** the *OK* button to move to the following screen:

```
┌──────────────────────────────────────────────────────────┐
│ ─             Create Executable                            │
├──────────────────────────────────────────────────────────┤
│ 1. Make sure the executable file name is correct.    ┌─────────┐│
│ 2. Select all dynamic libraries.                     │  OK     ││
│ 3. If additional resources are required, specify a resource file. └─────────┘│
│ 4. Click OK to create executable file.               ┌─────────┐│
│                                                      │ Cancel  ││
│ Executable File Name:                                └─────────┘│
│ ┌────────────────────────────────────────────┐      ┌─────────┐│
│ │ c:\demos\book\demo.exe                      │      │  Help   ││
│ └────────────────────────────────────────────┘      └─────────┘│
│ Dynamic Libraries:                                   ┌─────────┐│
│ ┌────────────────────────────────────────────┐      │ Change..││
│ │ c:\demos\book\demo.pbl                      │      └─────────┘│
│ │                                             │                 │
│ │                                             │                 │
│ │                                             │                 │
│ └────────────────────────────────────────────┘                 │
│ Resource File Name:                                             │
│ ┌────────────────────────────────────────────┐      ┌─────────┐│
│ │                                             │      │ Files...││
│ └────────────────────────────────────────────┘      └─────────┘│
└──────────────────────────────────────────────────────────┘
```

This screen allows you to specify any resource files or libraries needed to create the executable. **Click** the *OK* button to continue. A short pause ensues as PowerBuilder creates the *.exe* file.

Close the application painter. You can now run the *demo.exe* file from within Windows. To distribute the application you would copy the *demo.exe* file and the PowerBuilder run-time files to a diskette. Consult PowerBuilder documentation for details on distributing the run-time library.

APPLICATION COMPONENTS

A PowerBuilder application can contain many different components, such as

> ✓ Windows
>
> ✓ DataWindows
>
> ✓ Controls
>
> ✓ UserObjects
>
> ✓ icons
>
> ✓ bitmaps

Most of these objects store in a PowerBuilder library, a *.pbl*, as you create your application. Some of the objects store in other types of files. For example, a bitmap can be stored in a DOS file named *name.bmp*, and an icon can store in a DOS file named *name.ico*.

By four ways, you can make the various components of a PowerBuilder application available when sealing off the application.

(1) You can include all the PowerBuilder objects, including bitmaps and icons, in a single executable file.

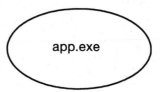

(2) You can include most of the PowerBuilder objects in the *.exe* file and provide one or more separate DOS files to hold bitmaps or icons. This can serve because bitmaps are graphics objects, possibly quite large. Leaving bitmaps in separate files can dramatically reduce the size of the *.exe* file.

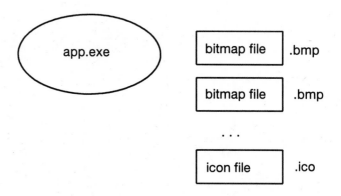

(3) You can use PowerBuilder Dynamic Libraries. A PBD can contain some of the objects used by the sealed off application. You can put some of the PowerBuilder objects into the *.exe* file with all the bitmaps and icons. Other objects remain in the PBD.

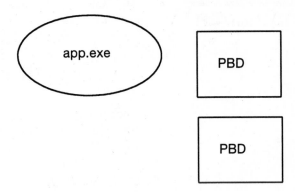

Last, you can use a combination of PBD files with external DOS files that hold icons or bitmaps.

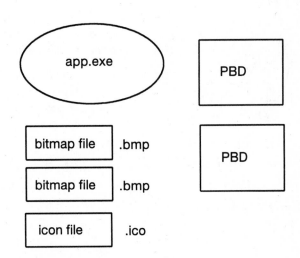

DISTRIBUTION OPTIONS

If you have used inheritance in building your application, you have two choices. You can put an ancestor object and all the objects that inherit from that ancestor in the *.exe* file. An alternative is to place the ancestor object and its descendants in one or more *.pbd* files. In this case the ancestor and descendant objects can scatter over several *.pbd* files.

To summarize, you cannot split an ancestor and its descendants between the *.exe* and *.pbd* files. The ancestor and all descendants can all stay in the *.exe* file. Or, the ancestor and all the descendants can stay in *.pbd* files.

POWERBUILDER DYNAMIC LIBRARIES

A PowerBuilder Dynamic Library is a DOS file that contains compiled PowerBuilder objects. The suffix *.pbd* marks these files. Running PowerBuilder application accesses the objects in a *.pbd*. The objects in the *.pbd* load into memory as needed by the running application, hence the name *dynamic library*. Libraries contain additional objects used by the running application.

You should use a *.pbd* to keep the *.exe* files as small as possible. If the number and size of the objects in your application make the *.exe* file larger than 1.2MB-1.5MB, use a *.pbd*. The libraries also should be small. Libraries should hold fifty to sixty objects and stay smaller than 800KB. If the objects for your application exceed this, split them into separate *.pbd* files.

A dynamic library allows several applications to share the same objects. If you have written multiple applications that use a similar set of objects, place those common objects into libraries. Separate applications can access the libraries and share the objects in the libraries.

Dynamic libraries simplify the compartmentalization of your application into smaller segments. These smaller segments make easier the management of the components of your application.

You can use libraries to distribute the components of an application selectively. This makes upgrading or repairing an application much easier. If there is a bug to fix, you could redistribute a single library rather than the complete application.

APPLICATION COMPONENTS

In addition to PowerBuilder Dynamic Libraries, you can distribute some types of objects in resource files. A PowerBuilder resource file is a DOS file with a *.pbr* suffix. The resource file can contain

✓ bitmaps (*.rle* or *.bmp* files)

✓ cursors (*.cur* files)

✓ icons (*.ico* files)

✓ DataWindow objects

A *.pbr* is useful for scripts in your application dynamically to assign resources to object attributes or object controls. Your application might assign a DataWindow object to a DataWindow control at run-time:

```
dw_control.DataObject = "dw_obj_name"
```

Or, it might assign a bitmap to a picture button at run-time:

```
picture_control.PictureName = "file.bmp"
```

Or, it might assign an icon to the icon attribute of a DataWindow control at run-time.

```
dw_control.icon = "name.ico"
```

You need not use a *.pbr* when you seal off your application. However, using a *.pbr* can help you reduce the number of files you need to distribute with your sealed off application. Instead of shipping the *.exe* file and several DOS files, you can ship one *.pbr* file with the *.exe* file.

Note that if you do not use a *.pbr* file, you must put dynamically-accessible DataWindow objects in a *.pbd*.

To create a *.pbr* file, use any editor of your choice, such as the Notepad supplied with Windows, to create an ASCII file. This file lists names of the objects for the *.pbr* file, such as

```
emp3.bmp
chart1.bmp
chart2.bmp
dist1.pbl (d_orders)
chart3.bmp
dw2.ico
```

Be sure to list only one object on any line. List all of the resources. Note that only one *.pbr* file is allowable within an application.

To include a DataWindow object in the *.pbr*, include an entry with the name of the library followed by the name of the object in parenthesis. The fourth line in the foregoing example shows this.

If the objects that you want to include in the *.pbr* are not in the current working directory, you must qualify each of the names to show the drive name and the complete search path to the objects. Note that if the name of the object in the .pbr includes the search path, the reference to the object in an application script must also include the search path.

When you seal off the application with the Application Painter, make sure that the application you want to seal off is the current application. Include all the *.pbl* files in the library search path for the application. If the application needs a *.pbr* file, assure that you have created it prior to sealing off the application.

A relational database management system usually includes various tools that supplement the database engine. You can use these tools, such as an SQL utility, to create and manipulate the tables in a database. You can also use the PowerBuilder Database Painter to perform various maintenance functions, including

✓ adding or dropping new tables
✓ adding or dropping columns within tables
✓ modifying columns within tables
✓ adding or dropping primary and foreign keys
✓ adding or dropping indices
✓ adding or dropping new views

Either the access permissions assigned to you by your database administrator or, in some cases, the capabilities of the Database Painter may limit the access to these facilities.

The vendor-supplied utilities often can supplement the DatabasePainter. In many cases, the vendor-supplied utilities can make more changes to the database than can the Database Painter.

EXTENDED COLUMN ATTRIBUTES

PowerBuilder allows you to create and maintain extended display and validation formats, edit masks and initial values for PowerBuilder applications. These are each extended attributes; they apply to columns as they will appear in a PowerBuilder application. They affect the appearance of on-screen columns.

For example, an edit mask can determine what characters the user can type into a field. Validation formats can assure the entering of only legal values.

PowerBuilder stores the extended formatting information in tables in the database. PowerBuilder can automatically add these tables to the database. PowerBuilder, not the database management system itself, creates these tables. PowerBuilder creates and manages the extended attributes. The database management system does not maintain or utilize these values.

DATA MANIPULATION TOOL

The Database Painter provides a data manipulation tool useful for adding, updating and deleting data held in the database. This tool provides a simple, facile interface for performing these operations.

DATABASE ADMINISTRATION TOOL

The Database Painter includes a database administration tool. This tool allows you to change access permissions, create SQL statements, and execute SQL statements.

USING THE DATABASE PAINTER

Start the Database Painter with the Database Painter icon on the PowerPanel or PowerBar.

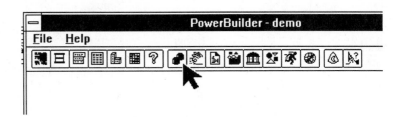

The Database Painter attempts to connect to the last database used. For the examples in this chapter, you should connect to the PowerBuilder supplied demonstration database.

If the connection works, the Select Tables window appears as shown in the following figure. This window shows the name of every table and view in the demonstration database.

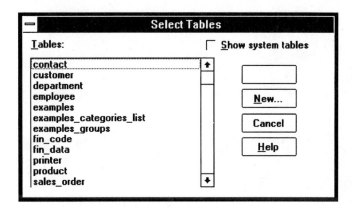

If the list of tables differs from the above list shown, you have
connected to the wrong database. Go back and connect to the
demonstration database before proceeding with this chapter.

SELECTING AND MOVING TABLES

The Select Tables window allows you to select any of the tables or views
highlighted in the Tables area. Clicking the _New_ button allows you to
create a new table.

Note the System Tables check box on the selection window, Checking
this box adds the names of the system tables in the database to the list
of file names displayed. If you check this box, you can see the names of
various system files including the system files PowerBuilder uses to store
extended attributes.

To select tables with the Select tables window, **click** the name of each
desired table, in this example _employee_ and _department_. The name of
each table you select will highlight. Then **click** the _Open_ button. You
can add tables the display one-by-one by **double-clicking** the name.
When you are done selecting tables, **click** the _Open_ button. The
Database Painter appears with the two tables you selected:

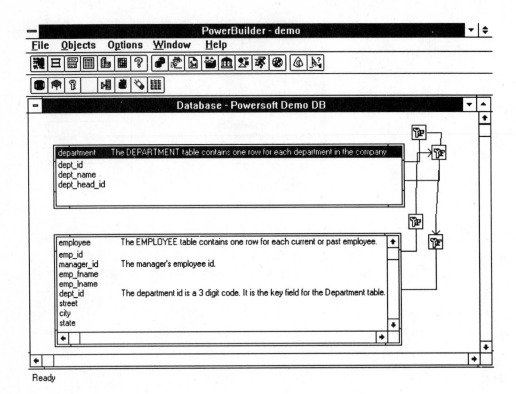

To move a table within the display, **left-click and hold** the cursor on the title bar above the table name. While holding the mouse button, **drag** the table to the new location. When the table is at the new location, release the mouse button. Try this now to make the screen appear as shown above.

The display shows each of the two selected tables. Each of the columns appears. Any foreign or primary key relationships also appear.

DISPLAYING KEY INFORMATION

Double-clicking the icon for a key displays information about that key. Double-click the primary key icon for the department table. The primary key is green.

Close the Primary Key definition window without making or saving any changes.

VIEW AND MAINTAIN A TABLE

To modify any of the attributes of a table, double-click anywhere inside the table. Alternatively, right-click the table name and select *Definition* from the popup menu. Double-click the employee table, and this window appears:

The definition for a table includes table-level characteristics and column-level characteristics.

Table Level Characteristics

The table-level characteristics presented in the Alter Table window are

- ✓ data, heading and label fonts
- ✓ comments about the table itself
- ✓ primary and foreign keys

Fonts

Clicking the Font button displays the Font window. With this window, you can assign fonts, font sizes and font styles. You can assign them separately for the

- ✓ data held in the table
- ✓ headings for columns
- ✓ labels for columns

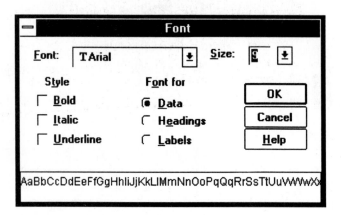

Comments

Clicking the comments button displays the Comments window. This window allows you to enter or to change a comment about the table. The comment you enter saves as an extended table definition. Since the comment is an extended table definition, it remains in a PowerBuilder-defined table in the database.

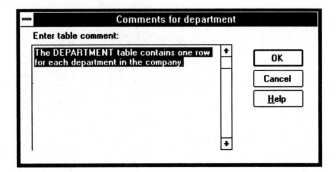

Primary Key

A primary key is a key composed of one or more columns that uniquely identifies any single row in the table. You select only one primary key from among the candidate keys for the table. (For further information on primary keys and candidate keys, consult Part Two of this book.)

Click the *Primary Key* button to open the Primary Key Definition window.

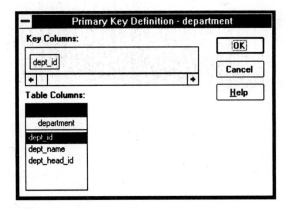

Do not change any primary key definitions for the demonstration database. Close the window.

To change the primary key, you would click the column names for the primary key. Click the names in the order they should appear within the primary key. Clicking a column name that already appears in the primary key removes it from the primary key. **Click** the cancel key to close the Primary Key Definition window.

As mentioned above, you can also display the Primary Key Definition Window by double-clicking the icon for the Primary Key shown on the Database Painter.

Foreign Keys

A foreign key is a combination of columns in one table used to reference one or more rows in another foreign table. A foreign key relates the information in one table to the information in another table. Any table can contain multiple foreign keys. The reason is that the information in one table can relate to the information in several other tables. For more information about foreign keys, consult Section Two of this book.

Click the *Foreign Key* button, and the Foreign key Selection window appears.

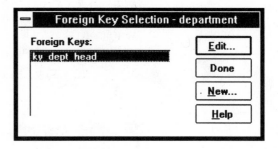

You may name one or more foreign keys. In this example, the foreign key, *dept_id,* is the only foreign key listed. **Clicking** the *New* button displays the Foreign Key Definition window.

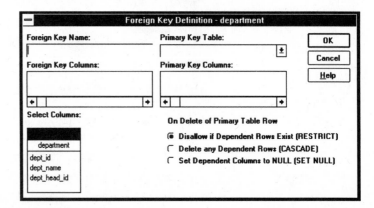

Do not define a new foreign key for the demonstration database. To define a new foreign key, you must provide a name for the key. You must select the foreign table that contains a primary key. Then you select the columns from the current table that should be included in the foreign key.

Click the *Cancel* button to close this window and to return to the Foreign Key Selection window. **Click** the *Edit* button to display the Foreign Key definition for the *dept_id* foreign key.

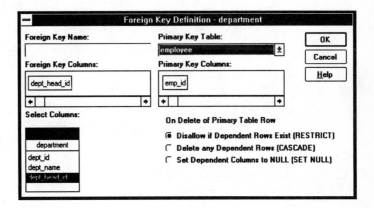

Click the *Cancel* button to return to the Database Painter.

Column Level Characteristics

You can use the Database Painter to specify many of the column-level characteristics of a table. You make these changes through the Alter Table window. The changes you may make vary between RDBMS engines, but generally include the name and data type of a column as well as whether the column can accept null values.

Extended Column Attributes

You can add extended column attributes to the database. These are definitions that are created and managed by PowerBuilder instead of by the RDBMS. Extended definitions include column headings and initial values. PowerBuilder maintains a repository of these values in tables in the database. Any PowerBuilder application that can access the database can access these extended column attributes.

The following table describes each of the extended column attributes that PowerBuilder supports.

Extended Column Attribute	Description
display format	Controls the format of the displayed data.
edit style	Controls the format of a column as the user is entering data.
validation rule	A formula or criteria that checks the validity of entered data.
header	A default column heading.
comment	A comment about the selected column.
justify	Default justification of left, right or center for a column.
height, width	Default height and default width of the column when the column displays in a DataWindow object. Values are in inches.
initial value	The default initial value for a column.
label	The default label for the column. Used when a label appears to the left of a column.

You can use the Alter Table window to change the values for any of these extended column attributes. When you click the *Alter* button, PowerBuilder generates any SQL statements needed to change any tables or extended column attributes.

The extended column attributes provide you with useful default values when building an application. This makes easier the creation of a standard appearance for DataWindow objects. It also makes it easier the building of DataWindow objects. You do not have to specify these characteristics each time you construct a DataWindow object. You can select the extended attributes once and reuse them for each DataWindow object. This allows you to share the extended attributes between objects in your application, or between applications.

DATABASE MANIPULATION

With the Data Manipulation tool in any single database table, you can

✓ retrieve data

✓ view data

✓ insert data

✓ modify data

✓ delete data

This tool handily and quickly changes to the data in a database table.

Make sure to **select** the employee table on the Database Painter window by **clicking** somewhere in the *employee table*. To access the Data Manipulation tool, **click** the *Data Manipulation* button on the toolbar as shown here:

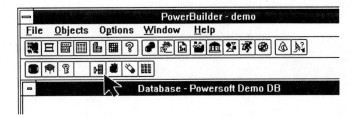

Alternatively, **select** *Data Manipulation* from the Objects menu. **Select** the presentation style of your choice. The next figure shows the Data Manipulation window with information from the employee table:

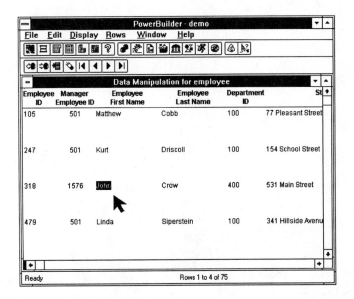

The control buttons for the Data Manipulation tool on the Painter Bar allow you to manipulate the displayed data:

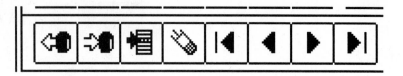

Each of these controls except *First* page and *Last* page, have a corresponding MenuItem. From left to right, the controls provide the following functions:

Control	Function
retrieve	Retrieves data from the database and displays it on-screen.
update db	Updates the database with any changes made to the displayed data.
insert row	Inserts a new row above the currently-selected row. Does not affect the database.
delete row	Deletes the selected row. Does not affect the database.
first	Move to the first page of data.
next	Move to the next page of data.
prior	Move to the previous page of data.
last	Move to the last page of data.

Two other MenuItems on the File menu provide for importing data from an external file or for saving the displayed data to an external file.

Try moving through the employee data, inserting and deleting rows. Do not save any changes to the database. **Close** the Data Manipulation tool and return to the Database Painter screen.

ADDING ELEMENTS TO THE DATABASE

With the Database Painter, you can add to a database:

✓ new tables

✓ indices

✓ display formats

✓ edit styles

✓ validation rules

Adding A New Table

To create a new table, you **use** the Create Table window. Three ways access the Create Table window:

✓ click the _New_ button on the Select Tables window
✓ click the _New Table_ button on the toolbar
✓ select _New_ from the Objects menu then select _Table_ from the cascading menu

The Create Table window appears.

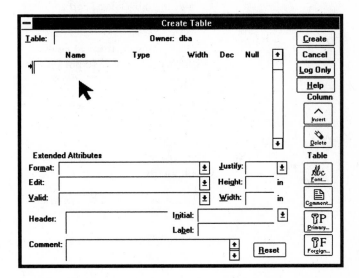

Do not create a new table. Just read the description given in the next paragraph.

To create a new table, first enter a name for that table. Once you have entered a table name, you can specify the font for the table or enter a comment with the Font or Comment controls.

Next, you can enter the information for each column in the table. The following illustration shows the entry and selection of column information.

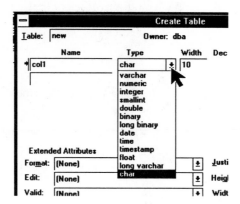

You can enter extended attributes for each column as you go along, or you can go back later and add them. The following sections describe these extended attributes.

When you have finished entering the columns for the table, select a primary key. If you do not select a primary key, a prompt will remind you to do so when you create the table.

Exit the Create Table window by clicking the *Cancel* key.

Adding A New Index

An index can increase performance. If you are unfamiliar with indexing, consult Section Two of this book. You should add an index to each column that is regularly used in a join.

To create an index, **open** the Create Index window. There are two ways to access this window:

✓ click the key button on the toolbar
✓ select *New* from the Objects menu and the Index

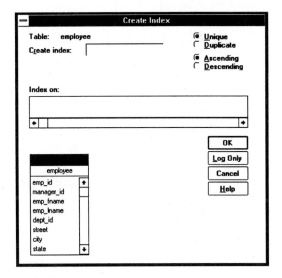

Do not create an index, just read along with the example. You would use this window to create any individual or composite keys. To create the index,

- ✓ enter the name for the index
- ✓ check one of the Unique or Duplicate choices
- ✓ check one of the Ascending or Descending choices
- ✓ select the columns to be included in the index
- ✓ click the *OK* button

Note that not all database engines support descending keys. Clicking the *OK* button creates then executes the SQL that adds the keys to the database.

Click the *Cancel* button to close the Index window.

DROPPING AN INDEX, TABLE, VIEW OR KEY

Use the Database Painter to drop an index, key, view or table. Do not drop any item now. From the Database Painter window, you would select an item by clicking it, for example, the employee table. Drop the element by clicking the *Drop* button on the tool bar, or by selecting Drop from the Objects menu. A prompt reminds you to confirm the deletion. To drop the selected element and continue, **click** the *OK* key.

USING EXTENDED ATTRIBUTES

You can define display formats, validation rules, or edit styles to the database with the Database Painter. These are each extended attributes. The following sections briefly introduce use of extended formats. For more detailed information, consult the PowerBuilder-supplied documentation.

You can create, delete or modify extended attributes with the Database Painter. Extended attributes remain in a repository accessible by any application that connects to the database. Last, you can use the Database Painter to assign any of the extended attributes to a particular column.

Note that whereas the extended attributes remain in tables in the database, they are not part of the database management system. The extended attributes are only used by PowerBuilder, not by the database management system.

You can also define extended attributes in the DataWindow Painter. Extended attributes defined for a DataWindow with the DataWindow Painter are available only to the window or its descendants.

When you are using the DataWindow Painter, you can

✓ accept the default display format assigned to a column with the Database Painter
✓ override the assigned display format with another display format from the repository
✓ create an unnamed format for use with a single column on a DataWindow form

Note that the extended attributes attach to the DataWindow object when you create a DataWindow object. The extended attributes stay with the DataWindow object. No link continues between the extended attributes for the DataWindow object and the repository.

Your changing the attributes in the repository DOES NOT automatically update the DataWindow objects. You need to recreate the DataWindow. PowerSoft also provides an extended attribute synchronizer with the Enterprise edition of PowerBuilder. This utility may also be available separately as well as from the PowerBuilder bulletin board. This utility is of some assistance in synchronizing a DataWindow object with changes made in the extended attributes held in the repository.

Display Formats

The advantage of the repository is that display formats are often a property of the data itself. For example, a zip code or social security number always appears with the same format.

A display format defines and names a particular style used for displaying a value. For example, you can create a display format useful for displaying currency amounts with a dollar sign and commas. You can define an edit style that shows dates with the name of the month spelled instead of shown as a number.

You can rely on each of these display formats when you create a DataWindow object. Creation of the DataWindow automatically applies the display formats. When the DataWindow appears in the running application, data displays with the display formats.

Note that you do not display formats when entering data into a DataWindow object. When the user tabs to an entry field, the display changes to the value without any formatting. To display formatting during data entry, use an edit mask as described in a following section.

Accessing The Display Format Painter

From the DataBase Painter, **open** the display for the desired table so the column names display. **Position** the cursor on the column name *zip-code* in the employee table. **Right-click** on the *department_head_id* to display a pop-up menu that includes extended attribute choices. This menu appears in the following figure. **Select** the Display MenuItem.

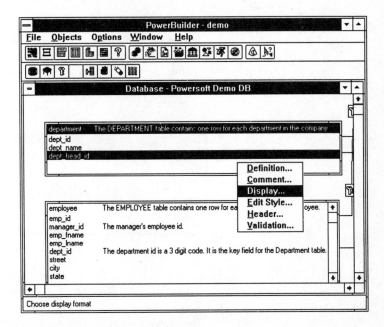

The Column Display format window appears here:

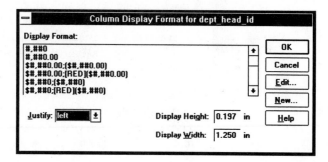

You can use this window to edit an existing display format or to create a new display format. To create a new display format, **click** the *New* button.

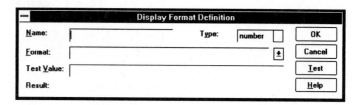

This window allows you to enter a name for the new format. You can then enter the mask for the display format. In the demonstration database, *department_head_id* is of type number. The following window shows a mask that allows the entry of up to four characters into the number field.

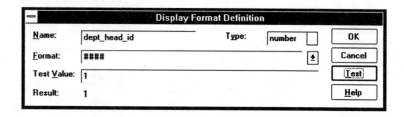

To test the mask, **enter** a value in the Test Value field and **click** the test button. As shown above, the result of the application of the mask to the Test Value field appears in the Result field.

For more help in using display masks, **click** the Help button shown on the window above.

Click the *Cancel* button to close the Display Format Definition window. **Click** the *Cancel* button to close the Column Display window.

Defining Display Formats

A display format carries a mask, the characters of which have a special meaning. Different mask characters can represent:

✓ numbers
✓ strings
✓ dates
✓ times

Take as an example a mask used to display a string. Each @ character in the mask shows where a character from the string appears in the output display. Other characters appear in the output display as themselves. So the mask

```
(@@@) @@@-@@@@
```

displays a U.S. telephone number. The telephone number 916-555-1212 would display as

```
(916)555-1212
```

A display format mask can have multiple sections. Each section corresponds to a form of the item being displayed.

For example, take a mask that will display positive and negative numbers differently. With the following mask, negative numbers appear in parentheses.

```
$##,##0;($##,##0)
```

There must be at least one section in a mask. Any additional sections are optional.

Display formats can combine in a single mask. Use a space to separate the elements for the different types. For example, the following useful mask displays a date and time:

```
mmmm-dd-yy h:mm
```

Consult the PowerBuilder User's Guide chapter on "Displaying and Validating Data" for more information on display format masks. The *Help* button for the display format window provides further instructions. Descriptions of the particulars of each type of mask for dates, strings, etc. is in the PowerBuilder on-line help. Search for "display formats" shown in the next figure.

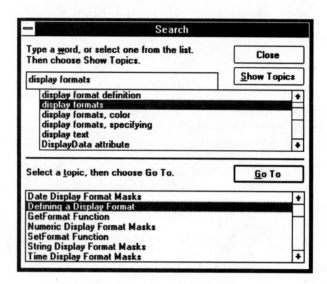

Examine the phone column in the employee table for an example of each of the extended attributes. Hint: you will have to check the "show system tables" box to see this database table.

For some further examples of display format rules, use the Data Manipulation tool in the Database Painter to look in the pbcatfmt table in the demonstration database. This table is the repository of display format styles is held.

Validation Rules

A PowerBuilder validation rule checks data as the user enters it. For example, the following validation rule can assure that an entered number is greater than zero:

```
@col > 0
```

As with display formats, you can create a validation rule and save the rule in the repository. As with any extended attribute, any validation rules in the repository connect to a DataWindow object when you create the DataWindow object and no link to the repository remains.

A validation rule in the repository is automatic when building a DataWindow object. Of course, as with any extended attribute, you can use the DataWindow Painter to override the rules in the depository.

PowerBuilder constructs and maintains validation. The database management system is unaware of these rules. For further information on validation formats, consult the on-line help.

A validation rule is an expression evaluated to a logical value of TRUE or FALSE. If the expression evaluates to TRUE, entered data survives. Evaluation of the expression to FALSE triggers the ItemError event.

Accessing The Validation Format Painter

From the DataBase Painter, **select** the display for the employee table so that the column names display. **Position** the cursor on the column name *emp_id* in the employee table. **Right-click** to display a pop-up menu. This menu appears in the following figure. **Select** the *Validation* MenuItem.

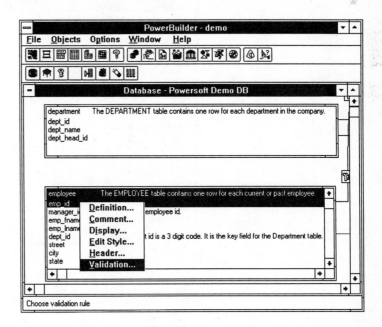

After you **select** *Validation*, this window appears:

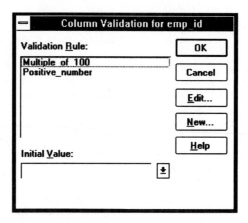

You can select or edit an existing style, or create a new style from this window. If you select to create a new Validation rule, **click** the *New* button. The Input Validation window appears.

Click the *Help* button for assistance in designing input validation edit styles. Also, examine the phone column in the employee table for an example of each of the extended attributes. For some further examples of validation rules, use the Data Manipulation tool in the Database Painter to look in the *pbcatvld* table in the demonstration database. This is the table holding the repository of validation styles.

Click the *Cancel* button to close the Input Validation window. **Click** the *Cancel* button to close the Validation window.

Edit Styles

An edit style affects both the display and presentation of data. For Instance, a column contains a coded value where the code is meaningful to the user. A status column could hold the values A, T or L to indicate an employee status of *active*, *terminated* or *on-leave*. In addition, you want a radio button with which to make the choice between the three options.

Employee tatus

   ⊂ Active

   ⊂ Terminated

   ⊂ On Leave

The following edit styles have support

- ✓ an edit box in which a user can type a value—the default
- ✓ a DropDownListBox
- ✓ a CheckBox
- ✓ RadioButtons
- ✓ EditMask specifying allowable characters
- ✓ a DropDownDataWindow

Examine the phone column in the employee table for an example. The description of each of these edit controls exceeds the scope of this text. Consult the PowerBuilder-supplied documentation for instructions on the use of these edit styles. In particular, consult the *User's Guide* chapter on displaying and validating data.

Maintaining Extended Attributes

From the Objects menu of the Database Painter, **select** any of (a) *Edit Style Maintenance*, (b) *Display Format Maintenance*, or (c) *Validation Maintenance*. You can use the window that appears to create a new entity (with the *New* button,) modify an existing entity, or delete an existing entity.

Close all the windows. **Close** the Database Painter.

1-13 MDI Applications

Many Windows applications use a style called MDI (Multiple Document Interface.) An MDI application opens a main window called the *MDI frame window*. Within the main window the application can open other windows called *sheets*. PowerBuilder is an excellent example of an MDI application.

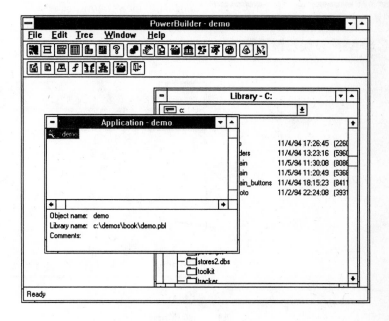

The illustration above shows PowerBuilder running with two painters open. The *MDI frame window* is the main PowerBuilder window—with a title bar, a menu bar and an icon bar. Two MDI sheets appear, one for the Library Painter, a second for the Application Painter.

Many large-scale Windows applications, like word-processing or spread-sheet applications, are MDI applications.

MDI applications are most handy for performing similar tasks in an application. A spread sheet may have multiple sheets open at the same time, or a word processor might have multiple documents open at the same time. In these examples, similar tasks are occurring. In other cases, the sheets may not be so similar, but they may still relate. For example, in an order-processing application, different sheets can serve for client maintenance, order entry and inventory control.

In either case, the user confronts a single, integrated interface. This makes using the application easier. If your application must support multiple windows and easily move among those windows, make your application an MDI application.

MDI COMPONENTS

An MDI frame window has several components—a frame, a menu bar, a client area, and optionally, a MicroHelp status area.

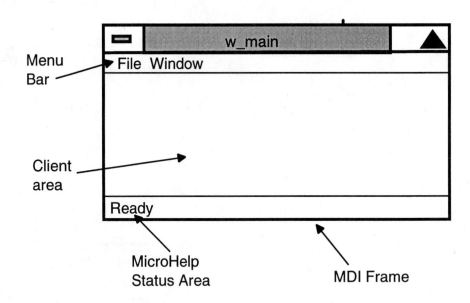

MDI Frame

The MDI frame is the main window for the application. The frame contains the client area. PowerBuilder supports two types of frames, *standard* and *custom*.

Every MDI frame automatically gets these two shortcut keys.

Key	Use
Ctrl+F4	Close the active sheet. Make the next sheet active. The next sheet is the immediately previous active sheet.
Ctrl+F6	Make the next sheet the active sheet.

Standard Frame

A standard MDI frame can optionally contain a *menu bar* or a *MicroHelp status* area. The client area displays any MDI sheets as they open. With a standard frame, only sheets are allowable within the client area.

Sheets within the MDI frame can inherit the MDI Frame menu. Alternately, each sheet in an MDI application can have its own menu. Any menu bar for the MDI application will always display on the frame menu bar, never on a sheet.

While you can write an MDI application without any menus, it is usually preferable to have at least one menu for the application. This makes managing the application easier with all the sheets closed.

When a standard frame opens, automatic sizing of the client area occurs. Any sheet opened by the application sizes to display within the client area.

Custom Frame

A custom frame also can display a *menu bar* and a *MicroHelp status area*. Again, they are both optional. Unlike a standard frame, the client area for a custom frame can contain other objects besides sheets. With a custom frame, the client area can contain other objects including buttons or StaticText.

With a custom frame, the application must size the client area. If the application area does not size properly, sheets displaying in the client area may be partially obscured.

MDI Client Area

In an MDI application, the client area displays various sheets. Opening the MDI frame creates automatically a control named *MDI_1*. This control identifies the client area of the MDI frame. With a standard frame, PowerBuilder manages the sizing of the MDI_1 frame. If you are using a custom frame, the application must include a script for the Resize event. This script must redraw the window to an appropriate size.

You can use the Object browser to examine the attributes and related functions of the MDI_1 frame. **Open** the browser from the PowerScript painter. **Double-click** on the name of the MDI window you would like to browse. The browser will display a list of controls for the window object. One of those controls will be the MDI_1 client area. **Select** MDI_1 then **click** either *Attributes* or *Functions*. Either the *attributes* of the client area, or the *functions* related to the client area displays, depending on your selection.

MDI Sheets

Sheets are also windows. When these sheets open, they display within the client area of the MDI frame. You can use any of the various types of windows as an MDI sheet, except another MDI frame. The OpenSheet function opens an MDI sheet.

A sheet allows a user to perform specific activities. For example, in PowerBuilder, separate sheets are for the painters. Multiple sheets can open at the same time. You can move between the sheets at will. You can have the Application Painter and the Library Painter open at the same time and move back and forth between them at will.

Activation

Only one application window can be active at a time. The active window has a highlighted menu bar. The active window receives any keyboard input. The input from the keyboard goes to the active application. The input from the mouse may also go to the active application, such as in selecting a menu item or in clicking a button.

When the user opens an MDI application, the MDI frame becomes the active window. The MDI frame continues as the active window until the user selects another application or opens an MDI sheet. When a sheet opens, the MDI frame and the sheet are both active. If multiple sheets are open, the frame and the selected sheet are active.

MicroHelp

Because a menu bar is limited in size, only a limited number of words can easily display. For example, a word-processing application can have menu items like *File*, *Edit*, *View*, *Text*, *Style*, *Page*, *Frame*, *Tools*, *Window*, *Help*. With this many entries, only one word is available for the title of each MenuItem. To assist the user, an MDI application can present additional information about a MenuItem on the MicroHelp status area.

When you create the MDI frame with the Window Painter you get two selections, *MDI frame* or *MDI frame with MicroHelp*. You must select the *MDI frame with MicroHelp* to display MicroHelp.

The Menu Painter can associate MicroHelp with each MenuItem. When the user selects a MenuItem in the running application, the MicroHelp text displays in the MicroHelp area of the MDI frame. For example, when you click and hold on the application icon in the PowerBuilder MDI frame, the text "Run application painter" appears in the MicroHelp area.

Menus

As described in an earlier chapter, you use the Menu Painter to create a menu. You then use the Window Painter to associate the menu with the window of your choice. This is the same for MDI applications.

In an MDI application, you can associate a menu with the MDI frame. This helps when the menu for the frame lists all the sheets that can display within the frame. For example, take a word-processing application. While you may wish to open several documents at the same time, the commands used for manipulating each of the documents are the same.

In other applications, each of the open sheets may serve a different purpose. In this case, you can associate a separate menu with each sheet. The menu for the sheet displays on the MDI frame menu bar, not on the sheet itself. When the sheet opens, the menu for the sheet displays on the MDI frame menu bar. No menu displays on the sheet.

The displayed menu is the current menu. If a sheet opens and lacks a menu of its own, the current menu applies. That is, the new sheet uses the menu displayed by the MDI frame of the preceding sheet.

BUILDING MDI APPLICATIONS

Creating an MDI application is much like creating any application. This chapter only presents an outline for creating MDI applications rather than a step-by-step example as in previous chapters. This is in part because MDI applications are much like other applications and what you have learned applies equally to them. Also, you should now be familiar with the painters used when creating an MDI application. So, in this chapter you find less close guidance.

MDI Frame

The steps you learned earlier to other applications apply to MDI applications. Start by creating an application object and application library. Next, create the MDI Frame. Use the Window Painter to create a new window. When the Window Painter appears with the new window, double-click in the window or select *Window Style MenuItem* from the Design menu.

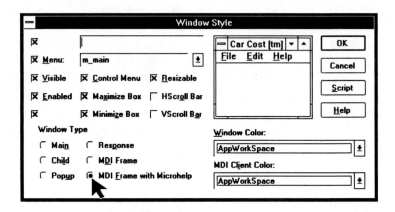

For the window style, select a type of *MDI Frame* or *MDI with MicroHelp*. I suggest always using *MicroHelp* unless you can find some overwhelming reason to the contrary. Save the new window into your application library.

Opening An MDI Frame

Once you have created the MDI frame, go back to the application painter and write a script for the application open event.

The following is a sample script for an application open event. This script looks in an initialization file of your application for database connection information. Since the path to the initialization file is not completely specific, the file must be in the DOS search path or in the current working directory.

The application tries to connect to the database. If the connection occurs, the script opens the MDI frame, in this case a window named *w_main*. Notice that the open function opens the MDI frame, just as in your sample application it opens the main window for the application.

```
// Sample script for MDI application open event
sqlca.DBMS = ProfileString("myapp.ini","sqlca","dbms","")
sqlca.database =
ProfileString("myapp.ini","sqlca","database","")
sqlca.userid =
ProfileString("myapp.ini","sqlca","userid","")
sqlca.dbpass =
ProfileString("myapp.ini","sqlca","dbpass","")
sqlca.logid = ProfileString("myapp.ini","sqlca","logid","")
sqlca.logpass =
ProfileString("myapp.ini","sqlca","logpass","")
sqlca.servername =
ProfileString("myapp.ini","sqlca","servername","")
sqlca.dbparm =
ProfileString("myapp.ini","sqlca","dbparm","")

connect;
if sqlca.sqlcode <> 0 then
  messagebox("connect","Unable to connect to database");
  Halt Close
end if

Open (w_main)
```

Create A Menu

Next create a menu for your application. You should group menu items in some logical fashion. It is also good to follow windows conventions. The following illustration shows the Menu Painter with a sample menu. Notice the MenuItems named *File*, *Window* and *Help*, which are common to most Windows applications.

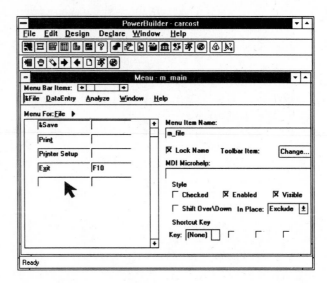

Notice in the illustration above the selection under the *File* MenuItem of the *Save* MenuItem. Note too, the specification of MicroHelp, in this case the phrase, *Save changed information*. Finally, notice that there are MenuItems for *Print*, *Printer setup* and *Exit*. Again, these are common MenuItems for any Windows application.

This script calls the Windows-supplied printer setup window:

```
//Clicked script for m_printsetup
if PrintSetup( ) = -1 then
   MessageBox("Error!","PrintSetup Failed")
end if
```

This is the script of the clicked event for the *Exit* MenuItem:

```
If MessageBox('Exit?','Exit
Application',Question!,YesNo!) = 1 then
   close (ParentWindow)
End If
```

This above script prompts the user for a confirmation with a MessageBox. If the user clicks *Yes*, the parentWindow closes, ending the application.

The illustration below shows the Window MenuItems. They are *Tile*, *Layer*, *Cascade* and *Arrange* Icons; all standard choices for a Windows application.

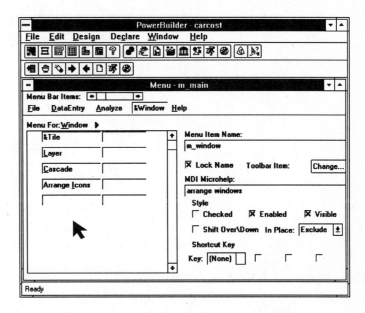

Here is the script for the Clicked event of the *Tile* MenuItem. The script calls the ArrangeSheets function with an argument of *Tile!*

```
//Clicked script for m_tile
ParentWindow.ArrangeSheets(Tile!)
```

The scripts for the other MenuItems are much the same; only the enumerated type is different. The enumerated types for the ArrangeSheets function call for the other MenuItems are

✓ Layer!
✓ Cascade!
✓ Icons!

Create A Sheet

Next, create an MDI sheet. Use the Window Painter to create a new MDI window. For a style, assign *Child*.

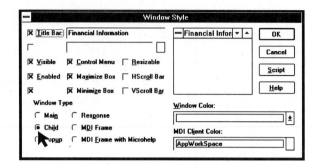

While this window will serve as an MDI sheet, it is still a regular window object. You can add any controls you wish, such as a DataWindow control.

User Defined Events

From the Window Painter, you can create your own events. From the Declare Menu in the Window Painter, select the *User Events* MenuItem. The following window appears:

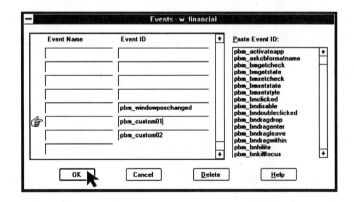

Create two events of your own. To create your own event, enter a name at the end of the list, such as *update_dw* according to the illustration. As soon as you enter a name, the list of events becomes available for selections. This list includes many Windows events not already available to PowerBuilder objects. It also includes a set of custom events you can use for whatever purpose you like. Create two custom events of your own. Name them *update_dw* and *print_dw*. Assign them custom event ids *pbm_custom01* and *pbm_custom02* as shown above.

Save the changes and close the Events window. If you start the script painter and pull down on the events menu you will see that the window now has two new associated events. Note that the events appear at the end of the list rather than in alphabetical order.

Here is a sample script to associate with the *update_dw* event:

```
f_update_dw(dw_financial,"financial")
```

Similarly, here is a script for the *print_dw* event. This script starts a print job and prints the window when the *print_dw* event triggers:

```
integer job_number
job_number = PrintOpen("Financial Information")
PrintDataWindow (job_number,dw_financial)
PrintClose(job_number)
```

Save the sheet and return to the Menu Painter for the menu of your application. Remember the Print and Update MenuItems under the File menu? Here is a sample script that triggers the update event for whatever MDI sheet is open. This script would function in the clicked event:

```
window  activeSheet
activeSheet = w_main.GetActiveSheet()
If IsValid(activesheet) then
 activeSheet.TriggerEvent("update_dw")
end if
```

The first line of the script declares a variable named *ActiveSheet* of type Window. The *IsValid* function returns the current active sheet. The next line triggers the *update_dw* event for the active sheet.

Now you see why the custom event you created is useful. Creating your own *update_dw* event for each sheet in the application makes simple updating any window. Similarly, here is a sample script for the *Save* MenuItem. This script triggers the *print_dw* event for the active sheet:

```
// clicked event for m_main.m_file.m_print
window activeSheet
integer job_number
string sheetTitle
activeSheet = w_main.GetActiveSheet()
If IsValid(activesheet) then
   activeSheet.PostEvent("print_dw")
end if
```

Note that this script posts the event instead of triggering the event. The difference is that a triggered event happens immediately. A posted event only happens when Windows gets around to it.

Open A Sheet

Now you are ready to add a script to your menu to open a sheet. Here is a script for the clicked event that would open a sheet named *w_financial*. You should consult the PowerBuilder on-line help and look at the description of the OpenSheet function to learn what each argument means. Note that there is a special function, *OpenSheet*, that opens a sheet instead of the *Open* function used for other windows.

```
OpenSheet(w_financial,"w_financial",w_main,4,Casc
aded!)
```

The following is a sample script that might appear in the open event for the *w_financial* window. This script executes as the sheet opens:

```
SetPointer(HourGlass!)
dw_financial.settransobject (sqlca)
dw_financial.retrieve( )

m_main.m_dataentry.m_financial.check()

// reset the height and width
w_financial.width = &
ProfileInt("carcost.ini","application","financialW",2000)
w_financial.height = &
ProfileInt("carcost.ini","application","financialH",1100)

// reset the position
w_financial.X = &
ProfileInt("carcost.ini","application","financialX",100)
w_financial.Y = &
ProfileInt("carcost.ini","application","financialY",100)

SetPointer(Beam!)
```

Setting the cursor shape to an HourGlass starts this script. This indicates to the user the application is performing some action that there may cause a delay.

Next, the script sets the transaction object. Then the *Retrieve* function retrieves data from the database into the DataWindow buffer.

The next line puts a check mark next to the MenuItem used to open the window. Whenever the user references the menu, the check mark indicates the window is open.

The next section resets the height and width of the window to the last size saved in the profile file for the application. Then the saved position resets the window to the position it had when last used.

The window is now ready for use, so the pointer resumes the default I-beam shape.

Finally, here is a sample script useful for the close event for the sheet:

```
f_close_sheet(w_financial,"financial")
m_main.m_dataentry.m_financial.uncheck()
```

This script closes the sheet then removes the check mark on the MenuItem:

Toolbars

A toolbar can make using your MDI application easier. The user can click icons on the toolbar as a shortcut instead of having to choose a MenuItem. You are familiar with toolbars now from the PowerBuilder painters.

To add a toolbar to an MDI frame is simple. When you define a MenuItem in the Menu Painter, you can associate a picture with the MenuItem. From the Menu Painter, **click** the *Change* button as shown below:

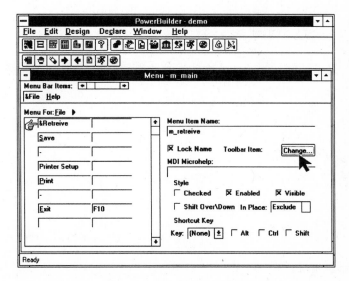

The following window appears:

```
┌──────────────────────────────────────────────────────────────────┐
│ ─                           Toolbar Item                           │
├──────────────────────────────────────────────────────────────────┤
│  Picture:    ┌────────────────────────┐    ┌──────────────────┐    │
│              │                        │    │       OK         │    │
│  Down Picture:┌───────────────────────┐    ├──────────────────┤    │
│              │         ▲              │    │     Cancel       │    │
│  Text:       ┌────────────────────────┐    ├──────────────────┤    │
│              │                        │    │  Change Picture… │    │
│                                            ├──────────────────┤    │
│  Space Before: │0│  Order: │0│  ☒ Visible  □ Display Down  Change Down Picture… │
│                                            ├──────────────────┤    │
│                                            │      Help        │    │
└──────────────────────────────────────────────────────────────────┘
```

Use this window to associate a picture with any MenuItem. You can use any standard Windows graphics software to create the picture as a *.bmp* or *.rle* file.

When you associate the menu with the Window in the Window Painter, enable the use of a toolbar. Use the Options menu to enable a toolbar. There are two choices, one for a color toolbar using pictures, another for a text toolbar.

For more information on toolbars, consult the PowerBuilder *User's Guide* chapter *Building MDI Applications*.

1-14 Debugging Your Application

PowerBuilder includes an interactive debugger. The Debug Painter allows you to stop a running application to examine scripts. By looking at a script when the application stops, you can locate script errors.

You use the Debug Painter to run the application instead of executing it directly. You use the debugger to set breakpoints in a script. A breakpoint, or Stop, marks a line in a script.

Execution stops at a marked line. When the program stops at a stop point, the debugger window replaces the running application. The Debug Painter window displays the script containing the stop point. You can then use the Debug painter to examine variables in the script.

The steps for debugging a program are

- ✓ open the Debug Painter
- ✓ set one or more stops in scripts
- ✓ run the program from within the Debug Painter
- ✓ examine or change program attributes or script variables
- ✓ add or modify stops to isolate the problem
- ✓ repair errors you find in your scripts

OPEN THE DEBUG PAINTER

Start the debugger with the Debug icon from the PowerBar or PowerPanel.

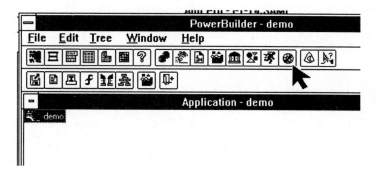

The Select Script window allows you to select an object type from a pulldown list:

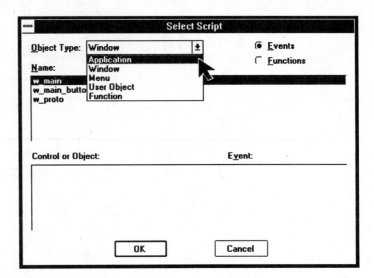

The pull down lists PowerBuilder objects that can have an associated script. Use this list to select an object type, for example, application:

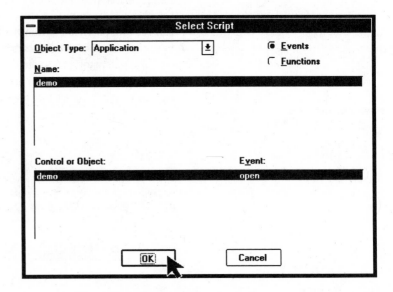

The window above lists any scripts associated with the object you selected. In this example, the application you have written there is only one script associated with the application object, the script for the open event. Click OK to see the following debug window:

SETTING STOP POINTS

Having clicked the *OK* button, the Debug window opens.

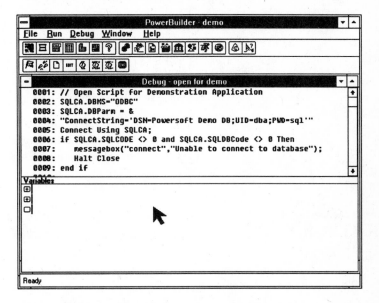

This debug screen allows you to set or remove stop points, that is, breakpoints. A breakpoint, or stop, is a place in the script where the application stops running when you are using the debugger. **Place** the cursor anywhere on a line in the script and double click. As shown next, this sets a stop point.

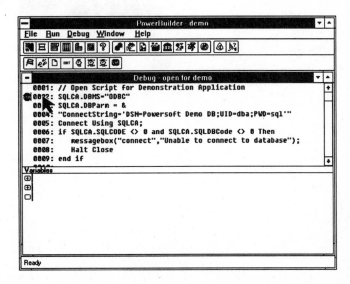

When you run the application with the debugger, the application stops at any line with a stop. The program stops just before that line executes.

Double-click the *line* a second time to remove a stop point. Each double-click adds or removes the stop point to the line at which the cursor points.

Note that you can only assign a stop to an executable statement. You cannot assign a stop point to a comment or variable declaration.

NOTE: DO NOT add a stop to a script for an *Activate* or *GetFocus* event. The *Activate* or *GetFocus* event triggers each time you return from the debugger to the application. This causes a recursive loop from which you cannot escape.

EDITING STOP POINTS

You can edit the stop points at any time. **Double-click** the *if SQLCA* statement to insert a stop. **Click** the *Edit Stop points* icon on the Debug Painter icon bar:

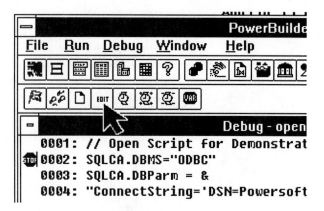

A new window appears. This window has a list of all the stop points you have set for your application.

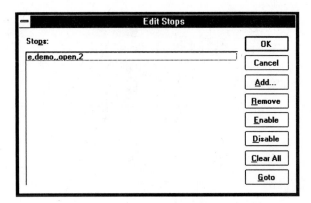

The controls for this window allow you to enable or disable stop points or to add or remove stop points. You can also clear all the stop points set for your application with the *Clear All* button.

Each line in the Edit Stops has five elements:

```
state, object, control, event, lineno
```

The state is *enabled* or *disabled*. Execution does not stop at a disabled breakpoint. Following entries indicate which object, control and event. The last line shows the line of the script on which the stop appears.

Click the *Cancel* button to close the window.

EXECUTING THE PROGRAM

Once satisfied with the stops you have set, execute the program from within the debugger. **Click** the leftmost icon on the PainterBar, the small flag, then select *Start* from the Run menu, or type *ctrl-T*.

The program starts to run from within the debugger. **When** you get to the first stop point, the running program disappears and the Debug Painter re-appears. In your sample application, this happens quickly, as there is a stop early in the open script for the application.

DISPLAYING INFORMATION WHEN STOPPED

Click the *Show Variables* icon on the painter bar, as shown below. *ctrl-V* or the *Show Variables* MenuItem on the Debug Menu also displays the variables window. Clicking the *Variables* icon a second time removes the variables display, as does the *Variables* MenuItem on the Debug menu.

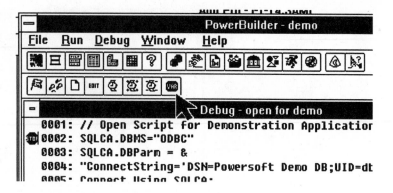

Note in the display a plus sign in the box to the left of the Global entry. This indicates further entries in this category. When the application is running from within the Debug Painter, you can **Double-click** the name *Global*, and a list of global variables appears. **Double-click** again the transaction *sqlca* entry. This causes each of the attributes of the transaction object to display:

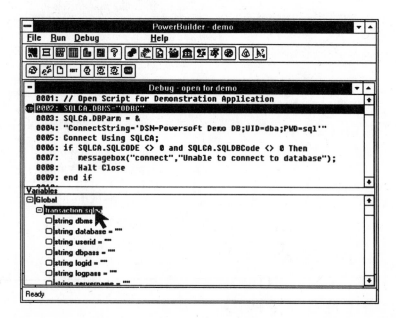

This display shows each of the attributes of the selected variable. As the program runs, and the values change, the display changes. Double-click on variables to add them or to delete them from the lower display. You can examine the contents of global variables, shared variables, variables local to the current script, or instance objects.

This is the heart of the Debug Painter. You can add breakpoints to scripts. When the application stops at the breakpoint, you can examine the values of variables. This visible path through the various program scripts, coupled with the variable display, allows you to determine errors in a script.

Close the Debug Painter. Congratulations! You have finished the tutorial portion of this book.

CONTINUING EXECUTION

Select the *continue* or *step* icons on the Painter Bar, or the same choices on the **Run** *menu*, or the shortcut keys *ctrl-S* or *ctrl-C* to continue the program or step to the next script line. To stop the debug process entirely, Exit the Debug Painter.

REPAIRING ERRORS

Carefully stop the Debug Painter before making any changes in your application. To repair an error, stop the Debug Painter completely, open the script editor for the appropriate script and make any needed changes. To check the repair, run the application, or again run the application within the Debug Painter.

For more information on the Debug Painter including watch lists and responses to serious errors, consult the PowerBuilder *User's Guide*.

1-15 Networking and ODBC

In the past, a central computer provided all data processing services for an organization. In this older model, a main-frame or mini-computer would be the sole processor in an organization. All programs would run on this machine. Users, even remote users, would use a terminal or a terminal emulator to access the central computer. All the work occurred on the central machine.

This chapter provides a purposefully-brief introduction to some basic networking concepts. Networks allow processing and data distribution around an organization or region.

For more information about networking consult the book *Computer Networks* written by Andrew S. Tannenbaum (Prentice-Hall, 1988, ISBN 0-13-162959-X). This superb book covers computer networking in great detail.

Many different types of networks from many different manufacturers exist. Each of these networks supports different hardware and software standards. This chapter introduces enough information about networking to help you get started writing PowerBuilder applications.

A computer network interconnects autonomous computers. The computers connect in order to transfer data.

Since the computers are autonomous, one computer on the network does not directly control another computer on the network. There is no master-slave relationship.

A network shares resources between host computers. It shares programs, data and equipment without regard to physical location. It increases reliability. If one resource is unavailable, others can serve instead. A network is cost effective. Connecting personal computers or workstations with a network is less expensive than purchasing and sharing a single large machine. Connecting to a wide area network is less expensive than connecting to a computer through the switched telephone network. Finally, a network is efficient through distributing tasks across resources.

A computer network connecting resources in close physical proximity is called a *local area network* (LAN.) Close proximity means usually only within a mile or so. A computer network connecting resources that are geographically widespread is called a *wide area network* (WAN.)

A computer network allows people to communicate from different places. For example, two people in different offices in different states can work together on a single report. A computer network also provides remote access to a database. For example, a single database server can hold all the reservations information for an airline. Computers anywhere on a wide area network can access this reservation information.

NETWORKS

One of the first major wide area computer networks was the ARPANET. Funded by the US Government, the Advanced Projects Research Administration built a network designed to provide reliable communications after a nuclear war. The terminology used in this chapter derives from that developed for the ARPANET.

The world's largest network, the Internet, evolved from the original ARPANET. Millions of users world-wide now communicate via the Internet. The new "information highway" depends upon the Internet.

A networked computer used for running application programs is called a host. There can be many host computers on a network.

Hosts can be clients or servers. Hosts that are servers provide data for other hosts on the sub-net. Hosts that are clients use data provided by a server.

Hosts connect by a communication subnet, or subnet for short. The subnet carries messages between the hosts. The subnet carries messages between users much as the telephone network carries conversations between users.

The subnet includes transmission lines and switching devices. Transmission lines are *circuits*, *channels*, or *trunks*. The network switch elements are specialized computers that connect two or more of the transmission elements. The switch element accepts data from an incoming transmission line and forwards it to the appropriate outgoing transmission line. Different names for the same network elements switching elements are *Interface Message Processors* (IMP), *packet switch nodes*, *intermediate systems*, or *data switching exchanges*.

There are two basic designs for a communications subnet:

✓ point-to-point
✓ broadcast channels

POINT-TO-POINT NETWORKS

In a point-to-point network, numerous cables or leased telephone lines connect pairs of IMPs. Communications between unconnected IMPs must route through other IMPs. A message, often referred to as a packet, goes from one IMP to another; intermediate IMPs first store then forward a packet until it arrives at the destination IMP.

A subnet that communicates in this fashion is a point-to-point store and forward network, or packet-switched network. Most wide area networks include store-and-forward subnets.

BROADCAST NETWORKS

Broadcast network systems rely on a single communications channel. All the hosts on the subnet share this single channel. An IMP broadcasts a packet over the network. The packet includes the address of the destination IMP. Every host reads every packet travelling on the sub-net. The destination IMP reads every packet that is broadcast over the net and selects those packets with its address.

Most local area networks are broadcast networks. In this case, the IMP is a single chip embedded on a controller card within the host computer. Here, only one host exists for every IMP. This is different than a wide area network where a single IMP may provide services for many hosts.

Andrew Tannenbaum provides an excellent analogy of broadcast systems.

> [You might] consider someone standing at the end of a corridor with many rooms off it and shouting, "Watson come here, I want you." Although the packet may actually be received (heard) by many people, only Watson responds.

STANDARD NETWORK MODELS

In order to reduce complexity, networks organize into a series of standard layers or levels. Each layer builds atop of the next-lower level.

The following shows the ISO (International Standards Organization) OSI (Open Systems Interconnection) Reference Model. This is an open model because it connects open systems, systems that can communicate with each other. The *OSI model* is its usual name.

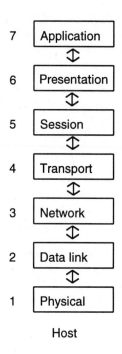

As shown in the figure above, the OSI model has seven layers. Each layer rests atop the next lower level. Each layer provides certain well-defined services to the next higher level. Each layer shields the layer above from the details of how the services are provided or implemented.

All the layers shown in the figure above comprise a protocol stack. A protocol stack runs on a single host. Each host runs a protocol stack of its own.

Conceptually, an individual layer on one host communicates with the same layer on another host. For example, level one on a host communicates with level one on another host.

In fact, no data transfers directly between the two similar levels on the two hosts, except for the physical layer. Each layer passes data and control information to layers below it until the lowest layer is reached.

A well-defined interface exists between adjacent layers. The interface defines the primitive operations and services that the layer can offer to the layer above. This set of layers and protocols is a *network architecture*.

Physical Layer

The physical layer encodes each packet of information onto the transmission medum. For example, the physical layer would translate packets onto an anolog telphone line or local area network.

Hosts each connect to some physical medium, like a co-axial cable or copper twisted-pair wire. Data travels across this physical media.

The physical layer of the OSI model concerns the connection to the physical media. It is the physical layer responsible for making sure a bit transmitted from one host arrives correctly at another host. The design of the physical layer deals with mechanical, electrical and procedural interfaces. Physical layer design is the job of electrical engineers.

Some of the more-common physical layer connections are Ethernet, ARCNET, and token ring.

Data Link Layer

The data link layer supervises transmission of packets. The data link layer confirms the checksum for each packet. It then addresses each packet. A duplicate of the packet then goes across the network. This layer keeps a copy of each packet until it receives a confirmation from the next host in the network that the packet has arrived correctly.

The data link layer transforms the raw transmission facility into a communications line free of transmission errors. The data link layer breaks the input it receives into a set of data frames. The data frames transmit sequentially to the physical layer. The receiving host transmits acknowledgment frames back to the transmitting host. The data link layer is responsible for acknowledging the receipt of these acknowledgment frames.

The physical layer only accepts and transmits a series of bits. The data link layer creates and recognizes the frame boundaries and patterns. The data link layer does this by adding special bit patterns to the beginning and end of the frame.

Noise on the physical media can corrupt a data frame. The data link layer is responsible for re-transmitting a corrupted data frame. The data link layer is responsible for solving problems created by lost, damaged or duplicate frames. The data link layer is also responsible for flow control. Flow control assures that a receiver will not be flooded with information it cannot process in a timely fashion.

The Network Layer

The network layer selects the route through which the message travels. The network layer breaks each of the segments of a message into packets. It counts each of the packets then adds a header to each packet. Each header contains the sequence number of the packet and the address of the receiving host.

The network layer controls the operation of the subnet. This includes determination of how packets route from their source to their destination. The network layer is also responsible for controlling network congestion. In broadcast networks where routing is simple, the network layer is often small or non-existent.

The Transport Layer

The transport layer protects transmitted data. It divides data into segments and creates checksum tests that assure correct transmission of data. It also makes backup copies of data if messages need retransmitting. The transport layer adds a header to each segment of a message containing the segment's checsum and an indication of its position in the message.

The transport layer accepts data from the session layer, and if necessary splits it into smaller units and passes the data to the network layer. it must ensure that all the pieces arrive correctly at the receiving end. it must isolate the session layer from changes in the underlying hardware.

Usually, the transport layer creates a single network connection for each transport connection requested by the session layer. If the transport connection requires high throughput, the transport layer may create multiple network connections. In this case, the transport layer can divide the data among the network connections to improve throughput.

The transport layer determines the type of service provided to the session layer. The most popular transport connection provides an error-free point-to-point channel that delivers messages in the order they were went. There are other transport services, however, that make no guarantee about the order of delivery. Determination of the type of service occurs when the connection happens.

The transport layer provides true source-to-destination, or end-to-end services. A program on one host converses with a similar machine on a destination host. with Message headers and control messages manage this conversation. The layers below the transport layer are instead responsible for communication between immediate neighbors and not the ultimate source and destination machines.

The Session Layer

The session layer starts communications. It sets boundaries, called *brackets*, that establish the beginning and end of each message. This layer also establishes message transmission as half-duplex or full-duplex. If messages travel half-duplex, the sending and receiving hosts take turns using the communications channel. In a full-duplex environment, both hosts can talk across the channel simultaneously.

The session layer allows users on different hosts to establish corresponding sessions. A session provides for ordinary data transport like the transport layer. It also provides enhanced services useful to some applications. For example, a session can allow a user on one host to log onto a remote host or to transfer a file between two hosts.

The Presentation Layer

The presentation layer translates a message into a form that the receiving computer can interpret. For example, the presentation layer would translate a message into ASCII for transmission to a remote host. This layer may also compress or encrypt transmitted data.

All the lower layers of the OSI standard provide services to move data reliably from one location to another. The presentation layer is responsible for the syntax and semantics of moving information between hosts. For example, the presentation layer is responsible for encoding data in a standard format, such as ASCII or EBCDIC. Programs transfer data as character strings, integers or numbers. Different hosts typically have different internal representations of these values. These internal values must have standard-format encoding for exchange between hosts. The presentation layer can provide other encoding services, like compression or encryption.

The Application Layer

The application layer is the only part of the communications heirarchy with which the user interacts. The application layer converts data into bits and then attaches a header that identifies the sending and receiving hosts.

The application layer provides commonly-needed protocols, such as when terminals from different manufacturers have different controls. The application layer can accept generic commands and translate those generic commands into terminal specific commands. The application layer can also provide file transfer functions. Electronic mail, remote job entry, or directory searches are all functions supported by the application layer.

COMMON NETWORKS

You might encounter a large variety of common networks when building PowerBuilder applications. These include TCP/IP and Novell.

PowerBuilder works with all the important networks you may encounter. The scope of this book does not cover any of these networks in detail. You will, however, find many excellent texts that describe whatever network you are using.

ODBC

Each database vendor provides its own database language or API (application programming interface.) Selecting a single vendor could restrict you to using the proprietary interface provided by a vendor.

A proprietary interface can make difficult the accession of data held outside of the DBMS or of data distributed somewhere across a network. While a vendor may provide import and export facilities, moving or accessing data can still be difficult.

Microsoft has provided a standard for accessing data held in RDBMS, non-RDBMS and non-database formats from Windows applications. This standard interface is *ODBC*, an acronym for *Open Database Connectivity*. ODBC is part of Microsoft's Windows Open Service Architecture (WOSA.) While several candidates compete for a database connectivity standard, ODBC currently the leads in the Windows marketplace.

The goal of ODBC is transparent access from any client to any server. ODBC provides ready access to data held in any RDBMS from all important manufacturers including Oracle, IBM, Sybase, and Informix. ODBC also provides access to data held in non-RDBMS files with products like dBASE. Finally, ODBC provides access to data held outside of databases including flat files or applications like spreadsheets and word processors.

ODBC is a standard based on the SQL Access Group Call Level Interface (CLI.) ODBC specifies a single API for concurrently accessing, modifying, or viewing database tables. With ODBC, an application can access a single API for simutaneous access to any number of different data sources held in various locations.

ODBC isolates an application from any underlying network, RDBMS, DBMS or application. Since the application decouples from any specific database manager or network, it isolates from any changes to the database manager or network. Because ODBC is available on a wide variety of platforms, applications are more easily portable to a variety of environments. Microsoft and other independent software vendors provide ODBC drivers for all important applications and platforms.

ODBC guarantees a minimum level of functionality for accessing any supported data source. This functionality lets you connect to a data source, send commands via the ODBC API, or transmit embedded SQL. ODBC commands can retrieve a data selection or return the results of a command.

ODBC standardizes error messages. It also standardizes the interface used to log-on to a remote data source, the data types that can be sent between hosts, and the grammar of SQL statements. This means an application can interpret the same error messages, use the same log-on sequence and the same SQL dialect for any host connection.

A host application can call to the ODBC API to perform database operations. The host application can also issue SQL statements through the API. The ODBC API translates these SQL statements into SQL understood by the remote host then transmits them to the host.

ODBC provides extended functions and an extended SQL grammar that supports advanced data types like dates, time, time stamps, and binary objects. Calls to the API or SQL statements access ODBC.

The ODBC interface supports scrollable cursors, asynchronous queries and array processing of fetches or updates. The SQL grammar includes full transaction support including rollback and commit statements. The extended grammar provided with ODBC supports the use of advanced data types including dates, times, time stamps and binary objects. The SQL grammar provides operators for outer joins and stored procedures.

An application can select from any number of ODBC sources as long as an ODBC compliant driver is available. Concurrent access to a variety of sources is possible. ODBC provides all the facilities needed for mission-critical on-line transaction processing systems and decision support systems.

THE DATA MANAGER

ODBC provides transparent data access through the ODBC data manager and database specific drivers. An ODBC compliant application running on a client machine calls to the ODBC API, that is, to the ODBC data manager. The data manager stands between the application and the drivers, and it manages exchanges between the application and a data source.

The data manager processes the calls to the API. This allows the data manager to perform argument checking. This also allows the data manager to load, and unload, specific ODBC drivers as needed. The data manager also translates the standard queries it receives into SQL native to the data source.

The data manager provides services to applications. In windows, the API is a windows dll (dynamic link library.) For example, the windows dll for the data manager is named *odbc.dll*. Each ODBC compliant application can call the data manager to communicate with more than one driver at the same time. Each application can access different data sources through the same API. The application does not need to change as data sources change.

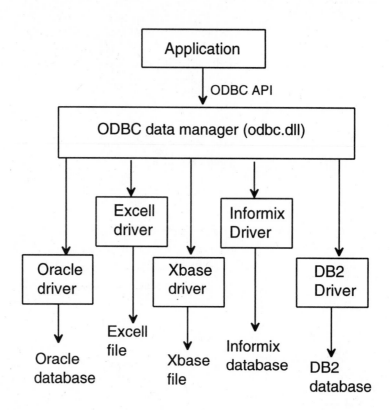

USING ODBC AND POWERBUILDER

A variety of vendors supports ODBC. Each vendor, such as Q&E or Microsoft, provides ODBC drivers. Any ODBC-compliant application, like PowerBuilder, can use an ODBC driver to connect a data source. You specify an ODBC connection to PowerBuilder. PowerBuilder then references the ODBC driver, a *.dll* file, to access that data source.

Since PowerBuilder knows how to make an ODBC connection, connecting to a new data source only requires the correct ODBC driver. PowerBuilder always references the ODBC interface; the driver interfaces with the target data source. ODBC drivers are available for all common data sources including all important database management systems, various flat file management systems like xBase, and other applications like spreadsheets.

The ODBC connection is transparent to your application. You only need to specify the data source; and if the correct ODBC driver is present, that connection occurs automatically.

Note that there may be a price to pay for using an ODBC connection. Since the ODBC interface is by intent a general interface, some specificity within a database may erode. For example, if you are using the Database Painter, there may be some functions unavailable that are available with tools supplied with the RDBMS. You may find that you can rename or reposition a column in a table with a tool supplied with the RDBMS, but not with the Database Painter.

PowerSoft also supplies software to make a native connection to the more popular databases. This may require drivers from PowerSoft and drivers from the database manufacturer. You may find that a native connection performs better than an ODBC connection. The reasonis that ODBC in some cases may sacrifice efficiency for portability.

Section Two

Database Concepts

2-1 An Introduction to Relational Databases

The many popular implementaions of a **relational database management system** (*RDBMS*) run on the largest mainframes and on the smallest personal computers. These systems all reflect relational database theory. Following chapters introduce this theory—just enough theory to help you write real-world programs.

Knowing at least some **relational database theory** helps you to write effective database applications. Understanding the theory is easy. Applying the theory is easy. What you learn here about the theory pertains to any commercial relational database system. This information applies to DB2 on an IBM mainframe, Informix, Sybase or Oracle on a mini-computer, or Access or Watcom on a personal computer. More complete or thorough information about relational database theory is in books suggested in Appendix C.

All relational database systems use **Structured Query Language** (SQL). This book does not teach SQL in depth.

WHAT IS AN RDBMS?

A relational database is a collection of tables that contain data.

For example, here is a database with two tables. The first table contains information about customers; the second table contains information about orders customers have placed.

Customers

cust_name	cust_num	state	city	zip
Ace Sports	1	CA	Coalinga	94303-003
John's Skiis	2	NV	Reno	87452-000
Runner's Shoes	5	UT	Salt Lake	78943-004
Sam's Sports	32	AL	Birmingham	04563-000

Orders

cust_num	order_num	order_date	ship_date	ship_via	ship_cost
1	1	1/3/94	1/15/94	FedEx	$1.50
1	2	12/20/93	1/15/94	UPS	$3.50
5	3	2/2/94		UPS	$2.75
1	8	2/2/94		UPS	$4.25
32	7	3/1/94		FedEx	$3.25
5	22	11/15/92	1/15/94	UPS	$2.25
32	4	12/12/92	1/1/94	FedEx	$1.75

A **relational database management system** automates the creation and manipulation of tables. It provides facilities for creating and destroying tables. It provides facilities for storing, retrieving and changing the data held in the tables.

A database management system includes facilities for

✓ creating a new, empty, database
✓ dropping an existing database
✓ adding empty new tables to a database
✓ removing existing tables from a database
✓ access to data in tables
✓ sharing data
✓ adding data to tables
✓ deleting data from tables
✓ modifying data in tables
✓ copying data between tables
✓ moving data between tables

Various database utilities provide these functions.

Or, Structured Query Language (SQL, pronounced *c-quel*) provides the functions in many cases. Descriptions of SQL appears in subsequent sections.

WHY USE AN RDBMS?

You can much more easily use the tools provided with an RDBMS than write your own programs. It is clearly easier to write an SQL query like

```
select * from customers
```

to get all the rows from a table than to write a program that does the same thing.

Databases can share data. Computer users throughout a network can access a database stored on a mainframe, mini-computer, personal computer or workstation.

The **RDBMS has important advantages**; it

    ✓ handles <u>multiple users</u> on a machine or network

    ✓ governs <u>concurrent access</u> to shared data

    ✓ harmonizes <u>sharing</u> by multiple users

    ✓ assures <u>data safety</u> in the data base

WARNING: Keeping multiple copies of data can be dangerous. If different users access different copies of a data set, they can make independent changes. As the several data sets diverge, managing the changes becomes increasingly difficult. The solution is a correctly-designed database that curbs, eliminates or prevents redundant data.

A **single database** keeps

    ✓ all data changes

    ✓ all data changes in a unique location

    ✓ all data sets consistent

Recent database management systems allow easy and efficient storage and retrieval of enormous amounts of data. As data grows, access speed correspondingly becomes more and more important.

A commercial RDBMS provides fast data access to even large volumes of data because it uses sophisticated data retrieval mechanisms.

A centralized database can help to organize information for a business. It more easily balances the needs of many users or applications.

Such a **centralized database**

    ✓ holds all the core business data for an enterprise

    ✓ provides a model of all the operations of the enterprise

    ✓ reconciles data for the entire enterprise, allowing each part of the enterprise to act on the same information

Moreover, a sophisticated RDBMS offers additional facilities for the user or programmer to access the database. These include report writers and screen managers and fourth-generation languages.

DATA LANGUAGES

A data-access language (for example, SQL) or sub-language accesses a database. This language must provide facilities for

✓ data definition
✓ data manipulation
✓ data control

Data definition statements

✓ create a database,

✓ create tables within the database and

✓ specify what data can be stored in the tables

Data manipulation statements change data; they

✓ add

✓ update

✓ modify

✓ delete

Data control statements

✓ govern access to a database
✓ maintain the integrity of the data
✓ enable data recovery
✓ sustain concurrency control

SQL provides a standard language for performing these database operations. SQL can also serve as a sub-language, its statements becoming part of a host language like C or PowerBuilder.

The same SQL statements can be interactive, or they can be embedded. For example, you can type interactively the following SQL statement:

```
select company-name from customers
```

Or, you can embed it in a program in another language. Here is that query in a PowerBuilder program:

```
select company-name
   from customers
   into :sc;
```

Database Vendors also provide their proprietary tools and languages, including

✓ database management utilities

✓ screen painters
✓ report writers

SQL AND RDBMS—SOME HISTORY

SQL is the industry-standard language for manipulating relational databases.

E.F. Codd, an IBM researcher, described the relational model for database management systems in "A Relational Model of Data for Large Shared Data Banks," *Communications of the ACM* (June 1970).

This article led to projects by many researchers. IBM's System/R project, started in 1974, produced a working relational database system in 1978. The developers of System/R created a language called Sequel (an acronym for Structured English Query Language).

IBM delivered the first commercial relational database, SQL/DS, in 1982. IBM released another relational database management system, DB2, in 1985. DB2 also includes SQL.

SQL has become an industry-standard language for accessing relational databases. The American National Standards Institute (ANSI) formally approved SQL in 1986 as ANSI X3.135.

Note that each manufacturer adds its unique extensions to SQL. Sometime, manufacturers perform the same operation differently. Otherwhile, manufacturers add their own proprietary features.

Developers outside IBM also produced commercial relational database management systems. An example is the Ingres project at U.C. Berkeley, which (before SQL/DS) pioneered products including Informix, Unify and Oracle.

Today, many manufacturers sell RDBMS for the numerous different operating environments. The relational model has replaced other earlier database models (*i.e.*, the network model and the hierarchical model). RDBMS dominate the marketplace.

CONTROLLING DATABASE ACCESS

A relational database management system needs to protect data from unauthorized access. It has

✓ permissions and passwords to control access
✓ commands to restrict database access to certified individuals or groups

DATA MODELING

Data modeling helps you to design the structure of a database.

The structure of a database should

✓ <u>reflect the structure</u> of the enterprise
✓ <u>model the data</u> of the enterprise

Any database system starts with the recognition of a need, usually a need to collect and manipulate data.

An example is a freight company needing to manage package-tracking information. The database

✓ <u>designer</u> models the structure to serve the end user
✓ <u>manager</u> maintains the database system
✓ <u>end user</u> handles the data

THE DATABASE LIFE CYCLE

Any **database project** involves

✓ a simple <u>description</u> of the problem
✓ an <u>outline</u> of means to solve it
✓ a <u>construction</u> of an appropriate database <u>in four phases</u>

1. planning

2. design

3. implementation

4. refinement

2-2 Relational Database Architecture

Three architectural views explain a relational database management system:

✓ the conceptual view
✓ the external view
✓ the internal view

A single database has

✓ only <u>one conceptual</u> view
✓ <u>several external</u> views
✓ only <u>one internal</u> view

Descriptions of the three views follow.

THE CONCEPTUAL VIEW

The **conceptual view** of the database is the complete logical structure of the database as the entire enterprise sees it.

Any database has only one conceptual view. All the users of the database share this common view.

The conceptual view **represents the enterprise-wide view** of the data in a database. Does the business have customers? What is interesting about a customer—name, address, phone number? Customers have orders. What is part of an order—an order number? A shipping date? How is a customer connected to an order?

The conceptual view **includes all the details about the structure and contents** of the database. This view defines the data and its logical relationships.

The conceptual view **exceeds a particular user's view** of the data. It avoids the constraints of a particular language or a particular operating system.

The conceptual view **appears as a *conceptual level schema*.** Hence, this text refers to the conceptual level schema as the *schema*.

Example: The following figure again shows the simple orders database. A real database would normally be more complex. This database has a table for customers and a table for orders. Customers can place multiple orders.

customers

cust_name	cust_num	state	city	zip
Ace Sports	1	CA	Coalinga	94303-003
John's Skis	2	NV	Reno	87452-000
Runner's Shoes	5	UT	Salt Lake	78943-004
Sam's Sports	32	AL	Birmingham	04563-000

orders

cust_num	order_num	order_date	ship_date	ship_via	ship_cost
1	1	1/3/94	1/15/94	FedEx	$1.50
1	2	12/20/93	1/15/94	UPS	$3.50
5	3	2/2/94		UPS	$2.75
1	8	2/2/94		UPS	$4.25
32	7	3/1/94		FedEx	$3.25
5	22	11/15/92	1/15/94	UPS	$2.25
32	4	12/12/92	1/1/94	FedEx	$1.75

Here is the (conceptual level) schema for this database written in SQL:

```
create table customer (
    cust_name char (30),
    cust_num serial,
    state char(2),
    city char(30)
    )
create table orders
    cust_num integer,
    order_num serial,
    order_date date,
```

```
ship_date date,
ship_via char(10),
ship_cost decimal(4,2)
)
```

The schema defines each of the tables, and each of the data elements types found in the database. This schema

✓ creates the two tables
✓ creates each of the columns in the tables
✓ defines the data type of each column.

Entity-Relationship modeling is a tool useful for desinging databases. ER-modeling is not detatiled in this text. ER-modeling is useful

✓ when <u>designing the structure</u> of a database
✓ when <u>designing the conceptual view</u> of the database.

THE EXTERNAL VIEW

External views are individual views of the database. Individual users each can have different views of the same database.

Example: An accounting clerk maintains information about customers, adds new customers, changes customer information or drops old customers. That accounting clerk only knows about customers. On the other hand, an order clerk in another department maintains orders. That order clerk knows about customers and orders. <u>Either clerkhas a different view of the same database</u>.

<u>Many external views</u> can exist, but only <u>one conceptual view</u> of a database exists.

<u>An external view is one user's view</u>, possibly incorporating only part of the schema.

Different programming languages can also represent different external views.

Example: The following data structure from a C program is an **external view of the orders table from the sample** database shown above.

```
struct orders {
    int cnum;
    int order_num;
    int order_date;
    int ship_date;
    int ship_via,
    int ship_cost
    };
```

Here is a data structure from a **COBOL** **program for the same table.**

```
01 ORD
    02 CUSTOMER-NUM PIC X(18).
    02 ORDER-NUM PIC X(20).
    02 ORDER-DATE PIC X(8).
    02 SHIP-DATE PIC X(9).
    02 SHIP-VIA PIC X(10).
    02 SHIP-COST PIC S9(2)v(2).
```

Each of the data structures has different names for the data items in the orders table. In the example, the C programmer has chosen *cnum* as an identifier for the customer number, and the COBOL programmer has chosen *customer-num*. Each of these data structures represents a different external view of the same table in the same database.

THE INTERNAL VIEW

Only **one internal view exists.** The following figure shows the components of the internal view, including a database manager, a file system, and a disk driver.

Components of the Internal View

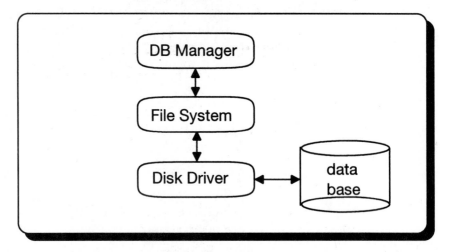

The internal view isolates the user from the storage methods and structures used by a particular machine or operating system. The internal view manages data representations and access. The user need not worry about storing or retrieving a number or character string because the internal view manages that.

Database Manager

A database is a user data-set managed by an RDBMS. The database manager gives the user access to this database.

The database manager

> ✓ <u>controls the interface</u> between the user and the internal workings of the computer
> ✓ <u>supervises requests</u> made at the conceptual view level
> ✓ <u>accepts high-level requests</u>; for example, "Find all the sales orders for Tuesday."
> ✓ <u>operates on tables and rows of data</u> within tables.
> ✓ <u>translates requests</u> for any operation on tables and rows into requests for operations on files and records

In many relational database management systems, requests to the database manager arrive as SQL statements.

In many client-server environments, the front-end system passes SQL statements to the back-end database manager.

For instance, the database manager can

> ✓ <u>access</u> a named table
> ✓ <u>retrieve</u> data from a table
> ✓ <u>remove</u> rows from a table
> ✓ <u>create</u> a new table
> ✓ <u>drop</u> unwanted tables

The database manager translates table-related requests into commands to the file manager.

File Manager

The **file manager manages** groups of files **and responds** to requests for operations on files.

The file manager

> ✓ <u>receives requests</u> for file operations and <u>processes these requests</u> for operations on files
> ✓ <u>uses any host operating system</u>, such as DOS, OS/2, the Mac or Unix. The RDBMS often uses this file manager supplied with the operating system. In many cases to improve performance, the manufacturer will supply its own file system to replace the native operating system. This is more common in larger Unix environments.
> ✓ <u>translates file manipulation requests</u> into commands understood by the disk manager

The file manager responds to requests like

✓ <u>create</u> a new file
✓ <u>erase</u> a named file
✓ <u>change</u> the name of a file
✓ <u>move</u> a file to a new location
✓ <u>retrieve</u> the first record from a named file
✓ <u>replace</u> a record in the named file
✓ <u>add</u> a record to a named file

Disk Driver

The **disk driver operates the low-level physical interface** between a disk drive and the operating system.

The disk driver

✓ <u>reads data</u> on the disk drive
✓ <u>writes data</u> to tracks on the disk drive
✓ <u>places data on</u> the physical disk drive
✓ <u>takes data off</u> the physical disk drive

The supplier usually includes the disk driver with the underlying operating system.

2-3 Relational Database Structure

In the past, programs used files, records and fields to store and retrieve data. Various software products evolved to speed the retrieval of data from these files. These included Indexed Sequential Access Method (ISAM), Keyed Sequential Access Method (KSAM), and many different hierarchical database systems. Relational database mangement systems have replaced these older systems.

INTRODUCTION

A relational datbase management system stores data in tables. These tables hold rows of data. Each row contains multiple data items.

The parts of a relational database management system resemble the data structures used in older systems. Tables are similiar to files; rows are similar to records.

These parts of a relational database have more formal names:

- ✓ a table is a *relation*
- ✓ a row is a *tuple*
- ✓ a data item is an *attribute*

Extended definitions of these parts appear in each of the later sections.

A *relational database* is a collection of tables holding data. It is relational because it relates data held in one table to data held in another table. It handily allows combining data from two tables to answer a single question.

Note: the term relational *does not signify that relating data is easy. Relational is a mathematical term describing relationships between sets. You probably do not want to get into this,as it leads to relational algebra.*

ATOMIC DATA VALUES

In a relational database, the smallest available data item is a single value, like an order number or zip code. These individual data values are atomic. They are atomic because they are the smallest available unit of data. *Atomic*, drawn from ancient Greek, means indivisible.

An atomic data value is the <u>smallest unit of data</u> that can be stored into, or retrieved from, a relational database. For example, there is no way to store only part of a customer number or retrieve only part of a customer number.

However, searching the database with part of an atomic value is possible. You could search for all customer names that start with the letter A. Each item fitting the search criteria appears in full, not in part. Your search for the letter *A* would call forth all customer names beginning with *A*.

DOMAINS

A *domain* is a set of all the data item's possible atomic values. For example, if customer numbers can assume values from one to 99999, the domain of customer numbers has 99999 values—all the integers from one to 99999. All of these possible customer numbers occur in the domain of customer numbers.

Domain of Customer Numbers

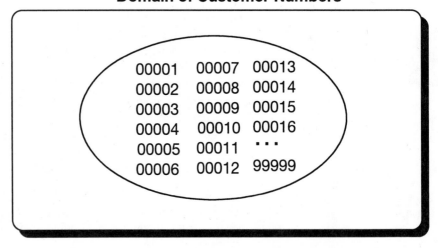

Not all values in the domain need to appear in the database. For illustration, take the domain of the names of states in the United States. There are fifty values in the domain of state names, one for each of the states. If a company ship to only two states, the names of the two states—no more— will appear in this database.

TABLES

A table has a heading and a body, as is shown in the following illustration. When calling this a *table*, remember that it is a *relation*.

Table—Heading and Body

cust-name	cust-num	telephone
sam	1003	512-3454
suszie	2004	445-4323
joan	1002	222-2343
jack	3006	343-2342

Head —
Body

ATTRIBUTES

The heading of a relation consists of one or more *attributes*. The attributes name the kind of data that will be held in the table. Each of the attributes is a name for an underlying domain.

Attributes

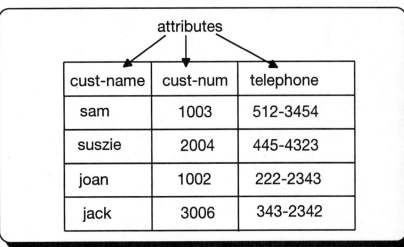

attributes

cust-name	cust-num	telephone
sam	1003	512-3454
suszie	2004	445-4323
joan	1002	222-2343
jack	3006	343-2342

Different attributes can be synonyms referring to the same underlying domain. For example, the attributes *tel-no* and *telephone-no* can signify the same underlying domain of telephone numbers. Each of the attributes must "exist over the same underlying domain." The next figure shows this.

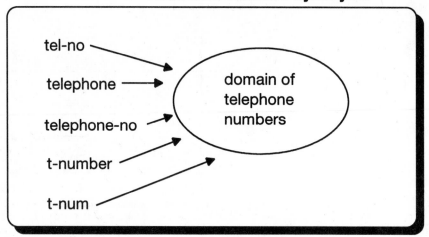

Attributes That Are Synonyms

Do not use synonyms in your database applications. When drawing data in different tables from the same domain, use the same attribute.

For example, when drawing data from the domain of zip codes, using the attribute *zip-code* in one table and *z-code* in another table confuses matters. This approach makes much more difficult the writing of programs that refer to the two tables. Keeping the same attribute in both tables avoids this confusion.

An attribute used in two tables has the unique identification of belonging to one of the tables with a qualifier. The qualifier is the table name. For example, *orders.zip-code* and *customers.zip-code*.

Attributes From Different Domains

Tables usually hold different kinds of data, such as customer names, order numbers and telephone numbers. Each of these kinds comes from a different domain. The attributes show what kinds of data the table holds. The following figure illustrates.

Attributes Drawn From Different Domains

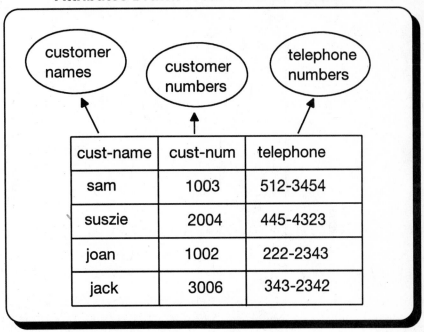

Attributes From The Same Domain

Multiple attributes in the same table can exist over the same underlying domain. Example: An orders table could have a ship-to zip code and a bill-to zip code. The following figure illustrates.

Here, both attributes—*ship-zip* and *bill-zip*—exist over the same domain. Use different attributes when drawing from the same underlying domain in a single table. Use names that show the difference in the use of the data, as in *ship-zip* and *bill-zip*.

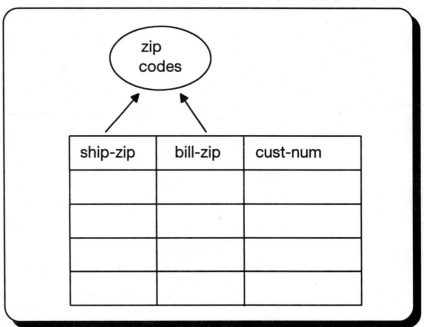

Attributes Drawn From The Same Domain

THE DEGREE OF A RELATION

The *degree* of the relation is the number of attributes found in the header.

A table that has one attribute is degree one or **unary**. A table that has two attributes is degree two or **binary**. A table with three attributes is **tertiary**. A table that has more than three attributes is called **n-ary**, for example 17-ary.

TUPLES

A table has two parts, a header and a body.

The **header** holds attributes.

The table **body** holds *tuples* (rhymes with *couples*,) or rows. Each tuple is made of pairs of attributes and data values. Here is an example.

Tuples

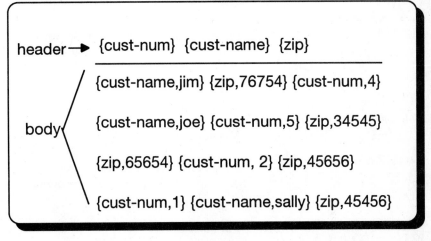

Each pair in a tuple has an attribute that corresponds to an attribute in the the header. Each attribute in a tuple associates with a data value. The **associated value** is either a <u>data value</u> drawn from the underlying domain, or a <u>null value</u> indicating no value has been selected yet. Here is the same table with some missing data.

Tuples With Missing Data

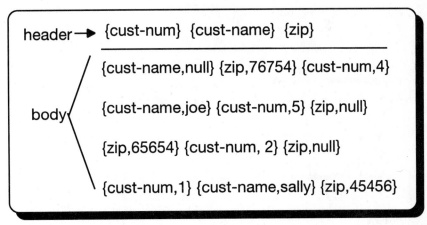

For ease of presentation, attributes appear in the header, not in each tuple. Also for ease of presentation, the data values all allign under the attribute in the header. Although showing a relation this way is easier, rows consist of tuples, that is, groups of attribute-data pairs.

Each of the tuples in the table must have the same number of attributes as the header. Every tuple has the same number of attributes.

A table at first is empty. Over time, added rows expand the table or deleted rows dimish it. The user can change data in the rows.

Attributes Are Not Ordered

Relations usually appear as neatly-ordered tables. An attibute heads each column. A column heading identifies all the same data in the table.

Attribute-data pairs may appear in any order in any row. Indeed, tuples have no order.

Tuples Are Not Ordered In A Table

A table changes over time, with rows being added and/or dropped. As rows are added/dropped, the row order changes. A relational database does not maintain the order of rows in a table as the table changes. You cannot maintain the order of rows during these changes.

NULL DATA VALUES

The null value is a well specified value indicating that no specific data is present from an underlying domain. This differs from an empty value. To a request for data from a table where no data has been entered, some indeterminate value might appear. The null value indicates that no element of the domain is available.

The null value produces predictable results in logical comparisons. An unspecified value will produce unknown and unpredictable results.

No standard governs the usage of nulls and three-value logic. You should consult the documentation provided with your system to see how nulls are used.

CARDINALITY

The cardinality of a relation is the number of tuples in the relation.

Example: A table with ten rows has a cardinality of ten.

NO REPEATING DATA IN ROWS

Attribute-data pairs make a row in a table. Each attribute can only have one associated data value. A data structure with multiple data items associated with an attribute is *not* a relation.

Here is an example of a data struture that is not a relation:

```
{cust-number}{order-number}
{order-number,193,231,33}{cust-number,1}
```

This data structure has a heading with attributes, just like a relation. The body of the table contains attributes. The attributes pair with data items. Since the cust-num attribute in the body has more than one associated data item, this is not a relation.

TUPLES DON'T CONTAIN REPEATING GROUPS

Rows of data make the body of a table. Groups of attribute-data pairs form each row. A single attribute can only appear once in a row.

Example: An order has a ship-to zip and a bill-to zip. The data structure has a heading, like a relation. It has a body, like a relation. The same attribute, *zip*, appears twice in the header. Because the attribute appears twice, this is not a relation.

```
{cust-num} {zip} {zip}
{cust-num,1}{zip,84392}{zip,94934}
```

RELATIONS DON'T CONTAIN DUPLICATE TUPLES

Rows cannot repeat in relation. Here is another example of a data structure that is not a relation:

```
{cust-num}{order-num}{cust-name}
{cust-num,1}{order-num,1}{cust-name,joe}
{cust-num,1}{order-num,2}{cust-name,sally}
{cust-num,1}{order-num,1}{cust-name,joe}
```

Relational database architecture uses the mathematics of sets. A domain, for instance, is a set. A set does not have duplicate elements. A relation is cannot have duplicate tuples.

Duplicate rows in table are unnecessary.

Example: Here is data about shipments that were made on the same day. The identical rows of data keep this data from being put in a relation.

```
ship-date   ship-zip
Jan 2, 1993    83222
Jan 2, 1993    83222
Jan 2, 1993    83222
Jan 2, 1993    83222
```

Adding an order number to the data makes each row unique. With the addition of an order number, you can put this data in a relation.

{order-num}	{ship-date}	{ship-zip}
{order-num,1}	{ship-date,2/2/94}	{ship-zip,93222}
{order-num,2}	{ship-date,2/2/94}	{ship-zip,93222}
{order-num,3}	{ship-date,2/2/94}	{ship-zip,93222}

Many systems do not enforce this restriction against duplicate rows. Although the relational model states clearly that duplicate rows are not allowed, most manufacturer's data base systems will allow duplicate rows.

Even when the RDBMS allows duplicate rows, it usually provides some secondary mechanism for prohibiting them. Be careful. It is your responsiblity with most systems to assure that duplicate rows will not be added to the database.

TUPLES ARE UN-ORDERED

The attribute-data pairs in a tuple are unordered. Just as attributes are un-ordered within a tuple, tuples are un-ordered within a relation. The tuples in a relation can appear in any order, and it is still the same relation.

Example: This is the same relation written three different ways.

{order-num}	{ship-date}	{ship-zip}
{order-num,1}	{ship-date,2/2/94}	{ship-zip,93222}
{order-num,2}	{ship-date,2/2/94}	{ship-zip,93222}
{order-num,3}	{ship-date,2/2/94}	{ship-zip,93222}

{order-num}	{ship-date}	{ship-zip}
{order-num,3}	{ship-date,2/2/94}	{ship-zip,93222}
{order-num,2}	{ship-date,2/2/94}	{ship-zip,93222}
{order-num,1}	{ship-date,2/2/94}	{ship-zip,93222}

{order-num}	{ship-date}	{ship-zip}
{order-num,3}	{ship-date,2/2/94}	{ship-zip,93222}
{order-num,2}	{ship-date,2/2/94}	{ship-zip,93222}
{order-num,1}	{ship-date,2/2/94}	{ship-zip,93222}

KEYS

As stated in an earlier section, each row of a table is unique. This is because duplicate rows are not allowable in a table.

Since no duplicate rows are in a table, any row has a unique identification to permit selection. A *key* permits this selection.

For example, look at the table above that holds order information. The order-number attribute is a key for this relation. It is a key because it uniquely selects any row from the table.

If a table have duplicate rows, there is no way to insure existence of a unique key. This is why relations may not have duplicate rows.

One or more attributes make a key. One attribute may uniquely identify any row in a relation, such as an order number. If this one attribute can uniquely identify and select any row, it can serve as a key.

Composite Keys

Sometimes, one attribute is not enough for unique selection of any single row in a table. If so, multiple attributes must combine to form a key. A key formed by multiple attributes is a *composite key*.

Example: One order can include more than one kind of stock. Here is another table that shows the stock used to fill an order.

Because a single order can ship with more than one kind of stock item, the order number is not unique.

order-number	stock-number
3	a1003
3	a3233
3	b4434
1	b5545
1	a4543
1	b2454
2	a1432

The same stock item can appear in different orders, so the stock number is not unique.

The order number is not unique, so it is not a key for this table.

The stock number is not unique, so it is not a key for this table.

A composite key made from the order number and stock number can uniquely identify and select any row in this table.

Candidate Keys

More than one possible key can open a table. In this case, each separate key is a *candidate key*. Often, multiple canditate keys for a table exist.

For a relation to be a relation, it has at least one candidate key. More than one candidate key can exist. Candidate keys can be individual keys, and composite keys, or a combination of both.

Candidate keys must be minimal.

Example: Take a table where a customer-number is a candidate key. Another key made from a customer number and a customer name is not a candidate key in this table. The reason is that taking the customer name away still leaves the customer number as a candidate key.

One key from among the candidate keys must be a primary key. This selection is arbitrary. The user can select any of the candidate keys as the primary key. Candidate keys not selected as the primary key remain secondary keys.

Keys provide the only addressing mechanism in the relation model. Only a key selects an individual row from a table. The only way to find a tuple is to know the name of the its table and the value of the primary key for that row.

Foreign Keys

Keys relate together the information in different tables. The primary key in one table can locate data in another table.

Example: Take the following two tables.

Stock			Orders		
order-number	stock-num		order-num	cust-num	ship-date
---	---		---	---	---
3	1003		1	32	1/3
3	3233		2	33	1/2
3	4434		3	17	1/4
1	5545				
1	4543				
1	2454				
2	1432				

The first table shows orders from customers. The primary key is the order number. The second table shows the stock items included in any order. The primary key is a composite key made from the order number and stock number.

When a customer orders, the stock table increases by one or more rows for that order. Every stock item that appears in the order gets a row. The person entering the row for the stock item into the table adds in the order number.

This simplifies finding all the stock items for a single order. Searching the stock table for an order number finds all the stock items for the order.

The order number is the primary key for the orders table. It is a foreign key for the stock table. A foreign key is a primary key from one table that is used to select data from a different table.

The foreign-key primary-key relationships are the glue that holds a relational database together.

Unlike some earlier database systems, no explicit relationships exist between the tables in a relational database. Tables related only by primary-key foreign-key relationships. These foreign-key relatioships allow data to be combined from multiple tables.

Note: A foreign key need not be part of the primary key of the relation. In the example above, the foreign key order-number happens to be part of the primary key. The foreign key does not have to be one of the candidate keys, either. In the example above, the customer number is not a candidate key for the stock table.

A primary key can be used as a foreign key into the same relation that holds the primary key.

INTEGRITY RULES

The relational model provides two rules that help insure data integrity. They are entity integrity and referential integrity.

The *entity integrity* rule states that null values cannot be in a primary key. The primary key would no longer be unique with values in the primary key. If a key is not unique, it cannot be a candidate key or a primary key. Foreign keys can contain null values. No requirement in the relational model holds that a foreign key be unique.

The *referential integrity* rule maintains the relationship between primary keys and foreign keys. Referential integrity states that a foreign key must exist in the table containing the primary key.

Example: Here is the small database about orders and stock again. The foreign key in the stock table is the order number.

Stock		Orders		
order-number	stock-num	order-num	cust-num	ship-date

```
 -------------        -------------------
 3       1003          1     32    1/3
 3       3233          2     33    1/2
 3       4434          3     17    1/4
 1       5545
 1       4543
 1       2454
 2       1432
```

Maintaining referential integrity in this database requires that there be an order number in the orders table for every order number found in the stock table.

Deleting the first row in the orders table would delete order number one. That would lose the referential integrity because now there would be stock items for order one in the stock table that do not relate to any existing order. To maintain referential integrity, you must drop all the stock items for order number one when the order is dropped.

Relational database software from many vendors does not enforce referential integrity or entity integrity. The responsible programmer must maintain referential or entity integrity. Any evaluation of a database system checks the support of referential and entity integrity.

NORMALIZING A TABLE

A normalized relation does not contain repeating data groups. Normalization changes an un-normalized data structure into a table.

A normalized relation is simpler than an un-normalized data structure. Changing a normalized table is easier than changing an un-normalized data structure.

Example: Adding a row of data to a table is easier than inserting data fields into an un-normalized data structure.

Here is a data structure with repeating data.

```
{cust-number}{order-number}
{order-number,193,231,33}{cust-number,1}
```

Following is the table that results from normalizing this data structure.

{cust-number}	{order-number}
{cust-numer,1}	{order-number,193}
{cust-number,1}	{order-number,231}
{cust-number,1}	{order-number,33}

WHAT IS A RELATIONAL DATABASE?

A relational database is group of normalized relations of various degrees. The set of tuples in the relations changes over time.

Normalizing the relations in a database is necessary. Each relation is empty when it is first created. The number of tuples added later determines the degree of each relation.

The degree of the relation as well as the set of tuples change over time. Tuples do not change in the relational model. Instead, a new tuple replaces the old tuple. In practice, most relational database systems change tuples.

This chapter introduces SQL data definition commands. Data definition commands create a database, create tables in the database, and create columns in the tables. The following chapters present SQL commands used for data access and data access control.

Note: these chapters do not completely present SQL. They give just enough SQL to start you building and accessing databases from a host language.

For a more complete introduction to SQL, see one of the many excellent avalable books or the documentation supplied with your database system.

THE DATABASE ENVIRONMENT

SQL looks in the current environment for a database. This database contains tables, and these tables contain data. No two tables in the database can have the same name.

DATA TYPES

No standard exists for the data types that can be stored in a relational database. Different relational database systems from different manufacturers can store different types of data. Commonly-available data types appear in the following table.

Optional portions of data type names are in brackets. For example, defining a decimal number could use dec(10,2) or decimal(10,2). Here is a list of common SQL data types.

SQL Data Types

`character[(length)]`	a string of one or more characters
`varchar(length)`	a character string of variable length
`numeric[(precision[,scale)]]`	a real number, usually a synonym for a float
`dec[imal][(precision, [scale]}]`	a decimal number
`numberprecision[,scale)]]`	same as numeric
`integer`	an integer
`smallint`	a small integer
`float[(precision)]`	a real number
`real`	a real number
`double precision`	a double precision real number

The length, precision, and scale listed as part of the datatypes must be positive integers. A length or precision must exceed zero. The default values for length and scale are vendor dependent. The default value of precision is implementation dependent.

The default precision of *smallint* and *integer values* are also implementation dependent. An integer can always hold a larger positive or smaller negative value than a smallint. A *double precision* number is also capable of holding a larger positive or smaller negative value than a float. You should consult your system-supplied documentation for the default precisions of these data types.

Note that numeric, decimal, integer and smallint datatypes are exact types. They store in such a fashion that they will always be exact.

In contrast to the exact types, the *float, double precision* and *real* are approximate data types. This is because the host computer stores float, double precision, and real numbers in such a fashion that their value may be inexact. When such numbers are very large or very small, the host computer may store them as an approximation.

The size and format of each of these data types varies from machine to machine and system to system. You should read the documentation for your system to find the format for these data types for your system. Other data types for dates, money and time are found in some implementations.

THE ELEMENTS OF SQL

SQL has a well-specified syntax. This syntax has various elements, including key-words, operators and identifiers. These elements combine to make SQL statements. The most basic elements are characters.

All SQL elements derive from a character set. These characters include the lower case letters *a* to *z* and the upper case letters *A* to *Z*. The character set includes the digits *0, 1, 2, 3, 4, 5, 6, 7, 8, 9*. The character set includes a new line marker and some special characters. The special characters must include

```
%  _  ,  ( )  <  >  .  :  =  +  -  *  /
```

and a character for a blank space. The complete character set and the sorting order for the character set are implementation dependent.

Literals

There are two types of literals: *strings* and *numbers*. A string is a series of characters enclosed in single quotes. Here are some examples of string literals:

```
'This is a literal'
'123456'
'customer'
```

Single quotes appear in a character literal as two single quotes in a row. For example,

```
'this is a quote '' in a literal'
```

Exact numeric literals are signed integer or decimal numbers, for example

```
1
1.2354
-3.3
.0002
```

Approximate numeric literals appear in exponential format. An exponential number has an exact literal, a capital E, and a second exact literal representing the exponent of the number; for example,

Literal	Value	
1.23E04	12300	
4E5		400000
25E-4	.0002	
-3E3	-3000	
-3E-4	-.0003	

TOKENS

Tokens are the basic syntactic units of the SQL language. Tokens include delimiters and non-delimiters.

A delimiter is a character string of one of the following special symbols:

```
,  (  )  <  >  .  :  =  +  -  *  /  <>  <=  >=
```

Non-delimiters are either a numeric literal, an identifier, or a keyword. Description of numeric literals is in the preceding section.

Any number of separators can follow a token. A separator is a space, newline marker, or comment. A separator or delimiter token must follow every nondelimiter token.

The user chooses an identifier for some object in the database, such as a column name or a table name. An identifier is a series of up to 18 characters. The first letter of an identifier must be a letter. The underscore character "_" can appear in an identifier, but never two underscore characters in a row.

Some identifiers are pre-defined by SQL. These are keywords. These keywords have a built-in meaning for SQL. The following figure shows a list of common SQL key-words. You should consult the documentation supplied with your RDBMS for a more complete list.

SQL Keywords

all	delete	into	references
and	desc	is	rollback
any	double	language	section
asc	end	like	select
authorization	escape	max	setavg
access	exec	min	smallint
begin	exists	module	some
between	fetch	not	sql
by	float	null	sqlcode
character	foreign	of	sum
check	fortran	on	table
close	found	open	to
cobol	from	option	union
commit	go	or	unique
continue	goto	order	update
count	grant	pascal	user
create	group	pl1	values
current	having	precision	view
cursor	in	primary	whenever
dec	indicator	privliges	where
decimal	insert	procedure	with
declare	int	public	work
default	integer	real	

SQL SYNTAX

Each SQL statement typically has more than one possible variation. A description of any SQL statement shows each of the possible variations.

This section presents the syntax of SQL statements. This book does not describe all ANSI-standard SQL statements or variations. Consult your system documentation for a complete listing of all available SQL statements and their possible forms.

Certain words must appear in a particular SQL statement for it to be interpreted correctly. These are key-words. Key words will appear capitalized LIKE THIS. Here is an example:

```
CREATE TABLE
```

When used in an SQL program, the key words do not have to be capitalized. This statement could be used to create a table:

```
create table orders
```

Some parts of an SQL statement are variable, chosen by the user. For example, the user must pick a name when creating a table.

```
CREATE TABLE table-name
```

The user can select any appropriate name for this variable part. Here are several examples:

```
create table orders
create table invoices
create table temperature
```

The name length has a system-dependent upper limit. Not all characters can occur in a name. Consult your system documentation for explicit naming rules.

Some portions of an SQL statement must appear yet can vary. For example, when creating a column in a table, the user must select the data type. This data type can be one of several choices. The user must select one of the data types.

```
CREATE TABLE table-name (column-name data-type)
```

Here are some examples:

```
create table example (fname char(10))
create table example (age integer)
```

Some portions of an SQL statement are optional. For example, the ANSI standard allows a column to be specified as unique or non-unique upon creation of a table.

In a column specified as unique, any single data value can appear only once. In that situation, the RDBMS will disallow a row in a table if the attribute to be placed in the unique column is already in the relation in another row.

This identification of the column as unique is optional. Optional portions of an SQL statement appear in brackets.

```
CREATE TABLE table-name
```

```
(column-name, data-type [UNIQUE])
```

Here are two legal SQL statements.

```
create table test (attr1 integer unique)
```

```
create table test (attr1 integer)
```

Some SQL statements provide a number of choices. These choices appear separated by vertical bars. In this example, a column can be UNIQUE or NOT UNIQUE:

```
CREATE TABLE table name
  (column-name, data-type UNIQUE | NOT UNIQUE)
```

Here is an example of each:

```
create table test (attr1, integer unique)
```

```
create table test (attr1, integer not unique)
```

Choices appear also with brackets. Optional parts of an SQL statement that do not have to be included in all cases appear with these brackets.

This example shows that a column can be specified as *not null* or as *not unique*. Specifying a column as not null prohibits the use of null values in that column.

```
CREATE TABLE table name
(column-name data-type [NOT NULL [UNIQUE]])
```

This results in two possible statements.

```
create table sales
  (customer-name char(10) not null)
```

```
create table sales
  (customer-name char(10) not unique
```

An SQL statement can allow repetition. Braces indicate the repeating portion of the statement. Ellipses indicate the repetition.

Note in this example that there is a comma after the closing brace and before the ellipses. So, the comma appears only when part of the statement repeats.

```
CREATE TABLE table-name
```

```
({column-name data-type [UNIQUE]},...)
```

This example shows that the *create table* statement can define multiple columns.

```
create table sales (
   customer-name char(20),
   customer-id char(20) unique,
   phone char(20)
   )
```

CREATE OR DROP A DATABASE

There is no standard SQL syntax for creating a database or dropping a database. Consult your system documentation for the syntax of the appropriate statement. Some systems use

```
CREATE DATABASE database-name
```

```
DROP DATABASE database-name
```

For example,

```
create database orders
drop database orders
```

CREATE A TABLE CREATE COLUMNS

The *create table* statement can create a new table. The create table statement also creates the columns in the table. The ANSI-86 standard for the creation of a table is

```
CREATE TABLE table-name
({column-name data-type [NOT NULL [UNIQUE]] |
UNIQUE ({column-name},...},...)
```

This statement often occurs in a less-complex form similar to

```
CREATE TABLE table-name
[({column-name data-type [NOT NULL [UNIQUE]] |
[UNIQUE]},...)]
```

The *create table* statement creates a table and, optionally, the columns for that table. Some implementations mandate having at least one column named when the table is created. As the brackets indicate in the statement above, a table can be created without columns. A second, following, *alter table* statement could then create columns in that table as described in a following section.

This example creates the orders table in the orders database

```
create table orders (
   customer-number char(10),
   order-number integer,
   customer-inv-number char(20),
   tax-rate real,
   ship-rate real
   )
```

Note that in the standard no two tables in a database can have the same name. Each table must have a unique name. Some implementations allow tables to have the same name if they are owned by different users.

DROP A TABLE

There is no ANSII standard SQL statement for dropping a table from a database. A common syntax for removing a table from a database is

```
DROP TABLE table-name
```

Any information held in the table will be lost. For example,

```
drop table sales
```

CREATE A TEMPORARY TABLE

The following statement will create a temporary table:

```
CREATE TEMP TABLE table-name
   ({column-name, data-type [UNIQUE]},...)
```

A temporary table can function to store information during the current session. A temporary table will disappear at the end of the current session.

The TEMP keyword is not a part of the current SQL standard and will not be found in all database implementations.

ADDING COLUMNS TO A TABLE

The *alter table* statement commonly adds columns to an existing table. This statement is not part of the ANSI-86 SQL standard. Here are three typical variations of this statement:

```
ALTER TABLE table-name ADD COLUMN column-name
data-type [NOT NULL] [DEFAULT {literal |
SYSTEM}]
```

```
ALTER TABLE table-name ADD (column-name
data-type) [NOT NULL WITH DEFAULT]
```

```
 ALTER TABLE table-name ADD column-name
data-type [NULL | NOT NULL]
```

This statement permits adding a column to an existing table. For example, to add a column to the customer's relation, use:

```
alter table customer
  add ship-weight real not null
```

Please note that no two columns within a table can have the same name; column names must be unique.

The preceding chapter described the SQL syntax for creating tables. This chapter describes the SQL syntax for accessing the data in those tables.

You can selectively retrieve data from tables. You can selectively print some or all of the columns and all of the rows. You can combine and display the information found in multiple tables.

This chapter shows how to perform these selections and combinations.

A following section describes each of the selection operations. The operations are

- ✓ Selection
- ✓ Projection
- ✓ Union
- ✓ Intersection
- ✓ Difference
- ✓ Join
- ✓ View

Conceptually, although not physically, each operation produces a new table. The first two operations, *selection* and *projection*, operate on a single table to produce a second new table. The operations *difference* and *join* combine multiple tables to produce a new table. A *view* creates a new table from one or more tables.

SELECTION

The *select* statement displays some or all of the rows from an existing table. The result of the selection is a new table containing the selected items. The following figure shows all the rows for order number one being selected from a table that contains three orders.

Original Table

order-number	stock-number
3	a1003
3	a3233
3	b4434
1	b5545
1	a4543
1	b2454
2	a1432

Here is the table that results from the selection.

order-number	stock-number
1	b5545
1	a4543
1	b2454

The following examples start with simple select statements and proceed to more complex selections. Here is the syntax for a simple selection:

```
SELECT *
    FROM {table-name | view-name}, . . .
```

The * (asterisk) indicates that all the columns of the table table-name will be selected.

This query returns all the records from the orders table.

```
select * from orders
```

Search Conditions

A search condition restricts the selection of records from a table.

```
SELECT *
FROM {table-name | view-name}, . . .
WHERE search-condition]
```

The search condition is of the form

```
[NOT] {predicate | search condition} }
[{AND | OR] [NOT] {predicate | (search
condition)}]...
```

Descriptions of searchconditions appear   more fully in following sections, but here are a few examples:

```
select * from customers
   where customer-number > 3

select * from customers
   where not customer-number = 1

select * from customers
   where customer-number = 3
   or customer-number = 4
```

The following query returns the records from the orders table where the customer number is equal to one. This is the selection that would produce the results shown in the preceding figure.

```
select * from orders
   where customer-number = 1
```

Typing the select statement in an interactive SQL system causes each of the three records to appear on-screen. This statement embedded in a host program also retrieves the same rows.Relational operators in a search condition can restrict a selection. Relational operators are in the following figure.

```
=     equals
!=    not equals
<>    not equals
<     less than
<=    less than or equal to
>     greater than
>=    greater than or equal to
```

Examples are

```
select * from orders where ship-rate = .65
select * from orders where ship-rate < .65
select * from orders where ship-rate >= .65
select * from orders where ship-rate <= .65
select * from orders where ship-rate != .65
```

Arithmetic statements can also restrict a selection. Here are the arithmetic operators:

```
+        addition
-        subtraction
*        multiplication
/        division
**       exponentiation
mod      modulus
```

Examples are

```
select * from orders where ship-rate = 3*.1

select * from orders where ship-rate = 3*.1+.5

select * from orders where ship-rate = 3*5/2+.5
```

The *precedence order* of the arithmetic operators determines the order of evaluation of an arithmetic expression as shown in the next figure. Multiplication and division appear higher on this list, so they are performed before addition and subtraction. Subtraction or addition is performed before exponentiation. Exponentiation is performed before the modulus operator.

```
Order of Precedence
       * /
       + -
       **
      mod
```

For example, in the expression

```
3*5+1**2
```

three is first multiplied by 5, resulting in a value of 15. One is added to 15, resulting in a value of 16. Finally, 16 is squared to produce a value of 256.

Parentheses can also determine the precedence of evaluation of an expression. In the example

```
3+(5*2)
```

five is first multiplied by two, resulting in a value of ten. The resulting value of ten is then added to three to yield a value of 13. In another example,

```
(3+5)*2
```

five is added to three to produce a value of eight, which is multiplied by two producing a value of 16.

BOOLEAN OPERATORS

There are three *Boolean values* in SQL—true, false and unknown. (Unknown or null are the same.) *Unknown* is a specific third logical value, like *true* or *false*, that indicates the value is unknown. This differs from an unspecified or undetermined value.

For example, many programming languages can refer to an uninitialized variable. This variable may contain a different indeterminate value each time the program runs or each time the program runs on a different machine. An unititialized variable might contain a value of ten one time or ten thousand the next time.

This differs from the Boolean unknown value. The value *unknown* is always the same each time a program runs or when a program runs on a different computer.

The two Boolean operators *and* and *or* combine two values to produce a value of true, false or unknown. For example, the following expression produces a value of true

```
true and true
```

There are three Boolean values--true, false and unknown. The operator "not" inverts the value of true or false. *Not true* is *false*. *Not false* is *true*.

The order of precedence of Boolean operators isnot

```
and
or
```

Parentheses can change this order. For example,

```
(not true) and true
```

The following figure shows how Boolean values combine with the operator <u>and</u> to produce a new resulting value of true or false.

AND	true	false	unknown
true	true	false	unknown
false	false	false	unknown
unknown	unknown	unknown	unknown

For example,

```
true and true
```

produces a value of true. The Boolean value of true combines with the second Boolean of true through the "and" operator. This results in a Boolean value of true.

The following table shows how two logical values combine with the Boolean inclusive or operator to produce a third logical value.

OR	true	false	unknown
true	true	true	unknown
false	true	false	unknown
unknown	unknown	unknown	unknown

For example, the expression *true or false* evaluates to a Boolean value of true.

The *not* operator changes the sense of a value. *Not true* has a value of false, and *not false* has a value of true.

Combining Expressions

The Boolean operators can combine arithmetic and relational operations. Here are some examples:

```
select * from orders
    where ship-rate != .65 and ship-rate .85

select * from orders
    where ship-rate .85 and ship-rate .45
select * from orders
    where ship-rate is not null
```

```
select * from orders
   where ship-rate is not .45
```

Here is a sample orders table:

Orders

order-number	stock-number
3	a1003
3	a3233
3	b4434
1	b5545
1	a4543
1	b2454
2	a1432

The following query returns all orders where the customer-number is greater than one but less than six.

```
select *
   from orders
      where customer-number >1 and customer-number
<6
```

The following table results from the selection.

new table

The next figure adds a shipping cost column to the orders table.

order-number	stock-number
3	a1003
3	a3233
3	b4434
2	a1432

orders

order-number	stock-number	ship-cost
3	a1003	$1.53
3	a3233	$2.24
3	b4434	$3.33
2	a1432	null
1	a3332	$1.56
1	b2323	null
5	c4343	$1.85
6	a3232	null

This query returns all orders where there is a shipping cost listed in the orders table

```
select *
   from orders
   where ship rate is not null
```

Parenthesis can determine the evaluation order of combined expressions. This appears in the following examples.

```
(ship-rate = .45 and ship-rate = .65) or
(ship-rate = .75 and ship-rate = .85)
```

```
((ship-rate = .45 and ship-rate =.65) or
(ship-rate = .75 and ship-rate = .85))
```

```
(ship-rate = .45 and ship-rate = .65) and
(ship-rate = .75 and ship-rate = .85) and
(ship-rate = .95 and ship-rate = .45)
```

THE ORDER BY CLAUSE IN A

By definition, the records in a relation in the table lack sorted order. The "*order by*" clause returns the records from a selection in ascending or descending order.

```
SELECT *
   FROM {table-name | view-name}, . . .
   [WHERE search-condition]
   [ORDER BY {column-name [ASC | DESC]}...]
```

Here is an orders table:

Orders

order-number	stock-number	ship-cost
3	a1003	$1.53
3	a3233	$2.24
3	b4434	$3.33
2	a1432	null
1	a3332	$1.56
1	b2323	null
5	c4343	$1.85
6	a3232	null

This query returns six records from the orders table where the order number is greater than one but less than five.

```
select *
   from orders
   where order-number >=1
   and order-number < 5
```

The following table results from the selection

New Table

order-number	stock-number	ship-cost
3	a1003	$1.53
3	a3233	$2.24
3	b4434	$3.33
2	a1432	null
1	a3332	$1.56
1	b2323	null

This select statement returns the records, in ascending order of stock number:

```
select *
   from orders
   where order-number >= 1
   and order-number < 5
   order by stock num
```

The following table results from the selection:

order-number	stock-number	ship-cost
3	a1003	$1.53
2	a1432	null
3	a3233	$2.24
1	a3332	$1.56
1	b2323	null
3	b4434	$3.33

This select statement returns the same records in descending order:

```
select *
   from orders
   where order-number >= 1
   and order-number < 5
   order by ship-cost desc
```

Sorting operations can combine. For example, this query orders the selected records in ascending order of customer number and descending order of ship rate:

```
select *
   from orders
   where order-number >= 1
   and order-number < 5
   order by cust-number, ship-cost desc
```

PROJECTION

Selection takes rows from of a table. *Projection* takes columns.

The following figure shows a projection of one of the rows of a table, the stock-number.

order-number	stock-number	ship-cost
3	a1003	$1.53
3	a3233	$2.24
3	b4434	$3.33
2	a1432	null
1	a3332	$1.56
1	b2323	null
5	c4343	$1.85
6	a3232	null

The selection list in the select statement produces a projection.

```
SELECT select-list
    FROM {table-name | view-name}, . . .
    [WHERE search-condition]
    [GROUP BY {column-name}]
    [ORDER BY {column-name [ASC | DESC]}...
```

Projection selects one or more columns of a table. For example, the query

```
select order-number, ship-cost from orders
```

projects just the order-number and ship-cost columns from the orders table. The next figure shows this.

order-number	ship-cost
3	$1.53
3	$2.24
3	$3.33
2	null
1	$1.56
1	null
5	$1.85
6	null

Projection selects just some of the columns of a table. Projection can also reorder the appearance of columns in the new table. (Remember, though, that there is no ordering of tuples in the relational model.) For example, this SQL statement produces the following projection.

```
select ship-cost, order-number from orders
```

ship-cost	order-number
$1.53	3
$2.24	3
$3.33	3
null	2
$1.56	1
null	1
$1.85	5
null	6

COMBINING SELECTION AND PROJECTION

Projections can combine with selections. This selection returns records with customer numbers between one and six, projecting two of the columns andselecting some of the rows.

```
select order-number, ship-cost
   from orders
   where order-number >= 1
   and order-number <= 5
   order by ship-cost desc
```

RETURNING DISTINCT RECORDS

The contents of data records can determine the results of a selection. You can group selected records based on their contents.

The keyword distinct eliminates duplicate records from the results of a selection.

```
SELECT [distinct] select-list
   FROM {table-name | view-name}, . . .
   [WHERE search-condition]
   [GROUP BY {column-name}]
   [ORDER BY {column-name [ASC | DESC]}...]
```

Following here is another table with data about orders.

orders table

order-number	stock-number	ship-cost
3	a1003	$1.53
3	a3233	$2.24
3	b4434	$3.33
2	a1432	$1.56
1	a3332	$1.56
1	b2323	$1.85
5	c4343	$1.85
6	a3232	$2.20

The sample table holds eight rows. The following projection selects all the order numbers from the table.

```
select order-num from orders
```

Adding the distinct keyword to the query returns only five order numbers, specifically the five distinct order numbers.

select distinct order-num from orders

order-number
3
2
1
5
6

AGGREGATING RECORDS

There are five *aggregate functions* in SQL. These functions operate on the rows returned by a selection. The result is a single value. For example, the query

```
select avg(ship-rate) from orders
```

returns the average shipping rate from the orders table. Summing all the values found in the shipping rate column and dividing by the number of records found in the table produces this average.

The five SQL aggregate functions are:

aggregate functions

maximum	returns the maximum value found among the selected rows
minimum	returns the minimum value found among the selected rows
sum	returns the sum of the value of the selected rows
count	returns a count of the rows selected
average	the arithmetic average of the returned rows

The distinct keyword can eliminate duplicate rows from a query. The distinct keyword can thus eliminate duplicate rows before application of one of these functions. For example, the query

```
select count(distinct ship-rate)
   from orders
```

will count each distinct shipping rate. This occurs because the query first returns each distinct shipping rate. Then the query counts each distinct shipping rate.

GROUP BY

The group by clause collects selected data into subgroups. One data value returnsfrom each subgroup.

```
SELECT *
FROM {table-name | view-name}, . . .
[WHERE search-condition]
[GROUP BY {column-name}]
[ORDER BY {column-name [ASC | DESC]}...]
```

Here is an orders table.

order-number	stock-number	ship-cost
3	a1003	$1.53
3	a3233	$2.24
3	b4434	$3.33
2	a1432	$1.56
1	a3332	$1.56
1	b2323	$1.85
5	c4343	$1.85
6	a3232	$2.20

The following query selects each order number from the orders table. The query then groups the order numbers. The table ensues.

```
select order-number
from orders
group by order number
   order-num
      3
      2
      1
      5
      6
```

Grouping is extremely useful when combined with aggregate functions. Without a group by clause, an aggregate function operates on all the records returned by a selection. A group by clause can divide the selected records into groups and allow the aggregate functions to operate on these groups.

For example,

```
select order-num, avg(ship-rate)
   from orders
   group by order-num
```

returns the average shipping rate for each of the order number groups selected. That is, grouping orders by order number occurs first. Computing the average shipping rate for each order-number group occurs next.

UNION

A *union* accepts two tables as input and produces a third (different) table as output. The union operation combines the rows of one table with the rows of another table to produce a third (new) table.

A union is an operation from the mathematical theory of sets. In a mathematical union, the elements of one set combine with the members of another set to produce a third set. This third set contains all the elements found in both the original sets.

The following figure illustrates the union of two sets. The first set, containing elements *x* is combined with the second set containing elements *y*. The resulting set contains all the elements of both sets.

the union of two sets

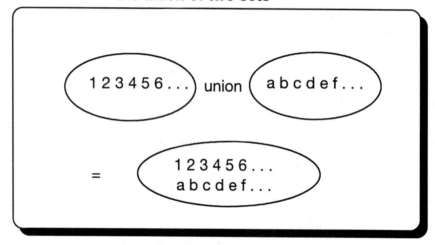

Tables must be union compatible to combine. Three conditions determine union compatibility. Here are the conditions and some examples.

First, every table must be of the same degree. If one table has three columns, so must the other.

Second, the attributes of each table come from the same underlying domains.

Third, attributes drawn from the same underlying domain must appear in the same order in each table heading. The attributes in the heading of one table must be in the same order in the heading of the other.

These three conditions insure that any union operation results in a relation. Without these rules, a union operation could produce a set but not produce a relation.

Using the union operator to combine two select statements produces a union.

```
SELECT *
    FROM {table-name | view-name}, . . .
    [WHERE search-condition]
    [GROUP BY {column-name}]
    [ORDER BY {column-name [ASC | DESC]}...]
    [UNION select-statement]
```

Take as an example a table that holds orders already shipped. Shipping an order moves the row from the orders table to the closed-orders table.

A union of the two tables, the orders table and the closed-orders table, produce a new table. This table contains all the rows from both tables. This query produces the union

```
select * from orders
union
select * from closed-orders
```

Note that the order numbers in the closed orders table have to differ from the order numbers in the orders table. A row duplicated in both tables would causethe union to contain duplicate tuples; the result would not be a relation.

A union does not return duplicate records. If the same row is in both tables it only appears once in the union. Some versions of SQL provide *all* as an operator that changes this. With the *all* operator, all the records from both tables appear.A union operation is associative. Unions performed in any order produce the same result. For example, (X union Y) union Z returns the same values as X union (Y union Z).

INTERSECTION

The *intersection* of two sets contains any elements that appear in both sets. The intersection of two tables contains any rows found in both tables.

Take as an example two sets, *a* and *b*. Set *a* contains the elements a, b, c, d, e, f, g. Set *b* contains the elements e, f, g, h, i, j, k. The intersection of the two sets contains the elements e, f, and g. The intersection of the two sets contains the elements found in both sets.

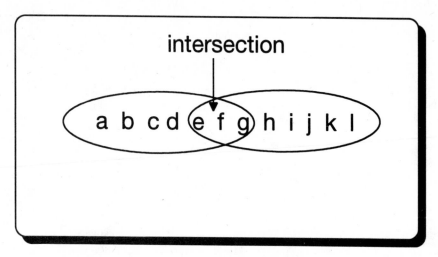

The intersection of these two sets contains the elements e, f and g. the intersection contains the elements common to both sets. The figure above shows this.

The intersect operator returns the intersection of two tables. The intersect operator is not part of the ANSII standard. The intersect operator is not in all SQL implementations.

The intersect operator combines two or more select statements. Following is the syntax of the intersect operator.

```
SELECT *
FROM {table-name | view-name}, . . .
[WHERE search-condition]
[GROUP BY {column-name}]
[ORDER BY {column-name [ASC | DESC]}...]
[INTERSECT select-statement]
```

Take as an example two tables. The first table contains rows about orders. The second table contains rows about back orders. The following query returns all the rows found in both tables:

```
select * from orders
intersect
select * from back-orders
```

As with the union operator, the two tables must be union compatible to form an intersection.

DIFFERENCE

A *difference* subtracts the members found in one set from the members found in another set. For example, take two sets *A* and *B*. Set *A* has the elements a, b, c, d and e. Set *B* has the elements d, e, f, g and h. with common elements f, g and h..

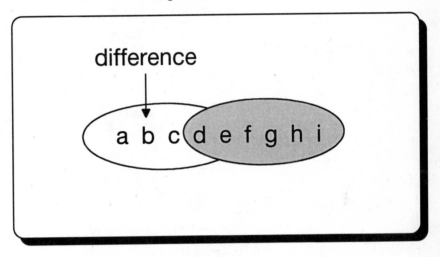

The difference A-B contains only elements that are found in set *A*, but not set *B*. The difference contains the elements, a, b, and c.

The difference operator combines two select statements. A table results from subtracting all the elements found in one table from the elements found in the other table. As with a union or intersection, a difference can only derive from union compatible tables. Not all SQL implementations support the difference operator.

```
SELECT *
    FROM {table-name | view-name}, . . .
    [WHERE search-condition]
    [GROUP BY {column-name}]
    [ORDER BY {column-name [ASC | DESC]}...]
    [MINUS select-statement]
```

For example, A minus B removes all the records from table A that are also found in table B. Take two relations A and B.

A	B
a	
b	
c	
d	d
e	e

```
f  f
   g
   h
```

The difference A minus B contains the elements a, b and c.

CARTESIAN PRODUCT

The *Cartesian product* joins one set with another. Every element in the first set joins every element in the second set. As an example, take two tables A and B.

```
Table A  Table B
-------- --------
   w            10
   x            20
   y            30
   z            40
```

The Cartesian product AxB of these two tables contains the following rows.

```
   AxB
   -------
w  10
w  20
w  30
w  40
x  10
x  20
x  30
x  40
y  10
y  20
y  30
y  40
z  10
z  20
z  30
z  40
```

Extended Cartesian products produce all possible combinations of the elements in multiple sets. As an example, here are three sets:

```
A    B    C
---  --   --
10   f    x
```

```
20   g   y
```

Here is the result of the extended Cartesian product AxBxC:

```
AxBxC
----------
   10 f x
   10 f y
   10 g x
   10 g y
   20 f x
   20 f y
   20 g x
   20 g y
```

JOIN

A *join* combines each of the rows in one table with matching rows in a second table. The *from* clause selects the tables to join. The *where* clause shows how the tables combine. Here is the SQL syntax for joining two tables.

```
SELECT *
   FROM {table-name | view-name},
   OUTER {table-name | view-name}, . . .
   [WHERE search-condition]
   [GROUP BY {column-name}]
   [ORDER BY {column-name [ASC | DESC]}...]
```

As an example, take a small database with two tables, orders and stock. Each order may have stock. Some orders do not have stock associated with them.

Stock		Orders		
order-number	stock-number	order-number	cust-number	ship-date
3	1003	1	32	1/3
3	3233	2	33	1/2
3	4434	3	17	1/4
1	5545	4	22	1/5
1	4543	5	17	1/4
1	2454			
2	1432			

Notice that some of the rows in the orders table do not have stock associated with them in the stock table. For example, order four does not have any stock associated with it in the stock table.

The following select statement joins the two tables.

```
select * from orders, stock
where order.order-number = stock.order-number
```

The join produces the following table:

New

order-number	cust-number	ship-date	order-number	stock-number
1	32	1/3	1	5545
1	32	1/3	1	4543
1	32	1/3	1	2454
2	33	1/2	2	1432
3	17	1/2	3	1003
3	17	1/2	3	3233
3	17	1/2	3	4434

Some of the rows in the orders table do not have corresponding entries in the stock table. An order without stock does not appear in the results of the *join*. A row in an inner table without a corresponding row in an outer table does not appear in the results of a the *join*. This is an *inner join*.

The two tables were joined by matching the order number. The selection of rows from the two tables rests on the order numbers being equal. Because the foreign key relationship rests on equality, this is called an *equi-join*.

The *join* command selects each row from the first table, one row at-a-time. This command searches the second table for a row with a matching order numbers. If a match is found based on the order number, the two rows combine and become part of the join.

The two columns used to join the two tables must exist over the same domain. The attributes *orders.order-number* and *stock.order-number* must exist over the same domain.

Note that the select statement fully qualifies the column names.This prevents any confusion when joining the tables, especially when attributes differ.

SELECTION AND PROJECTION

Selection and *projection* can modify the results of a join. An *equi-join* joins two tables based on equality between columns in two tables. Joins can also rest on inequalities. An in-equality selects some of the rows from a join. For example,

```
select * from order, stock
where order.order-number = stock.order-number
and order-number < 3
```

Any valid selection criteria restrict the results of a join.

Projection can select some of the columns returned by a join. The *natural-join* is a projection of the equi-join operation. The foreign key only appears once in the results of the join.

Here are two tables:

Stock			Orders		
order- number	stock- number		order- number	cust- number	ship- date
---------------	---		------------------------	---	---
3	1003		1	32	1/3
3	3233		2	33	1/2
3	4434		3	17	1/4
1	5545		4	22	1/5
1	4543		5	17	1/4
1	2454				
2	1432				

Here is the SQL for a natural inner equi-join of these two tables:

```
select
   orders.order_number,
   cust_number,
   ship_date,
   stock-number
from orders, stock
where orders.order_number = stock.order_number
```

Here is the result of the natural inner equi-join. Note that the order number only appears once in the resulting table.

order- number	cust- number	ship- date	stock- number
--------------	---	---	--------
1	32	1/3	4543
1	32	1/3	4543
1	32	1/3	2454

2	33	1/2	1432
3	17	1/2	1003
3	17	1/2	3233
3	17	1/2	4434

EXTENDED JOIN

Remember from the foregoing that an extended Cartesian product unites more than two sets. An example is the extended Cartesian product A x B x C (a times b times c.) An extended join returns as a result a sub-set of the extended Cartesian product.

When performing an extended join, the innermost table first joins to the next table. This produces another table. This new table then joins to the next outermost relation, and so on.

For example, this statement joins three tables:

```
select * from x,y,z where . . .
```

Another example joins three tables in an extended join:

```
select *
from a, b, c
where a.key1 = b.key1 and b.key2 = c.key2
```

This statement evokes an equi-join between tables a and b, resulting in a new table. An equi-join then occurs between the new table and table c. Note that table c is the outermost table.

OUTER JOIN

With an *inner join*, each row in the inner table must have a corresponding row in the outer table for anything to appear in the results of the join. In the *outer join*, every row from inner table appears in the results, even lacking a match with the outer table. If there be no match, some columns in the new resulting table are empty.

Here are two tables containing data:

Stock			Orders		
order-number	stock-number		order-num	cust-num	ship-date
3	1003		1	32	1/3
3	3233		2	33	1/2
3	4434		3	17	1/4
1	5545		4	22	1/5
1	4543		5	17	1/4
1	2454				
2	1432				

The outer key word added before the outer table name specifies an outer join. Here is an example:

```
select
    orders.order-number,
    cust-number,
    ship-date,
    stock-number
from orders, outer stock
where orders.order-number = stock.order-number
```

This table results from this outer join:

order-number	cust-number	ship-date	stock-number
1	32	1/3	4543
1	32	1/3	4543
1	32	1/3	2454
2	33	1/2	1432
3	17	1/2	1003
3	17	1/2	3233
3	17	1/2	4434
4	22	1/5	
5	17	1/4	

The results of the outer join contains every row selected from the inner table.

The outer join is highly useful. It is not, however, available in all SQL implementations. Nostandard prevails for the syntax of an outer join.

INCREASING ROWS

The insert statement increases records in a table.

```
INSERT INTO {table-name | view-name}
    [({column-name},...)]
    VALUES({literal | NULL},...) |
                    select-statement
```

An insert statement that has a values clause inserts a single row. Following are two examples:

```
insert into tablea
    values (1,2,"A3",.6,.2}
insert into orders (
    order-number,
    cust-number,
    ship-date)
    values (2,1,"12/14/93")
```

A select clause can take records from one table and insert copies into the target table. For example,

```
insert into target
select *
from source
```

The select clause chooses all the records from the table named *source*. A copy of each row selected then appears in the target-table.

The select clause can project columns for insertion into the target table.

```
insert into target
select a, b, c
from source
```

The select clause can gather information from more than one table.

```
insert into target
    select a.c1, b.c2, c.c3
from a, b, c
```

Finally, you can restrict the select clause. Here is an example:

```
insert into target
select a, b, c
    from source
    where c1 < 100
```

DELETION OF ROWS

The *delete* statement deletes rows from a table. Here is the syntax of the delete statement:

```
DELETE FROM {table-name | view-name}
[WHERE search-condition]
```

Omitting the *where* clause deletes all the rows from a table. This example deletes all the rows from the orders table.

```
delete from orders
   where 1 = 1
```

A *where* clause can selects the rows to delete. Here is an example:

```
delete from orders
where cust-number > 1
```

CHANGE OF ROWS

The *update* statement modifies the rows of a table. Here is the syntax of the update statement:

```
UPDATE {table-name | view-name}
SET {column-name = expression | NULL}
[WHERE search-condition]
```

An *update* statement that omits the *where* clause changes all the records in a table either to null or to a value given in a set clause.

```
update orders set ship-rate = null

update orders set ship-rate = .6
```

A *where* clause in an update statement changes rows if the *where* clause evaluates to true. This following example will update all rows where the ship-rate is .86 to be .95.

```
update orders
   set ship-rate = .95
   where ship-rate = .86
```

VIEWS

A *view* creates a new virtual table assembled from the one or more existing tables. Once the view is created, you can access it just like a table.

This mechanism makes easy thecreation of a different way for a user to look at a database. A view can be created that presents to the user just the information needed.

A view also provides data protection. A view can present just some of the data in a table. This hides the rest of the data in the table from the user.

With a view, a selected part of an existing table appears as a separate table with a unique name. A view can also come from columns in several tables. Here is the syntax used to create a simple view:

```
CREATE VIEW view-name
[({view-column-name},...)]
```

Here is an example that creates a view named *ship_info* from the existing orders table:

```
create view ship_info
   (order-number, ship-date
   Orders

order-  cust-   ship-
number  number  date
------------------
1       32      1/3
2       33      1/2
3       17      1/4
4       22      1/5
5       17      1/4
```

Here is the view that results from the create view statement:

```
Ship_info
order-  ship-
number  date
------------------
1       1/3
2       1/2
3       1/4
4       1/5
5       1/4
```

The view function as any other table. You can search for, select, and view differently selected data as if it were a table. You can also drop views.DROP VIEW view-name

Any *select* statement can create a view. This example shows how a view can be made from a join:

```
create view backlog (
```

```
select
   orders.order-number,
   cust-number,
   ship-date,
   stock-number
from orders, stock
where orders.order-number = stock.order-number
)
```

Since any select statement can create a view, a view can combine selections, projections and joins.

Vendors implementations may limit the functionality of views. For example, many vendors do not provide facilities for updating through a view that includes a join. You should consult documentation shipped with your system for more detailed information about views.

CURSORS

Cursors can only function within a program written in a host language, for example, within a C program.

You create a cursor with a *declare cursor* statement.

```
DECLARE cursor-name CURSOR FOR
select-statement [{UNION | UNION ALL}
   select-statement . . .
[FOR UPDATE OF {column-name}, . . .] |
[ORDER BY {{column-name | integer}
   [ASC | DESC]},...]]
```

The *declare cursor* statement includes a *select* statement. You must declare a cursor before using it. When the program needs the cursor, an *open cursor* statement opens the cursor. The *open cursor* statement executes the declared *select* statement. The *select* statement creates a thread through the selected data.

The host program can then fetch items from the selected data. That is, the cursor can be moved from one selected item to another.

In some systems, the cursor can move forward. Other systems provide greater control. Some systems allow cursors to move backward as well as forward. Other systems allow relative or direct cursor movement.

The thread through the selected data is dynamic. This is because different data may be selected each time the cursor is opened. Here is an example of a cursor:

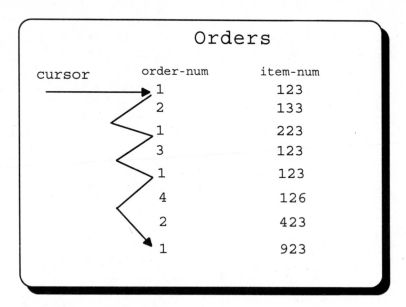

Here is the statement that declares the cursor shown in the figure:

```
declare c-order cursor for
   select * from orders
      where order-num = 1
```

A declare cursor statement can only function within a host program. The host program defines the cursor with the *declare cursor* statement.

Follow these several steps when using a cursor within a host program. First, define the cursor with a *declare cursor* statement. Later, when the host program is ready to use the cursor, the *prepare cursor* statement dynamically compiles the cursor.

The program opens the cursor when data is needed. Opening the cursor selects a dynamic set of rows from the database.

The host program can then access rows with the open cursor one-at-a-time with a *fetch* statement. Lastly, the cursor closes when the data no longer is needed. Here is an example in a hypothetical host language:

```
program sample
define record item-selected
   order_num integer,
   part_num integer;
define select-statement char(512)
   let select-statement =
```

```
        "select * from orders
           where order-num = 1"
      declare c_order
        cursor from select_statement
      prepare c-order
      open cursor c_order
      while SQLCODE <> 0
         fetch c-order into item-selected
         {statements to process returned data}
      end while
      close c_order
  end program
```

The use of cursors varies widely from system to system. You must consult the documentation supplied with your database management system and your host language. Here is some typical syntax for cursor manipulation statements.

The *prepare* statement compiles a previously-declared cursor.

```
PREPARE statement-name FROM :host-variable
```

The *open* statement opens a compiled cursor.

```
OPEN cursor-name
   [USING :host-var, . . . |
    USING DESCRIPTOR :host-var]
```

The host program then retrieves individual items selected by the cursor with the *fetch* statement.

```
FETCH cursor-name
   USING DESCRIPTOR host-variable
```

Some implementations support scrolling cursors. With a scrolling cursor, the host program can move back and forth through the selected items rather than just from beginning to end. For example, the first, last, next or previous items can be selected.

The *close cursor* statement closes a cursor:

```
CLOSE cursor-name
```

A relational database management system must provide facilities for maintaining data integrity. Data access control statements provide for integrity. These statements control access to a database or part of a database.

Data access control statements protect the database by limiting access to data held in the database. They grant or deny certain users access. Different users can gain different permissions. Data access control statements can prevent users from simultaneously accessing the same data.

TRANSACTIONS

A transaction is a unit of work that results from one or more changes to a database. You can group several inserts or modifications into a transaction.

You can either accept or discard all the work within a transaction at the end of that transaction. SQL statements govern accepting or discarding the work performed within a transaction. The transaction mechanism assures that either all the transition work is complete, else it discards all the changes.

Consider a sales order entry system. The entry of a new sales order might cause changes to several tables. The changes to all the tables might need discarding if there is some error during the data entry process.

A transaction helps assure that the data entered into the database is correct. A transaction starts as the order entry starts. At the end of the order entry process, the transaction passes or fails. If entry of the data is correct, the transaction passes. If the order entry has failed in some manner, the transaction fails. If the transaction fails, the database saves no changes.

LOGGING AND COMMIT

Transactions help to maintain the integrity of the data in a database. A log can store transactions as they happen. If the database is lost for any reason, you can add the logged transactions to the most recent backup copy of the database to restore the database to its most-recent state.

Hardware or software failures can damage data integrity. Failure of the computer in the middle of a transaction may corrupt data. A good RDBMS provides recovery facilities that allow restoration of a database after hardware or software failures.

The *commit* and *rollback* statements control transactions. The *commit* statement applies to the database all the work accomplished during a transaction. The *rollback* statement discards the transaction.

```
commit [work]
```

```
rollback [work]
```

Some database management systems provide a separate *begin work* statement. This statement begins transaction processing.

PERMISSIONS

Permissions control access to a database. Each permission grants a user the privilege to perform some operation. The permissions and the privileges they grant are

Permission	Privilege Granted
alter	change table structures
delete	remove rows from a table
insert	add rows to a table
select	select rows from a table
update	change rows in the table
all	all permissions
index	create or remove index

The grant statement provides a user one or more of the permissions shown in the above table.

```
GRANT {ALL | ALL PRIVILEGES |
{ALTER | DELETE | INDEX | INSERT | SELECT |
UPDATE[({column-name},...)]},...}
  ON {table-name},...
  TO {user-id | PUBLIC},...
  [WITH GRANT OPTION]
```

This *GRANT ALL* clause assigns all possible permissions to a user:

```
grant all on sales-order to john
```

The *public* keyword grants permission to anyone accessing the database. The following statement grants all permissions to anyone using the customers table.

```
grant all on customers to public
```

Grants of individual permissions are by name. To grant three separate permissions to the user Sally, write

```
grant insert, select, update
   on customers to sally
```

Usually, only the creator of a table or the database administrator may grant permissions. Adding the clause *with grant option* to a grant statement can change this. When a user obtains a permission with a grant statement that has a *with grant option* clause, that user may in turn grant that permission to other users; for example,

```
grant all on customers to sam
   with grant option
```

After this statement successfully runs, Sam can grant any permission to any other user. The *with grant option* clause does not apply if a permission has already been granted to the public. If a permission has already been granted to the public, every user has that permission already.

The *revoke* statement takes permissions away from users.

```
REVOKE {ALL | ALL PRIVILEGES |
{ALTER | DELETE | INDEX | INSERT | SELECT |
UPDATE},... }
   ON {table-name},...
   FROM {user-id | PUBLIC},...
```

Here are two examples of the *revoke* statement:

```
revoke all on customers from public

revoke index, insert, update
   on customers from sam
```

Revoking a permission from the public removes the permission from all users at large. The revoke statement can also revoke permissions for an individual user.

If an individual user has a permission with a earlier grant statement, a revoke statement for the public does not revoke that individually-assigned permission.

The revoke statement is not part of the ANSII standard. The syntax of the revoke statement varies from system to system.

TABLE LOCKING

Any user or transaction with permission to access a table can temporarily lock that table. While the table is locked, only the user or transaction that locked the table can access the table.

This locking mechanism provides concurrency control for the database. Concurrency control prevents separate transactions or users from colliding with each other.

Take as an example two order entry clerks responsible for updating orders. The first clerk accesses the order. This clerk has just found out that one of the back ordered items is now in stock. A customer calls the second clerk and asks for the status of the order. The second order-entry clerk accesses the order and sees two items on back order. Both clerks now have a copy of the order at which to look. They can access the same table at the same time. The first clerk updates the database indicating that the back ordered item is now available. The database now shows the item as available. The first clerk, at the customers request, then removes the back ordered item from the order. This updates the database by deleting the requested item from the order.

The two clerks have collided when accessing the table. If the first clerk had locked the table before making any changes, the second clerk would have been denied access to that table during the posting. The second clerk would have been unable to access the table until the updated order indicated the item in stock.

This is an example of concurrency control. Concurrency control applied with the lock statement would have prevented the two users' colliding with each other.

Execution of a commit statement or a rollback statement automatically unlocks a table. Ending a program or transaction also removes any locks.

The lock table statement prevents other users or transactions from accessing the locked table. Two different users cannot concurrently update a locked table.

The lock table statement is not part of the ANSI standard. The following syntax commonly prevails:

```
LOCK TABLE {table-name | view-name}
IN {SHARE | EXCLUSIVE} MODE
```

The user can lock a table in two different modes. Another user can read but not update a table locked in share mode. Another user can neither read nor write to a table locked in exclusive mode.

A locked table can dramatically slow the performance of a multi-user database. Once one user locks a table, all other users have to wait until removal of the lock. A user might lock a table then go to lunch. All the other users interested in the table must await the return of that user from lunch and the removal of the lock before they can access the locked table.

The end of a transaction or end of a program releases all locks.

LOCKING ROWS

A select statement with a for update clause locks all the selected rows. This prevents other users from changing these rows until a following update is complete.

```
SELECT *
    FROM {table-name | view-name}, . . .
    [WHERE search-condition]
    FOR UPDATE OF {column-name}, . . .
```

Some database engines provide more sophisticated locking mechanisms than just row level locking. Some engines can lock all the data selected with a cursor while allowing other users to access any other data not selected by the cursor.

Here is an example of a select statement that will lock rows until the completion of the following update statement.

```
select * from orders
    where customer-number = 151
    for update of customer-number

update orders
    set customer-number = 152
    where customer-number = 151
```

All the rows selected by the select statement are locked until the completion of the update statement.

PERFORMANCE AND INDEXING

The design of a database should always start as an accurate logical representation of the data appropriate to that database. Often, the most logical structure for the data does not provide the best or even adequate performance.

The logical database design results in a schema that represents the logical structure of the data. The physical design represents the way data is physically stored. The logical design often changes in the creation of the physical design in order to improve performance.

This section describes some of the techniques used to optimize the performance of a database.

Suppose you had someone's telephone number and a telephone book. Finding the name of the person with that phone number by looking in the telephone book is difficult because the listings are by name, not by number. To find the name, you would have to search the telephone book sequentially until you found the number.

It is easier to find the person by name because the listings are in name order. Finding the name if you have the number is difficult although the information is still there. Certainly, no one would want to search sequentially for the number throughout the book.

By definition and in practice, the rows in a relation do not reside in any particular order. As in the telephone number example above, finding a particular row would require a sequential search of the table.

An index can speed access to the rows of a table. A database index works like the index in a book.

A book index is a list of key information about various subjects held in sorted order. The index points to information on various topics.

Consider, a index of topics makes it easy to find information about a particular service or product in the yellow pages. Take the index entries for automobiles in the yellow pages, including those for automotive repair, renting, body work and such.

Next to an entry in the index, say, *automobiles rental*, is a page number. The page number points to the section, or sections, containing the indexed data. Searching the index avoids searching the entire book.

A database index similarly references data in the database. Finding the index entry speeds access to the data indexed.

The following table has two entries, *customer number* and *part number*. This could be a representation of all customers who have ordered a certain part.

cust-num	part-num
1	20
2	21
3	30
4	22
5	20
6	22
7	19
8	20

Finding anything in this table by customer number is easy because the customer numbers are in increasing order. If the table is not in order, as real tables rarely are, finding a customer number is more difficult.

Here is the same information in a new table where the customer numbers are not in any particular order. This table has also a row number that gives the address of any row of data.

row	cust-num	part-num
1	1	20
2	4	21
3	8	30
4	2	22
5	5	20
6	7	22
7	6	19
8	3	20

Finding a particular customer number in this table is more difficult. An index makes easier locating any customer number in the unsorted table. Here is an index to the customer numbers in this table

cust-num	location
1	1
2	4
3	8
4	2
5	5
6	7
7	6
8	3

This index again makes easy the finding of any row by customer number. To find the row for customer number four, search the customer number column in the index. Customer numbers are easy to find because they are in order in the index. Once you find the desired customer number, the index provides the physical location of the row in the previous table. The location in the index allows direct access to the desired row.

The index can also sort the data held in a table. Instead of moving each row, the index sorts. Selecting each indexed item in order selects data from the table in order.

Selecting the indexed entries in reverse order selects data from the table in reverse order. The following index makes easy selection of data in reverse order.

cust-num	location
8	3
7	6
6	7
5	5
4	2
3	8
2	4
1	1

An index can be used to speed access to any column in a table. Finding anything in the original sorted table by part number is difficult because the part numbers lack any particular order. An index eases and speeds finding information by part number. The following table indexes the parts that appear in the original sorted table.

part_no	order_num
19	7
20	1,5,8
21	2
22	4,6
30	3

Finding every customer that uses a certain part is now easy. Find the part number in the first column of the index. Every customer who uses that part appears in the second column.

For example, part number *20* can be found at locations *1*, *5* and *8*. Finding all the data values of *20* is easy through the locating of one entry in the index instead of each entry in the data table. With the index, all the entries for a particular data item are available without a search of the entire table.

Note that this indexing plays no part in the relational model. The location is an address that is internal to the RDMBS.

An index provides a space-time tradeoff. Allocating space to the index reduces the time needed to search for data. Taking the time once to compile an index reduces the amount of time needed for later searching.

The advantage of a database index is that it speeds access to the data in a table. Its disadvantage is that adding data is slow because the index must updated with the adding of data.

The statement

```
CREATE [UNIQUE] INDEX index-name
    on table-name
    ([column-name {ASC  DESC}]...)
```

creates an index.

The statement

```
DROP INDEX index-name
```

removes an index.

You can create an index for one column in a table or create a composite index for a combination of columns in a table.

An index does not save time when the table only has a small number of records. This changes dramatically as the table gets bigger. As the table gets bigger, using the index becomes faster and searching through all the rows becomes slower.

WHEN TO USE AN INDEX

An easy practical test determines when you should add indexes to a database: if your application is running slowly when searching for data, consider building an index.

An appropriate index will greatly speed searches or joins. If you frequently search a table on a column, build an index for that column. If you have two tables frequently joined on the same column, build an index for each table on that column.

If your application must search the customer-numbers table frequently for customer numbers, build an index for customer-number.

You should not build an index on any table that contains fewer than several hundred records. The index does not help; in fact, it may slow access to the database.

The index for a data-element can take nearly as much storage space as the data being indexed. This varies widely from system to system and depends heavily on the index scheme chosen by the DBMS implementor.

Consult the documentation provided with your database system to find the overhead for indexing. Indexing schemes vary from system to system and so does their overhead.

KEYS BASED ON MULTIPLE COLUMNS

SQL allows a single index from multiple columns—a *multiple-column index* or *composite index*.

The multiple-column index can exceed candidate keys. In many cases, access to the database improves with a multiple-column index.

This statement creates an index on the parts table in the sample database based on the two fields weight and cost:

```
create index ix
on parts (weight, cost)
```

The created index would assist the finding of all the parts of a specified weight within a weight range. This index would make faster the finding of all the parts that weigh more than one pound but cost less than $100.

DATA INTEGRITY

An index can prevent entry of duplicate data values in a table. If the operator *unique* appears in the create index statement, the table rejects entry of duplicate values. The statement

```
create unique index c_idx
    on customers (customer-number)
```

prevents the same customer from entry more than once in the customers table.

TYPES OF INDEXING

This section describes briefly the internal structures used with two common indexing schemes, *hashing* and *B-trees*. For a complete, in-depth discussion of B-trees or hashing read *The Art of Computer Programming*, by Donald Knuth.

B-Trees

An index speeds the search for data in a database although the index itself must be searched. Searching a huge index can take a long time. The searched goes faster if you build another index: an index to the index. This scheme of indexing the index is *multi-level indexing* or *tree-structured indexing*.

You can construct many levels of indexes to indexes. In practice, rarely are there more than three levels of indexing.

Various indexing methods exist for data stored within a computer. No one best storage structure applies to all types of indexes. The most-suitable index depends on the given application.

In general for most relational database applications, B-Trees work effectively. A B-Tree is a particular sort of multi-level or tree-structured index. B-Trees are the most-commonly available indexing method in commercial relational database management systems.

With B-Trees, the tree-structured index constantly updates to stay in balance. The B-Tree updates with every change to the index so it automatically stays in balance.

A B-tree minimizes the distance from the beginning of the index tree-structure to any specific index item. Balancing the tree-structure minimizes the time needed to access any individual item in the index.

Hashing

In hashing, an index provides direct access to an individual record. A hashing function transforms a data value into an address. A data value passes through the hashing function to produce an address.

Here is a sample hashing function:

```
address = remainder(customer-number/13)
```

Here is a list of customer numbers and their addresses generated by the hashing function. For example, *13* divides into *1000 76* times with a remainder of *12*.

cust-num	cust-num/13	remainder (address)
c1000	76	12
c1200	84	108
c1300	100	0
c1400	107	125
c1500	115	5

A table with addresses from *0* to *128* would have an address for each of the customer numbers in the example. The DBMS would use the hashing function to compute an address for each record based on the customer number. The DBMS would then store each record at the computed location. The record for customer number *1000* would appear at address *12*.

To later retrieve the record, the DBMS would compute the hashing function. The result points to the record address in the table.

Hashing has difficulties. Enough advance reserve space is necessary for all the possible address values that may result from the hashing function. This usually leaves a considerable portion of the reserved space empty. Hashed tables are usually sparsely populated when compared to the total reserved space.

Hashed records do not store in any sorted order by the hashing function. Unlike the B-tree, no ready way retrieves the records from a table in sorted order.

In practice, the hashing function is rarely perfect. The function must improved to account for the occasions when two data values produce the same address. This is a collision.

You must find a hashing function that generates addresses within the range of available storage while minimizing collisions. This can be difficult. As the size of the hashed file increases, the possibility of collisions increases.

Finally, a single table can take only one hashing structure. This limits the table to a single index. This differs from B-Trees where multiple indices on a single table are available.

2-7 Logical Database Design

Redundant data is usually undesirable in a database. This chapter presents guidelines helpful in building databases without redundant data.

Redundant data is undesirable because it makes the database more difficult to update or change. A database with redundant data is likely to have update problems or query problems. For example, in a database table holding both orders and customer address information, changing the address for a customer would mean changing every order in the table. Moving the customer addresses into a separate table makes it much easier to update supplier addresses when they change. Only one address record has to be changed instead of every order.

Each table in a database should only contain data about a single entity. For example, a table about orders should only have columns that contain data about the order. A table of customers should only contain customer information.

The process of assuring data singularity (as well as the corresponding process of removing redundancies from data) is called normalization. This chapter describes the process of normalization.

To design a normalized database, you first need to understand the structure of a relation, as described in an earlier chapter. In addition, you will need to become familiar with the three types of data dependencies—functional, transitive and multivalued—described in this chapter.

This chapter describes normal forms. The normal forms are guidelines useful for building a well-structured database. The basic normal forms are

✓ first-normal

✓ second-normal

✓ third-normal

✓ Boyce-Codd normal

✓ fourth-normal

The guidelines presented in this chapter will help you build databases that allow accurate updates and queries.

REDUNDANT DATA AND UPDATING

Deletion anomalies happen when the deletion of a single row in a table causes the loss of more than one fact. A database with update anomalies requires several records to be changed as a new fact enters the database.

Redundant data is minimized in a table when the data in the non-key columns of a table only contain data that is about the primary key of the table. For example, here are a customers table and orders table:

customers

cust-num	telephone	cust-name
2	234-3423	Johnson Supply Co.
1	343-2341	Redmond Feed
3	232-3343	Sasquatch Pet Supply
6	343-4443	Laredo Feed
4	955-5675	Autrey Barn Supply
3	333-4343	Poodles are Us
7	434-4434	Cats and Dogs

orders

cust-num	order-num	weight	cost
1	4	11.2	45.54
4	5	25.3	65.55
4	33	14.5	55.34
7	54	35.8	126.34

The primary key in the customers table is the customer number. All the other rows in the table contain data about the customer. The company name is the name of the customer. The telephone number is the telephone number of the customer. Each of the non-key attributes is about the primary key.

The primary key in the orders table is the order number. Each of the other columns in the orders relation contains data about this key. The customer number shows which customer placed the order. There are a weight for the order and a cost for the order. Each of these facts is a fact about the primary key. Each of these facts is about the order.

Here is the same information from these two tables combined into a single table:

combined

cust-num	telephone	cust-name	order-num	wt	cost
2	234-3423	Johnson Supply Co.	4	11.2	45.54
1	343-2341	Redmond Feed			
3	232-3343	Sasquatch Pet Supply			
6	343-4443	Laredo Feed			
4	955-5675	Autrey Barn Supply	5	25.3	65.55
4	955-5675	Autrey Barn Supply	33	14.5	55.34
3	333-4343	Poodles R Us			
7	434-4434	Cats and Dogs	54	35.8	126.34

This single table now contains all the information the two tables contained. This table is much more difficult to change or update.

This table is more difficult to update because it contains redundant information. For example, the telephone number for company number four occurs in two rows in the table. If the telephone number for a this company changes, several records in this table need to be changed. With the separate tables shown earlier, only one record has to change in the customer table when the phone number changes.

The primary key for this combined table is now the order number. Much of the information in the table is no longer about the primary key. For example, the phone number is about the company, not about the order. The company name is about the company, not about the order.

This single table is more difficult to search or modify. This single table is not so highly normalized as the two separate tables.

The following sections all help to formalize the common-sense notions that the non-key columns in relation should only hold information that is about the primary key.

The secret to building normalized databases is designing databases where tables are simple and tables where non-key columns only contain facts about the key column.

NORMAL FORMS

A relation must, by definition, have a primary key. The normal forms codify (no pun intended) the common-sense notion that all the other columns in a table should only contain information directly related to the primary key.

Certain rules help to verify that tables have this property. These rules are expressed as the normal forms described below. The normal forms help to establish well organized tables.

A table that is in one of these normal forms is called *normalized*. A schema where the tables are in normal forms is also called normalized.

Normalization changes an UN-normalized table into a normalized table. There are simple methods, described below, for changing a table that is not normalized to a table that is normalized.

Normalization is reversible. A relation can be converted to a higher normal form. It also be converted back into a lower normal form. This is because there is no loss of information during normalization. The transformation is lossless.

For example, look at the following simple table with two columns, name and extension. There is only one candidate key in this table, *name*. The structure of the data is simple. Each individual uses a certain phone and users may share a phone.

name	phone-ext
Paul	10
Susan	10
George	14
Sabrina	16
Bill	18
Karen	20

A simple diagram shows the relationship of the extension to the name. The diagram shows that the extension number depends on the name of the person and that each person possesses an extension.

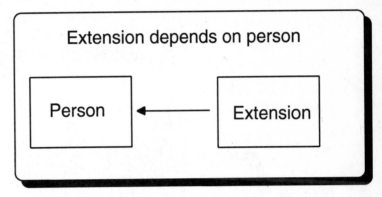

This example table is normalized because the information in the non-key column *extension* is directly about the information in the primary-key column *name*. The column *extension* contains information that is directly about the key *name*. The extension is information directly related to the individual.

Adding a third column makes the table less normalized. In this example, only certain phones are authorized for long distance calls:

name	phone-ext	long-dist
Paul	10	yes
Susan	10	yes
George	14	no
Sabrina	16	no
Bill	18	yes
Karen	20	yes

In the first table, the extension number is a fact about a person. The column *extension* is a fact about the primary-key *name*. The extension is a number used by the individual.

Only one candidate key is in this table, *name*. The structure of the data is simple. Each individual can use a certain phone, and users can share a phone. Some extensions have authority for long-distance calls.

Long-distance is not a fact about the user. Long-distance is a fact about the phone. The phone is authorized for long-distance, not the user. Another diagram makes the relationship between these three items more clear:

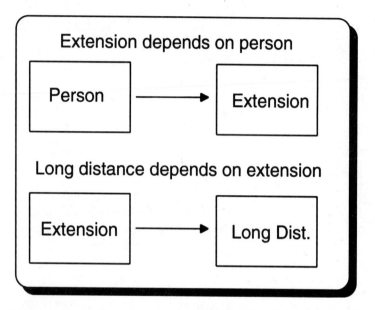

In a normalized table, all non-key columns of the table should contain information about the primary key. In this example, the column *Long-distance* is not about the primary key *name*. This means that the table is not normalized. The rules of normalization show this table should be split into two separate tables.

users

name	phone-ext
Paul	10
Susan	10
George	14
Sabrina	16
Bill	18
Karen	20

authorizations

extension	long-distance
10	yes
14	no
16	no
18	yes
20	yes

Splitting the original table into two tables leaves each resulting table in a more normalized form. With two tables, each non-key attribute in a table only contains data about the primary key in that table.

Less redundant data is in two tables. This makes the two tables, and the database as a whole, easier to update. If the long-distance authorization for a number changes, only one record needs changing in the authorization table. In the previous table, multiple records need changing each time an authorization alters. Each of the two relationships shown in the last dependency diagram now apply to a separate table.

In this example, one complex table was made into two simple tables. This is normalization. The normalization rules show that the table could be better organized to reduce redundant data. The normalization rules also show how to change the table to create a more simple schema.

Normalization results in a database that reflects the underlying nature of the data, has simplicity, and contains little redundant data. Certain steps, described below, can always normalize an un-normalized database. Removing repeating groups of data can change an un-normalized table of data to an equivalent normalized table.

Each of the normal forms constrains a database to be more organized than the last. Each normal form must be in force before the next one can be applied. A series of steps can apply successive levels of normalization to an UN-normalized database.

NORMAL FORMS AS GUIDELINES

Note that the normal forms are a set of guidelines for constructing a schema. There is nothing in a schema, or SQL, or the relational model, or an RDMBS that enforces normalization. (Unique indexes can be used to help maintain normalization, though.) The rules of normalization have been developed in addition to the relational model. Building a database that is not normalized is easy.

WHEN NOT TO NORMALIZE

A logical database design should always start with an attempt to comply to the normal forms described below. Once such a design is available, it can be de-normalized to handle any physical or operational constraints. For example, you might find that a fully-normalized database will run too slowly or that a fully-normalized database adds too much overhead in the construction of programs or reports.

Usually, a working database should be in at least third normal form (third normal form is described below.) In practice, many real-world well-designed databases do not even gain this goal.

Normalizing a database is not always appropriate. For example, the next table contains the author's address information.

address

name	city	street	state	zip
Paul Smith	San Francisco	1 Main St.	CA	094102

This table has five columns, name, street, city, state and zip. In any record where the city is San Francisco, the state will be California. This table is likely to have many duplicate city names.

Splitting this single table into two tables, a zip table and a name table, eliminates duplicate city names.

name

name	street	zip
Paul Mahler	1800 Market St #257	94102

zip

zip	state	city
94102	CA	San Francisco

When using the data in this database, the street, city, and state will almost always go together. For example, if this data is used to print a mailing list, all these fields will always appear together. Printing all the information from both tables will require joining the two tables together each time the combined data is needed.

Also, zip codes do not often change. Separating the zip, city and state into a separate table eliminates all the duplicates of city names and zip-codes found in the one combined table. Since the zip-code for a city is unlikely to change, there is no operational advantage in eliminating the duplicate data.

Rarely will it be necessary to change the zip-code for a city. The combined table will seldom change because a city has a new state. The duplicate city names are not likely to change. The duplicate information does not often change, so updating is less of a problem.

Reducing the redundancy of the data to improve the speed of updating when there is no updating has no point. In theory, breaking the one table into two simpler tables would reduce data redundancy and improve performance. In these circumstances, it will only introduce additional overhead.

This example shows that the normal forms are only an aid to the database designer. They are suggested guidelines for logical database design; it is not always appropriate to follow the guidelines.

FIRST NORMAL FORM

Chapter three described the first normal form. The first normal form (1NF) states that a table cannot contain repeating groups. That is, no repeating groups of data are allowed in a table. Each record must have the same number of attributes. Each row must have the same number of columns. For example, take the following table of data about compact disk albums that has several repeating groups:

not a relation

Perfomer	Album Name
Talking Heads	Speaking in Tongues,
	Little Creatures,
	Stop Making Sense

Changing a table with repeating groups to a table without repeating groups is simple. Replace the repeating groups with complete rows. For example, making each repeating group in the table above into a separate row makes the table into a 1NF (first normal form) relation:

relation

Perfomer	Album Name
Talking Heads	Speaking in Tongues
Talking Heads	Little Creatures
Talking Heads	Stop Making Sense

FUNCTIONAL DEPENDENCE

Functional dependence shows the logical relationships of data. Functional dependence means that the values for two columns logically associate. For two columns A and B, the value of B will always be the same for a particular value of A. The value of A determines the value of B. If B is functionally dependent on A, then A is the determinant of B. The following figure exemplifies "A functionally determines B":

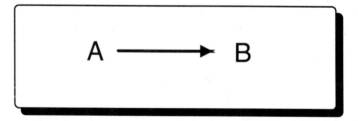

This can also refer to the containing relation. In this example, the functional dependence reads "R1 dot A functionally determines R2 dot B.

For example, take an organization where each individual may only work for a single boss. It is important to the logical structure of the schema that an individual be associated with a single boss. The logical design of the schema must somehow show that the boss depends on the employee.

Look at the following simple table with two columns, employee and supervisor:

employee	supervisor
Paul	Sam
Susan	Sam
George	Sam
Sally	Judy
Harry	Judy
Jerry	Judy

In this example, the value of the data in the column named *supervisor* depends on the value of the data in the column *employee*. Selecting any value for *name* uniquely determines a value for *supervisor*. For example, if the value of *name* is *Paul* then the value of *supervisor* is always *Sam*. *Employee* is the determinant of *supervisor*.

A simple dependency diagram shows this functional dependence.

employee ⟶ supervisor

If a person can work for two supervisors, this functional dependence is lost. For example, *Paul* can work for two different people, *Sam* and *Judy*. The table could look like this:

employee	supervisor
Paul	Sam
Susan	Sam
Paul	Judy
George	Sam
Sally	Judy
Harry	Judy
Jerry	Judy

A relation still exists because a candidate key exists. The candidate key is now composed from the two columns *employee* and *supervisor*, {employee,supervisor}. It is still in first normal form, since there are no repeating groups, no duplicate rows. It remains a table

The supervisor is no longer functionally dependent on the employee, though. For a single value for the column employee (Paul) there are two possible values for the column supervisor (Sam and Judy).

Note that the functional dependence is part of the structure of the data, not part of the relational model. If Paul can only work for one supervisor, the data in this table is wrong. The data in the table is wrong in that it is inconsistent with the logical structure of the enterprise.

The table no longer is an accurate model of the real world. Nothing in the data makes it inconsistent with the relational model. The data still fits nicely into a table—but it does not model the real world.

FUNCTIONAL DEPENDENCE AND COMPOSED COLUMNS

A column can be functionally dependent on two or more other columns taken together as a composite key. For example, look at the following table:

supervisor	employee	department
Judy	Paul	a
Judy	Sam	a
Judy	Joe	a
Bill	Paul	b
Bill	Susan	b
Bill	Samantha	b

In this example, the department is not functionally dependent on the supervisor name because Paul is now working for two supervisors in two different departments.

Putting two columns together, that is, composing two columns, achieves functional dependence. The department is functionally dependent on the composed columns {employee, supervisor}.

Another functional dependence diagram shows this in the following figure. The department is functionally dependent on the supervisor and employee taken together. The structure of the data specifies that any one person can only work for any one supervisor in a given department. That is, the department depends on the employee and the supervisor.

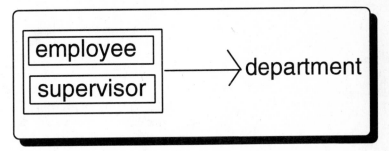

KEYS AND FUNCTIONAL DEPENDENCE

Every other column of a table functionally depends on a candidate key. A candidate key is a determinant for all the non-candidate key columns of a table. A candidate key determines any non-candidate key column. The reason is that selecting an individual candidate key always selects the same values for the non-key columns.

Please note that nothing in the definition of functional dependence says a determinant must be a candidate key or primary key. Any column can functionally depend on another column that is not a candidate key. For example, here is another simple table.

number	x	y
1	a	1
2	a	1
3	a	1

In this table, the column x is obviously not a candidate key. Still, y is functionally dependent on x because y must have the value of *1* whenever x has the value of *a*.

FULL FUNCTIONAL DEPENDENCE

Any column is fully functionally dependent on a composed column when it is functionally dependent on the composed column but not functionally dependent on any part of the composed column taken separately. Here is an example.

supervisor	employee	department
Judy	Paul	a
Judy	Sam	b
Judy	Joe	c
Bill	Paul	d
Bill	Susan	e
Bill	Samantha	f

In this example, the column named *department* functionally depends on the composed column pair {supervisor, employee}. In this data set, each employee only works in a single department. Since the *department* also functionally depends on the column *employee*, it does not fully functionally depend on the composed columns {supervisor, employee}.

Here is another example.

last-name	first-name	department
Mahler	Paul	1
Mahler	Susan	2
Mahler	Joe	3
Mahler	Kathy	4
Mahler	George	5
Jones	Paul	2

Here the column *department* functionally depends on the composed column pair {last-name, first-name}. The column *department* does not functionally depend on either the column *last-name*, or the column *first-name*. Since the column *department* functionally depends on the composed pair of columns, but not on either taken by itself, it is fully functionally dependent.

Dependencies show the structure of the data in a database. The fact that the department fully functionally depends on the composed last name and first name means that each individual is in just one department. (It also means that there are no two people in the organization with the same name.) Since it is important to the structure of the data that an individual is in a single department, this structure must be represented somehow in the schema of the database. The structure of the data in a database can be specified by stating the functional dependencies

SECOND NORMAL FORM

For a table to be in second normal form (2NF), it must be in first normal form and every non-key column must fully functionally depend on the primary key.

The example below shows a table used earlier with two columns, name and extension.

name	phone-ext
Paul	10
Susan	10
George	14
Sabrina	16
Bill	18
Karen	20

This table is in first normal form; there are no repeating groups. This table is also in second normal form because the non-key column *extension* is a fact about the key column *name*.

The next example adds another column to this table that is also about the primary key—a column about the individual's starting time. This column is called *early*. The column *early* indicates if the individual starts work early or late.

name	phone-ext	early
Paul	10	yes
Susan	10	no
George	14	yes
Sabrina	16	yes
Bill	18	yes
Karen	20	yes

This new column contains information that is about the primary key. An individual has authorization to start work early or late. This means that adding the new column to the table has not changed it from being in 2NF.

Here is the table with the long-distance column added again.

name	phone-ext	long-distance
Paul	10	yes
Susan	10	yes
George	14	no
Sabrina	16	no
Bill	18	yes
Karen	20	yes

This table is no longer in 2NF. It is no longer in 2NF because the column *long-distance* is not about the primary key *name*. The column *long-distance* is about the extension. The column *long-distance* does not fully functionally depend on the column *name*.

Projecting the original 1NF table into two tables eliminates any non-fully functional dependencies. This projection changes the 1NF table into two 2NF tables. The projection creates two 2NF tables, wherein each 2NF table has a primary key and columns about that primary key. This normalizes the 1NF table. Each of the new tables has simpler functional dependencies. The result appears in the following two tables.

phone

name	phone-ext
Paul	10
Susan	10
George	14
Sabrina	16
Bill	18
Karen	20

authorization

phone-ext	long-distance
10	yes
14	no
16	yes
18	yes
20	yes

The functional dependency diagram predicts the change from one 1NF table into two 2NF tables.

Each of the two dependencies moves to its own table. The 1NF table has two different functional dependencies. Splitting the 1NF table creates a new table for each of the dependencies.

Note that this decomposition is lossless, that is, there is no loss of information. The two resulting tables can easily re-combine into a single table.

THIRD NORMAL FORM

In a 2NF table, all the non-key columns must be fully functionally dependent on the primary key. A table must be in 2NF form before it can be in 3NF form.

In a 3NF table, all the non-key items must be mutually independent. The non-key columns are all mutually independent if none of them is functionally dependent on another. For a table to be 3NF, none of the non-key columns can functionally depend on any of the other non-key columns.

Here is a new table with three columns, supplier, status, and city.

supplier	status	city
s1	10	Detroit
s2	20	Boston
s3	20	Boston
s4	30	Dallas
s5	40	Dallas
s6	10	Detroit

In this set of data, each supplier is in a certain city. Each city has a specified status. The status depends on the city. The city depends on the supplier.

Because the city depends on the supplier and the status depends on the city, the status also depends on the supplier. If you know the supplier, you can determine the status, but only by going through the city. The status only depends on the supplier transitively through the city.

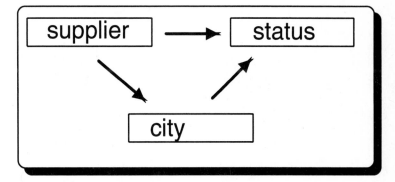

This kind of transitive dependency complicates updating the table. If the status changes for a city, every record for a given city must be changed.

Inserting a new record can be difficult. Adding a record to note that a certain city has a particular status is impossible until there is a supplier for that city. For example, you cannot add the information that San Francisco has status 70 until there is a supplier for San Francisco.

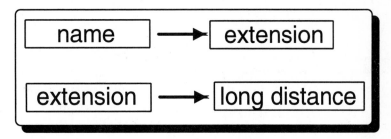

Deleting the only row for a particular city loses two items of information: (1) the information that a supplier is in a certain city, and (2) the information that a city has a certain status.

Projecting the 2NF table into separate 3NF tables solves this problem. The projection separates each of the functional dependencies into its own table. The two resulting tables look like this.

supplier	city
s1	Detroit
s2	Boston
s3	Boston
s4	Dallas
s5	Dallas
s6	Detroit

status	city
10	Detroit
20	Boston
30	Dallas

Each of these two tables is in 3NF. Each table is in 1NF because there are no repeating groups. Each table is in 2NF because all the non-key columns are functionally dependent on the primary key. Each is in 3NF because no non-key column is functionally dependent on another non-key column. It is in 3NF form because each of the columns is mutually independent.

In general, you can more easily manipulate tables with simple dependencies. They are easier to update. This is the benefit of the normal forms. The normal forms help you assure that tables, and a schema, are structurally simple.

CHOOSING A DECOMPOSITION

You cannot decompose some tables into independent components. These tables are called *atomic*. You can decompose some tables, but you should not necessarily do so.

There is often more than one possible decomposition of a table. Examine the following table. In this example, shipments are made from a warehouse and each warehouse has a status of open or closed.

shipment	status	warehouse
s1	open	CA
s2	closed	NV
s3	open	CA
s4	closed	NV
s5	closed	NV
s6	closed	NV

The entry under *status* depends on the entry under *warehouse*. Each *warehouse* entry has a *status* entry of *open* or *closed*.

The entry under *warehouse* depends on the number under *shipment*. Each *shipment* item ships from a single site under *warehouse*.

The status depends on the shipment number. Each shipment has an associated status of open or closed. Note that this probably is not part of the logical structure of the data. It is reasonable for the warehouse to have a status of open or closed. It is not reasonable for a shipment to have a status of open or closed. The following dependency diagram shows the dependencies of this table.

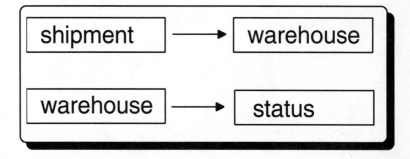

TRANSITIVE DEPENDENCE

Status and *warehouse* interdepend. Hence, the status transitively depends on the shipment number. The status depends on the shipment number through its relation to warehouse.

This projection normalizes the sample table into 3NF tables.

status

warehouse	status
CA	open
NV	closed

warehouse

shipment	warehouse
s1	CA
s2	NV
s3	CA
s4	NV
s5	NV
s6	NV

A different projection also normalizes the sample into two 3NF tables. This second projection decomposes the relation around the transitive dependence. As an exercise, draw for yourself the diagram for this projection.

In the first example, each projection is independent. Updating one table does not require updating the other table (except where the city changes). The status for a warehouse can change independently of the warehouse for a shipment.

In the second example, the projections are not independent. Changing the status for a warehouse requires updating both the tables in the second example.

In the first example, as long as the uniqueness of the keys persists, you can rejoin the two tables at any time into a 2NF relation. Even after various updates, you can join the two separate tables into a valid 2NF table.

In the second example, an update to just one relation can make it impossible to join the two relations back into a 2NF table with an inner join. Here is an example.

Warehouse

shipment	warehouse
s1	CA
s2	NV
s3	CA
s4	NV
s5	NV
s6	NV

Status

shipment	status
s1	open
s2	closed
s3	open
s4	closed
s5	closed
s6	closed

Deleting the first record from the status table makes it impossible to recombine all the records from both tables into a single table with an inner join. There would be no record for shipment one in the results of the join.

```
select shipment.shipment,status,warehouse
   from warehouse, status
   where warehouse.shipment =
      status.shipment
```

Here is the table resulting from the join.

shipment	status	warehouse
s2	closed	NV
s3	open	CA
s4	closed	NV
s5	closed	NV

Because the functional dependence of status on warehouse does not occur within a single table, an interrelational constraint exists between the two relations. This makes it easy to see that a decomposition where the projections are independent is preferable to one where they are not.

Tables are independent only if the functional dependencies of the original table can be logically deduced from the functional dependencies of the decomposed tables. Also, the attributes that are common to the two tables must be a candidate key for at least one of the resulting tables.

The tables in the first projection are independent. The common attribute *shipment#* is the primary key for the warehouse table. Every functional dependency in the original table either appears in the two projections or can be deduced from them.

In the second example, the projections are not independent. The functional dependence of status on warehouse cannot be deduced from the functional dependencies in the resulting tables.

BCNF

A table is in Boyce-Codd normal form (BCNF) when all functional dependencies are on candidate keys. This is a stronger requirement than 3NF, wherein the non-key columns just have to be mutually functionally independent. There are no functional dependencies on columns that are not candidate keys in a BCNF table. A relation is in BCNF when every determinant in a relation is a candidate key.

BCNF provides for normalization of a 3NF table that has all of the following properties

✓ multiple candidate keys
✓ composite candidate keys
✓ columns shared between the composite keys

Here is an example. The following table contains data about students and teachers.

student	subject	teacher
smith	reading	frank
smith	writing	sally
jones	reading	frank
jones	writing	jane

There are three logical constraints on this table

✓ A student takes a subject from one teacher only
✓ Each teacher teaches one subject only
✓ More than one teacher can teach a subject

There are two candidate keys for this table. Each is a composite key.

```
        Candidate Keys
    {student,subject)
    (student, teacher)
```

The functional dependencies appear in the following dependency diagram. The composite key (student,subject) is a determinant for *teacher*. The attribute *teacher* is a determinant for *subject*. The composite key (student,subject) is a determinant for *teacher*.

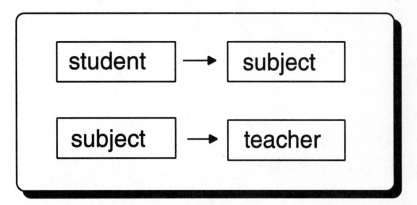

If the primary key is (student,subject), the relation is in 1NF because there are no repeating groups. The relation is in 2NF because the teacher is fully functionally dependent on the primary key (student,subject). There is only one non-key attribute, teacher. The relation is in 3NF because the non-key attributes are independent.

If the primary key is (student,teacher), the relation is in 1NF because there are no repeating groups. The relation is in 2NF because the subject is fully functionally dependent on the primary key (student,teacher). The relation is in 3NF because there is only one non-key attribute subject, so all non-key attributes are mutually independent.

The table is not in 3CNF because there are three determinants, (student,subject), (student,teacher) and teacher, but teacher is not a candidate key.

Projection into two BCNF tables normalizes this 3NF relation.

TS

teacher	subject
frank	reading
sally	writing
jane	writing

ST

student	teacher
smith	frank
smith	sally
jones	frank
jones	jane

FOURTH NORMAL FORM

Some tables cannot be normalized on the basis of functional dependencies. The fourth normal form rests instead on multi-valued dependencies. A table is in forth normal form when there are no multi-valued dependencies.

Here is an example where a teacher can teach more than one course. More than one textbook is used for a course. A course must be taught with all the required textbooks.

teacher	course	book
Frank	reading	Catcher in the Rye
Frank	reading	Justine
Frank	reading	Red Badge of Courage
Sally	reading	Catcher in the Rye
Sally	reading	Justine
Sally	reading	Red Badge of Courage
Frank	writing	Cry of the Wolf
frank	writing	The Man in the Iron Mask

There is only one candidate key for this table, (teacher,subject,book). There are no functional dependencies because all the columns are in the candidate key.

The table is in BCNF. Even so, it is clearly difficult to update. If another teacher, Jim, starts teaching reading, three records must be added to the table, one for each textbook. These three records are

```
jim  reading    Catcher in the Rye
jim  reading    Justine
jim  reading    Red Badge of Courage
```

A course does not have a single teacher. The teacher is not dependent on the course. However, a well-defined set of teachers teaches each course. The same set of teachers always teaches any single course. Selecting a course always results in the same set of teachers who teach the course. In the example if the course is reading, the teachers are always Frank and Sally. This table is difficult to update because of multivalued dependencies. The teacher is multidependent on the course. The text is multidependent on the course.

Here is the table after the addition of the new teacher.

teacher	course	book
Frank	reading	Catcher in the Rye
Frank	reading	Justine
Frank	reading	Red Badge of Courage
Sally	reading	Catcher in the Rye
Sally	reading	Justine
Sally	reading	Red Badge of Courage
Frank	writing	Cry of the Wolf
Frank	writing	The Man in the Iron Mask
Frank	writing	The Scarlet Letter
Jim	reading	Catcher in the Rye
jim	reading	Justine
jim	reading	Red Badge of Courage

Imagine a relation with three attributes, x, y, and z. The attribute z can only be multivalued dependent on x if the set of values selected by a given value of the attribute pair (x,y) depends on the value of x and does not depend on the value of y. This definition requires that a relation must have at least three attributes to be multivalued dependent.

For example, selecting the course *reading* selects the set of teachers *Frank*, *Sally* and *Jim*. Selecting the values of (reading,People) for the attribute pair course and textbook also selects the set of teachers *Frank*, *Sally* and *Jim*. This example shows that the set of teachers selected depends on the course alone, not on the combination of course and book.

A projection into two tables normalizes the single table.

```
    teacher
course  teacher

    text
course  text
```

Separating the multivalued dependencies into two tables makes the schema more simple. After the projection, the database is easier to update. After the projection, there are no multivalued dependencies. A table is in 4NF only when there are no multivalued dependencies.

OTHER NORMAL FORMS

Dependency theory is the theory of normalization and topics related to normalization. There are other normal forms. For example, there is a fifth normal form (5NF) and a (3,3)NF.

These further normal forms are beyond the scope of an introductory text. The normal forms presented in the previous sections illustrate problems you are likely to confront in real database applications.

You are unlikely to confront the problems illustrated by higher normal forms in an actual database. The application of the normal forms described above, particularly through BCNF, should create a well-designed database.

SUMMARY

This chapter has introduced the concepts of functional dependency and normalization.

Functional dependency demonstrates the logical structure of the data in a database. Data dependency diagrams can assist in determining the various data dependencies within a table.

The normal forms offer guidelines for structuring a database with simple data dependencies. In the various normal forms introduced, each form is more organized than the one before. Each normal form constrains a schema to have less complex data dependencies within tables. A shown series of steps successively reduced the complexity of a schema.

Eliminating repeating groups of data can reduce tables not in 1NF form to 1NF tables.

You can project a set of 2NF tables from 1NF tables with non-full functional dependencies on key columns.

You can project a collection of 3NF tables from 2NF tables that have inter-dependencies between non-key columns.

You can reduce by projection a 3NF table to a BCNF form. By projection, you can reduce a BCNF table to 4NF form.

REDUNDANT DATA AND UPDATING

Normalization concerns the meaning of the data in a database. The normal forms are guidelines to help the database designer design the logical structure of the data for an enterprise into the schema of the database.

It is better to have less-complex tables and thereby a less-complex schema. A schema will be simple when all the non-key columns in any table only contain information that is about the primary key of the containing table.

Appendix A—Database Glossary

The following glossary lists a few terms used in relational database, networking and object-oriented development. This glossary does not include terms specific to PowerBuilder, as this information is in the PowerBuilder documentation.

API—application programming interface.

attribute—a name that refers to a domain.

cardinality—the number of tuples in a relation.

B-tree—a particular type of index that minimizes any search through the index.

candidate key—one of the possible combinations of attributes that can make a key.

cartesian product—a combination of each of the elements of one set with every one of the elements of a second set.

CASE—Computer Aided Software Engineering.

network—see computer network.

class—the definition or prototype of an object.

client—a personal computer or workstation that accesses data on a remote server.

composite key—a key made from multiple attributes.

computer network—an interconnected collection of autonomous computers.

conceptual level schema—the representation of the structure and contents of the database.

conceptual view—the view of a database containing all the information about the schema.

concurrency control—the way to prevent multiple users from accessing data at the same time, thus protecting the database.

data modeling—the process of discovering the structure of data for an enterprise.

DBS—database management system.

degree—the number of attributes in the header of a relation. A relation with two attributes is a second-degree relation or binary.

difference—subtracts the elements of one set from another set.

DLL—data link library.

domain—the set of all possible values for a single type of data item; for example, the domain of all possible zip codes.

network—see computer network.

encapsulation—the holding of data and methods for an object within an object, protected from other objects or messages.

equi-join—a join where the foreign key relationship is an equality.

event—something that happens in the application environment; for example, a window opening or a mouse button click.

external view—a single user's view of part of the schema.

cardinality—the number of tuples in a relation.

entity—some person, place, thing or event.

functional dependence—the logical relationship between two elements wherein the value of one of the elements depends on the value of the other.

hashing—a storage intensive indexing method.

host—a networked computer used to run application programs.

inheritance—when a new object gains the properties of an existing object.

internal view—the view of the storage of data by an RDBMS.

intersection—the elements in common between two sets.

ISO—International Standards Organization.

key—one or more attributes that uniquely select any row of a table.

LAN—see local area network.

local area network—a network wherein all resources have physical proximity to each other.

logical schema—see schema.

method—an operation on the data within an object or on the object itself.

network—see computer network.

network architecture—the definition of the interfaces and protocols connecting a network.

normal form—a rule used to help establish a normalized database.

normalization—alterations to the design of a database that minimizes redundant data.

normalized—a normalized database is a database where the amount of redundant data has been minimized.

object—a thing within the PowerBuilder environment; for example, a button, a window, or an application.

ODBC—open database connectivity.

operator overloading—the condition wherein the same function can call different types for a single argument.

OSI—open systems interconnect.

outer join—a join wherein records appear when no matching records are in one of the tables.

permission—a status granting a user the capability to perform certain operations on a database.

polymorphisim—the condition wherein, for an object-oriented environment, different objects can accept the same message.

precedence order—the order in which operators receive evaluation.

primary key—a key that uniquely selects any individual row in a table.

RDBMS—Relational Database Management System.

referential integrity—the requirement that for any foreign key there must be a corresponding primary key.

schema—the representation of the structure and contents of the database.

SQL—Structured Query Language

server—a computer that provides data management services for other computers.

tuple—an attribute combined with a data value drawn from the domain over which the attribute exists

transaction—one or more operations on a database grouped together as a unit.

union—the combination of the elements of two sets into one set.

WAN—see wide area network.

wide area network—a network wherein all resources lack physical proximity.

Appendix B-Naming Conventions

Writing readable, useful applications are much easier if you adhere to certain naming conventions. This appendix suggests naming conventions for objects, controls and variables.

Naming Conventions For Objects

The following conventions are for the objects stored within a PowerBuilder library.

Object	Convention	Example
DataWindow	d_	d_employeeList
Function	f_	f_mortgage
menu	m_	m_mainMenu
Structure	s_	s_mortgage
Query	q_	q_employee
UserObject	u_	u_response
Window	w_	w_main

Naming Conventions For Controls

The following suggested conventions name controls that can appear on a window or DataWindow or can appear within a user-defined object.

Control	Convention	Example
CheckBox	cbx_	cbx_test
CommandButton	cb_	cb_close
DataWindow	dw_	dw_employee
DropDownListBox	ddlb_	ddlb_styles
Editmask	em_	em_zipcode
Graph	gr_	gr_territories
GroupBox	gb_	gb_salaries
HScrollBar	hsb_	hsb_cost
Line	ln_	ln_long
ListBox	lb	lb_salaries
MultiLineEdit	mle_	mle_comment
Oval	oval_	oval_large
Picture	p_	p_house
PictureButton	pb_	pb_update
RadioButton	rb_	rb_next
Rectangle	r_	r_large
RoundRectangle	rr_	rr_picture
SingleLineEdit	sle_	sle_comment
Statictext	st_	st_mainTitle
UserObject	uo_	uo_mortgage
VscrollBar	vsb_	vsb_percent

Naming Conventions For Variables

Naming conventions for variables may compound to specify the type and the scope of the variable. Examples appear at the end of the section.

Prefixes

Scope	Prefix
local	l
global	g
instance	i
shared	s
argument	a

Data Type Qualifiers

Data Type	Prefix
Window	w
MenuItem	m
DataWindow	dw
Structure	str
UserObject	uo
Integer	i_
Unsigned Integer	ui
Long	l
Unsigned Long	ul
Boolean	b

Data Type Qualifiers, Continued

Data Type	Prefix
String	s
Double	d
Real	r
Decimal	d
Time	t
DateTime	dt

Examples

Description	Example
Global Integer	gi_num_recs
Shared Structure	sstr_graph_data
Instance Unsigned Long	iul_test
Local Boolean	lb_complete
Argument data Window	adw_data_source
Global String Array	gs_buffer1[ ]
Shared DateTime	sdt_startTime
Instance Double	idb_final_cost
Local Window	lw_choices

Index

Index

Index

Datawindow Painter
    changing display, 187
    introduced, 52
    previewing datawindow, 188
    saving datawindow, 190
    saving datawindow object, 184
    selecting database fields, 180
    shortcut keys for, 198
    starting, 176
    tab order for fields, 196
    update characteristics, 191
Debug Painter
    described, 289
    introduced, 56
    running an application, 293
    starting, 289
    stop points, 291
    stop points, editing, 292
Decompostition
    choosing, 414
Difference, 367
Disk Driver, 322
Display Formats
    defining, 269
    using, 267
Distinct, 360
Do Loop, 95
Domains, 324
Dot Notation, 91
Duplicate Tuples
    prohibited, 331

E

Edit Control, 170
    manipulating contents of, 173
Embedded Sql Statements, 106
Encapsulation
    introduced, 41
Event Driven
    described, 71
Events
    as triggered by user, 28
    associated with an object, 28
    associated with application object, 28
    open application, description of, 29

    related to application object, 74
    relation to scripts, 73
    user defined, 284
Exit Statement, 97, 99
Extended Attributes
    using, 266
Extended Column Attributes, 251, 259
Extended Join, 372
External View, 317, 319

F

File Manager, 321
First Normal Form, 403
Flow Of Control, 92
Focus
    defined, 160
For Next Statement, 98
Foreign Key
    defining a, 258
Fourth Normal Form, 420
Function Painter
    compiling scripts with the, 239
    starting, 234
    writing scripts with the, 238
Functional Dependence, 404
    and composed columns, 407
    and keys, 407
    full, 408
Functions
    actual arguments of, 237
    calling a, 241
    compiling, 239
    described, 107, 233
    example of a, 240
    formal arguments of, 237
    global, 235
    introduced, 37
    scope of, 233
    scripts for, 238
    types, 108
    used with controls, 147
    useful with data windows, 173

Index

Index

Index

Index

What is on the Disk

Examples

The Disk contains files you will need when working through the examples in Part One of this book.

Create a directory on your hard disk to hold the files. Copy the files on the diskette directory "a:\examples" to the directory you created.

Nexgen Si, Inc. Class Libraries

The diskette also includes a sample version of the NexGen SI, Inc. class library. This library will assist you in constructing professional applications, as will the full library. The instructions for installing the class library are given in the diskette file named `a:\readme.txt`.